Mathematical Theory of Expanding and Contracting Economies

Mathematical Theory of Expanding and Contracting Economies

Oskar Morgenstern
New York University

Gerald L. Thompson
Carnegie-Mellon University

Lexington Books
D.C. Heath and Company
Lexington, Massachusetts
Toronto   London

Library of Congress Cataloging in Publication Data

Morgenstern, Oskar, 1902-
   Mathematical theory of expanding and contracting economies.

   Bibliography: p.
   1. Economics—Mathematical models. 2. Economic
development—Mathematical models. I. Thompson, Gerald Luther,
1923- joint author. II. Title.
HB135.M67   330'.01'51   76-2308
ISBN 0-669-00089-2

Published simultaneously in Canada

Printed in the United States of America

International Standard Book Number: 0-669-00089-2

Library of Congress Catalog Card Number: 76-2308

To Dorothy and Dorothea

Contents

Preface

This book was begun with the idea of presenting in a single place the various research results that we have obtained in the areas of expanding and contracting economy models over the past 20 years, some of which have been published in diverse places. However, the writing of this book, which has occupied us for the past two and one half years, has been much more than an expository exercise. For in going back over our earlier work we found that we were able to solve several previously unsolved mathematical problems, and to complete the formulation of some models that we had begun but were previously unable to finish. Thus while about half of the material in this book has been published previously, the rest is new.

The origin of expanding economy models is contained in John von Neumann's paper presented in 1932 in Princeton and again in 1936 in Vienna, published in German in 1937, and translated into English in 1945. Our own work began, with John G. Kemeny, in the summer of 1955, and resulted in our paper, published in 1956, now widely known as the KMT model, [48].[a] Our subsequent work appeared in 1967, 1969, 1971, 1972 (in the Proceedings [9] of the 1970 Vienna Conference) and in 1974 (in the Proceedings [66] of the Warsaw Conference).

We note the importance for the history of both economics and mathematics of the Mathematical Colloquium run by Karl Menger in Vienna in the 1930's and at which was presented not only von Neumann's paper and Menger's own work on utility theory, but also the important economic works of Abraham Wald. Moreover, the two International Conferences on expanding economy models, the first held in Vienna at the Institute for Advanced Studies in 1970 and the second held in Warsaw at the Computing Center of the Polish Academy of Sciences in 1972, marked a decided quickening of interest in large scale economic models in both eastern and western economies. These models have been much more widely accepted in eastern than western countries, perhaps because of the socialist emphasis on economic planning. But the reader will see in the text that the kinds of models we discuss have relevance to the economy of any given country, entirely independent of the particular political, cultural, or psychological characteristics of that country.

There are, however, at present only a handful of researchers interested in these models in the United States, but many more in Western Europe, and still more in the Eastern countries. We hope that the present book will contribute to the furthering of interest in this approach to economics, and to the start of applications of the models.

The slow penetration of von Neumann's ideas into economic science is

[a] The numbers in brackets refer to those in the bibliography.

partly due to their novelty and their mathematical unfamiliarity. It is also partly due to the fact that large computers are needed for computation, as well as to the fact that considerable algorithmic and software development is needed for such computations. Furthermore extensions of the original model had to be made in order to remove some of its initial limitations.

Combining well-known computer hardware development of recent years and the corresponding software developments in the mathematical programming area, with our new models, we feel that a new branch of economics, which we call *Mathematical Programming Economics*, can properly be said to have been initiated. This area will belong neither to micro- nor to macro- economics, since the computation and algorithmic power now exists to perform the necessary computations on unaggregated data, to whatever extent of detail may be needed. Indeed (in Chapters 5 and 13) we have included a number of remarks on the pitfalls of the aggregation of economic data. Lacking for true economic applications are the necessary data for important countries in the world. Once gathered, the needed computations can be made and actual economic decisions can be based on the results.

In this work linear programming is raised from the current wide and important applications to transportation, packaging, scheduling, etc., to truly large scale uses involving entire economies, to issues of national and world wide scope. This is a big step. But it was necessary to take it. We do not want to diminish the significance of the special linear programming models and applications, but here we go farther. Instead of dealing with *given* resources we have expansion or contraction, i.e., a change in the very problem to which linear programming is being applied. In other words we make use of parametric linear programming of a special kind.

Game theory plays a dual role in this book: as already shown in 1956 in the KMT paper, game theory is used as a technique for proving theorems, and because of its implication of linear programming it is a device for computation also. This was then, and still is, a noteworthy and quite unexpected feature of game theory. In the present book we go beyond this: game theory appears in its own right as a model of economic activity where there is interaction among players—whoever they might be—intent on seeking their advantage, sometimes opposed to each other, sometimes cooperating and in the cooperation determining the imputations, i.e., the division of the proceeds of their cooperation. This is the originally intended function of game theory while in most economic textbooks the limited idea still prevails that it applies only to situations of oligopoly. In fact game theory is a fundamental challenge to contemporary neo-classical economics as such. The present work can be viewed in the light of the preceding.

Our results relate to the basic properties of *any* economic system, regardless of its formal organization: whether based on individual, corporate or government decisions, whether free market or centrally directed, inputs of goods and services are needed to obtain outputs of goods and services. Whether true prices are formed on markets or whether they are only units of accounts, prices must be determined in order to have the economy function, either in expansion or contraction. Hence the theorems, algorithms and future large scale computations are suitable for all types of economies as should be the case of a truly general theory. The same applies, of course, to game theory. It is only natural that there must exist a theory that explains what is basic to all economic activity. The specific organization of countries is a superstructure that can be maintained only if the kernel is not destroyed. Chapter 10 gives methods for discovering the nature of the kernel.

In our models there are no traditional production functions, no chance factors built in, and no money. All this is deliberate and not a fault of the theory. In the future we hope it will be possible to account in the model for stochastic elements in production and demand. We note, incidentally, that conventional theory does not systematically treat them either.

Regarding money, the matter is similar to the relation between the theory of mechanics and the theory of light: The introduction of light does not require the modification of the basic theorems of mechanics. Although we now possess a theory of light, it is not needed to build most machines, but the theory is necessary when we go beyond the domain of mechanical theory. For instance when bodies move near or with the speed of light classical mechanics is of no help; we then have to go to relativity theory. Similar situations may arise—though that is by no means certain—when money is introduced into our models. Whatever money may do to our models there is no way of getting away from the fact that a technology always underlies economic activity. Technology may progress, the economy must adjust to it and, in spite of technological progress, the economy may want to reject it or may even have to fall back on an earlier one previously discarded because of new constraints being imposed. In Chapter 8 we illustrate such added constraints.

In general it would be easy to demand of a method or a model more than it can deliver at a given time. Frequently such demands are made without any hint being given as to how additional features could be incorporated. Such criticisms therefore would then have no value.

The reader will find a number of novel concepts and results in the book. For instance, the idea of profitable industries supporting unprofitable (e.g., certain service) industries, the inclusion of expansion in the definition of comparative advantage, the identification of control variables and their uses in describing such phenomena as technical change and controlling economic growth, contraction and compression of economies, long term planning models, world expanding models, trading blocks, international transactions, subeconomies in both open and closed models, consumption (private and public) of excess production and excess value, balance of profits as well as balance of trade, the spending of profits of profitable industries on defense and pollution abatement, etc.

The new results of this work (previously unpublished) are scattered throughout Chapters 2, 3, and 4, the last half of 5, the last half of 6, all of Chapters 7, 8, 10, 11, 12, and 13.

We suggest that a reader begin the study of this book by reading Chapter 1, most of Chapters 2 and 4 and the first half of Chapters 5 and 6. He can then go on to read Chapters 8, 10, 11, and 12 rather easily. These chapters contain some of the most interesting results of the book. On the second time through he should work some of the exercises at the end of most of the chapters. Excercises that may seem hard, as well as the more demanding Chapters 3, 9, and 13, can be deferred for further intensive study.

While joint work is never exactly equal, it should be noted that the second named author (Gerald L. Thompson) is responsible for Chapters 3, 8, and 13, Appendices 1 and 2, and the exercises that appear at the end of some of the chapters.

We began the writing of this book on March 8, 1973 in Pittsburgh, Pennsylvania, and made the final changes in the manuscript on November 11, 1975 in Princeton, New Jersey. During the two and one half years in between we have had numerous writing sessions in Princeton, Pittsburgh, New York City and Blue Mountain Lake, New York. While various obstacles arose during this period, we have enjoyed watching the manuscript grow, at times seemingly out of our control. The reader will note many places where additional work might have been done, but we found it necessary to limit ourselves from following every possible path in order to complete our work within a reasonable time.

In the course of our work we have been supported by many persons and institutions. For the last phases of this work we acknowledge with pleasure the valuable assistance rendered us in various ways by Eleanor Balocik, Bonnie Chwast, Radu Filimon, Dietrich Fischer, Delores Hall and Julia Martinez. We also thank our universities for placing at our disposal their important facilities.

Special thanks are due to the Office of Naval Research which has supported our studies over several years through grants to Carnegie-Mellon University and New York University.

Oskar Morgenstern and **Gerald L. Thompson**
November 11, 1975

Mathematical Theory of
Expanding and Contracting
Economies

1 Scope and Method of Investigation

1. Origin of the Expanding Economy Model

There are two ways in which science advances: *first*, by small, numerous steps, by the contributions made by many diligent and able workers. Gradually, though, one observes significant transformations that have, by cumulative effect, provided new insights; *second*, by the appearance, seemingly from nowhere, of a new thought, a new concept, or the discovery of a new phenomenon that forces a complete reorientation of the existing scientific outlook.

It is no exaggeration to say that von Neumann's short paper of 1937 (cf. Appendix 3) belongs to the second category. We do not in any way want to diminish the great contributions to economics made by earlier mathematical economists such as Cournot, Walras, Edgeworth, Fisher, Pareto, Zeuthen and others. But, excepting von Neumann's game theory, there is no piece of mathematical writing in economics—though seemingly dealing with a very restricted problem—which is as profound and has started so many new trends and in some sense has synthesized so much previous thought and effort as this paper. The depth of mathematical analysis in this paper stands out uniquely and has ushered in a new epoch in economics.

Economists have always been concerned with the problem of how to model a whole economy. The first such effort is the "Tableau Economique" of 1759 by François Quesnay, the founder of the physiocratic school. Later work by Adam Smith, David Ricardo and others was less explicit, and no attempt was made by them to quantify economic relations. Karl Marx postulated some interdependence of economic activity and attempted a limited, indeed primitive, algebraic description. He mainly postulated, but by modern standards did not prove, the existence of an evolutionary element. It was Léon Walras who finally set up a system of simultaneous equations purporting to show the interdependence between prices and production. However, his system was completely static. He did not prove his case even measured by the mathematical standards of his time (1872). He merely asserted the existence of an equilibrium by postulating an equality in numbers of equations and unknowns. Léon Walras and his followers took this equality to be a "proof" of the existence of a solution. Later, Walras' successor, Pareto, refined these ideas without, however, advancing any fundamentally new ideas. Other mathematical economists studied essentially partial equilibria, and when they discussed a general equilibrium, it was basically the same Walrasian system.

A fundamental change within that framework occurred when in 1935 Abraham Wald [133,134], encouraged by the mathematician Karl Menger, published the first mathematically rigorous proof that, for a suitably transformed Walrasian system, a solution in non-negative prices and quantities produced existed. He went further than that in one crucial respect, because he showed that it is necessary to determine which processes should be used, which should be abandoned, and which goods should have positive prices. This work, which we shall however not study any further, is a landmark in economic science. It has exercised decisive influence on all later work that has restricted itself to Walrasian static conceptions. By producing a rigorous existence proof of a definitely nonelementary mathematical character, it has raised standards for the entire field. It took several decades for this work to be appreciated and to make its influence felt in the literature: in some sense a measure of its originality and importance.

All this work related to stationary processes under very strict, but not always explicit, limiting assumptions, such as complete mobility of all factors, instantaneous adjustment, absence of uncertainty, etc. There was also the tacit prohibition for individual members of the economy to combine to their advantage, if such advantage existed and could be recognized. This situation prevails to this day in the writings of those who have continued and expanded the basic Walrasian ideas of a general equilibrium. This line of thought will not occupy us in what follows.

While the Walrasian *static* system evolved, a different current of thought began to appear. As already stated more or less vaguely, defined elements of thinking about economic growth or expansion can be traced back fairly long in the history of economics. They were, however, as is unavoidable, at first largely of a descriptive-historical nature, *not* analytical. For example, in 1913 J. Schumpeter developed a verbal theory of the role of an entrepreneur who, by introducing innovations into the economy, is thereby assumed to drive the system to higher levels, a push into "noncapitalistic spaces." On the other hand, in 1918 G. Cassel, a follower of Walras and whose mathematical system he drastically oversimplified, proposed the idea that the economy might expand at a uniform rate. However, not much was done with this idea; it was not developed mathematically and no theorem of any kind was even postulated. Nor does there seem to have been any development of this scheme in subsequent literature.

It was in 1932 in Princeton that an entirely new event occurred when John von Neumann, already recognized as one of his generation's great mathematicians[a], gave a lecture on a model of an expanding economy. This lecture was repeated in 1936 in Vienna in Karl Menger's Colloquium and, at Menger's insistence, was published in 1937 in the "Ergebnisse eines Mathematischen Kolloquiums" [105]. The model is that of a uniformly expanding closed economy for which it is proved that the expansion factor is equal to the interest factor. This fundamental result was obtained from a number of economically plausible assumptions, such as that goods are produced from each other, that processes that are unprofitable will be abandoned, and that goods produced in excess will have zero price. It was also assumed that every good entered in some amount, no matter how small, into the production of *every* other good. This strong assumption was necessary to ensure that the economy would not break apart into disconnected pieces.

It is the theory developed in von Neumann's paper which represents one of those rare discrete steps in the development of a science to which allusion was made in the first paragraph of this chapter. It is also the theory on which the present work is based and from which far reaching generalizations and extensions are obtained.

The unique place that von Neumann's work occupies in the history of mathematical economics is due to its broad underlying concept, the power of its mathematical analysis, and the possibility it offered for generalizations and expansions of the main idea. The model is of great mathematical interest; indeed, it was a vehicle used to arrive at a generalization of Brouwer's fixed point theorem, already used by von Neumann in his original 1928 paper on game theory. The economic significance of the model lies in the fact that it deals rigorously with the question of the production of commodities from commodities, a principal concern already of the classical economists.

Newton's *Principia* needed both the vast amount of observations by Tycho Brahe and his own invention—or better: discovery—of the differential calculus in order to establish the science of mechanics. For von Neumann's theory there was no corresponding body of economic data and only common knowledge of an economy went into the model. The mathematical innovation was a big step forward in topology, it generalized one of its most important devices: Brouwer's fixed point theorem, a theorem that was also fundamental earlier for the theory of games and from which the way led to the theory of convexity, now of great value in modern economics.

Von Neumann's paper remained unknown for many years. This may be due to the fact that it was published in a highly specialized mathematical

---

[a] The reader who wishes to learn more about von Neumann's role in mathematics should read the accounts by J.M. Ulam [132], Morgenstern[88], and H.W. Kuhn and A.W. Tucker[60].

journal of limited circulation among mathematicians only; that it used mathematics unfamiliar to mathematical economists of that time; and that it appeared shortly before the outbreak of World War II. The only reference to it of which we are aware, before its translation into English in 1946, is in a 1941 paper by Oskar Morgenstern[b] on J.R. Hicks [83 pp. 369 and 371-372] in which, among other things, it was pointed out that in economics one is confronted essentially with inequalities rather than with equalities and that, even apart from the inadequacy of a mere counting of equations and unknowns—obviously meaningless when inequalities are given—quite different mathematical problems were involved. In particular, it was the demonstration of the *implicit* nature of the problem, i.e., that one half is only solved if the other half is solved, and *vice versa*. This was a completely unfamiliar phenomenon for economists at that time and is not generally appreciated even today.

Von Neumann's paper appeared in an English translation by George Morgenstern[c] in 1946 [105] presumably because it was again mentioned in *The Theory of Games and Economic Behavior* (1944) in connection with the minimax theorem, which is fundamental to game theory. The translation[d] was accompanied by a paper by D.G. Champernowne [14], which attempted to present the main economic content of von Neumann's paper in nontechnical language—a difficult undertaking. It also raised some criticisms, especially about the treatment of labor inputs, points that we will consider in the present work (cf. Chapters 6 and 7).

2. Generalizations of the Model

The matter lay dormant again, save for occasional references to the model[e] until 1956 when there appeared a paper "Generalization of the von Neumann Model of an Expanding Economy," [48], by John G. Kemeny, Oskar Morgenstern, and Gerald L. Thompson, later to become informally but widely known as the *KMT Model*, as it will be repeatedly referred to here in this work. This paper brought a vast generalization, removed the assumption in the original model—that every good must be used or produced in every production activity—(found economically objectionable

[b] At that time (1941), von Neumann and Morgenstern were already beginning work on their joint book on game theory [1944], where the next reference to the von Neumann paper appears.

[c] No relation to Oskar Morgenstern. That author later changed his name to Morton.

[d] The original paper is reprinted with some minor corrections in English in Appendix 3.

[e] Von Neumann presented his model in 1950 at an economic seminar at Princeton University, only to find a total lack of interest among the faculty. When, already mortally ill in 1956, he was shown the KMT model with its vast generalizations, he expressed deep satisfaction with this development and urged that further efforts be made by the authors.

unless the model of the economy studied were highly aggregated), and used game theory as an analytical tool. The possibilities offered by game theoretical procedures also cleared up the important point made by von Neumann [Appendix 3, p. 245, Footnote 2] and von Neumann and Morgenstern [106, p. 154] that the appearance of the minimax theorem, both in game theory as well as in his model of an expanding economy, deserved further exploration. The KMT model accomplishes, among other things, precisely this: The von Neumann model can be presented and analyzed in terms of matrix game theory and, as we will show in Chapter 3, also by linear programming procedures (due to the well-known correspondence between them). Thus at least one avenue is opened up toward explaining this interrelationship.

The KMT model replaced the restrictive von Neumann assumption, that every good must enter in no matter how small an amount into the production of every other good, by the economically acceptable and conceptually simple condition that *something of value* must be produced by the economy. This merely means that total output must have a positive "value," i.e., that the sum of products of goods produced times corresponding prices must be positive. This is fully described in Chapter 2. We also show how outside demand can be introduced, along with its varying effects on growth rates and interest rates. Technological progress may appear in the form of a new demand which requires new goods and/or new, more efficient, processes or services. In Chapter 8 we give a concrete example to show how technological progress can be introduced gradually in a constructive manner.

The consequences of this generalization were that the expanding economy would not break apart, but might operate a number of interrelated *subeconomies*, each one having its own expansion factor that is equal to its interest factor. The number of these rates is finite and placed between determined bounds. In addition, for outside demand it was shown how variations influence growth rates and interest rates. Furthermore, the generalized model described in Chapter 5 explains the possibility of technological progress in the form of new, more efficient processes as well as the possibility of aggregation and the consequences for the change of expansion and interest rates (described in Chapter 2).

There have been attempts in the economic literature to come to grips with the intuitive notion that in an economy there exist *subeconomies*. These are conceived as leading lives of their own while embedded in the larger unit. The question is: How can such a dual role be described, and what forces separate the subeconomies and yet still hold them together? Nowhere were there any theorems. However, the KMT model of Chapter 2 provides such theorems, and in Chapter 5 additional insight is shown regarding the possible sizes and various relationships among subeconomies. The matter is far from being simple, but the underlying theory is powerful enough to provide valid answers. The existence of sub-economies is closely tied up with the problem of aggregation, see Chapters 5 and 13. We note here in general that the tendency in economics to form all kinds of aggregates, almost with abandon, runs counter to the tendency in other sciences to make increasingly finer distinctions which is tied up with their great progress.[f]

The ability to distinguish subeconomies has far reaching significance. A subeconomy is a subset of the goods and processes of the original economy which has the same solution and expansion coefficient as the original economy. There can be many subeconomies of various sizes, and it is possible to determine their interplay with one another. Thus we are not dealing with the conventional aggregation and its many-neglected problems. Our aggregation procedure is derived from the theory and is operational. Subeconomies are entities that can cooperate with each other or be in conflict, yet still belong to the same general economy. Subeconomies therefore play a considerable role in the subsequent chapters as our theory unfolds.

In a subsequent paper by Morgenstern and Thompson in 1967 [90], a further generalization was made, introducing savings and investments into the von Neumann model as modified in the 1956 KMT work. Both of these activities could be carried out by private and/or government agencies. These activities may change preferences, a factor that had not been studied before for this model; even for other models there were no rigorous theorems (cf. Chapter 6). The mathematical analysis revealed, among other things, that the frequently made assumption that an expanding economy must automatically go to one "efficient point" is not, in general, true since, as we have shown, no such point[g] even needs to exist, a result which is as important as it is unexpected. An outside agency, e.g., the government or an ideologically controlled board would have to determine in which of alternative directions the economy should be made to expand. *Thus the idea that there always is an efficient point—and allegedly a unique one!—is*

---

[f] It is interesting that the 18th Century economist R. Cantillon [12] had a clear idea that it matters, in monetary expansion, *where* in the economy the new money is injected in what quantities, since the sequence of price rises depends on such detail. This sophisticated approach to inflation has for the most part still not been appreciated.

[g] An "efficient point" means the following: given the vectors $x, y, x \geq y$ means $x_i \geq y_i$ for all i.
Definition: A production vector x is an *efficient point* if
(a) x is a feasible solution vector,
(b) for any other feasible vector x' we have $x' \not\geq x$. In other words, an efficient production vector x is a feasible solution with the property that no other feasible production vector is better or equal in every component. The similarity with the notion of a Pareto optimum deserves to be noted; and what is proved in Chapter 6 is exactly that this need not hold for every economy. There are, at any rate, also other objections to the indiscriminate use of the Pareto optimum found in the literature (cf. Morgenstern [86]).
The notion of an "efficiency point" is often unclearly treated in the literature. Some authors, like Malinvaud, vary their definition as does Koopmans. This is well treated by Truchon [128].

unwarranted. This is a great, indeed fundamental, difference from conventional economics.[h] There is, on the other hand, a welcome similarity to the solution concept in game theory, where for an essential *n*-person game, there are, in a solution, several, possibly infinitely many, imputations (or in some cases an *n*-person game and a corresponding economy may have *no* solution of a specified kind).

Both these results—the existence of subeconomies with individual, discrete but bounded expansion rates, and the possible nonexistence of efficient points—show the power of mathematical analysis, which yields economically meaningful results that could not have been anticipated intuitively nor be found by non-mathematical reasoning. In this there is a profound lesson; others are provided by game theory.

In Chapter 4 we generalize further by making the model *open*, i.e., by allowing the economy to be embedded in the "world", which here is not further specified. Later in Chapter 11 we describe a "world" consisting of several open economies which interact with each other in a complicated manner. At first we merely assume that there exists a world market for different goods such that the open expanding economy can import and export freely, provided the prices are right and the balance of payments condition is met. Thus the outside world affects the internal price structure: the internal equilibrium prices have to lie between the import and export prices. Furthermore, it has been possible to discuss subeconomies of the open model (cf. Chapter 5), and to add consumption to the open model (cf. Chapter 7), thus making it even richer.

We find that the fact of openness, when achieved, also produces interesting and unanticipated changes: for example, the expansion rates of certain subeconomies, while still being bounded, can now vary continuously rather than only in a discrete manner. Openness is achieved when at least one good is exported and one is imported. It is remarkable that in connecting the economy to the "world" by only one single export good and one single import good, plus adding control variables, this interesting transition to continuity occurs. Normally, continuity is the consequence of going over to large numbers, e.g., by introducing asymptotic behavior. We will show how a segment of expansion rates, over which particular expansion rates may vary continuously, is contained in the whole span of permissible expansion rates.

Furthermore, an important issue is resolved, one that has been a very restrictive feature of the von Neumann model, and, as a matter of fact, one of all linear models whether we consider stationary or expanding systems. This is the condition wherein if more is produced than can be sold profitably, the prices of these commodities must drop to zero. This is an objectionable condition if the excess production of a commodity can be sold in

---

[h] We comment in Chapter 6 on the far reaching implication of this discovery.

the export market at a positive price. In our *open* model the overproduced commodities can be sold on the world market and therefore their price will not drop to zero. Thus this objection does not apply. (Cf. Chapter 4).

In the present generalization we allow for the existence of unprofitable activities that are maintained at the expense of the profitable ones. Indeed, many production processes need free goods for technological reasons, e.g., air, and, obviously, government services. For initially strictly mathematical reasons, it became necessary to introduce a "balance of profit" condition (cf. Chapter 4). But the addition was fortuitious because it led to a theory of public goods, e.g., governmental services, private services, "law and order," and so on, with their prices and costs to become a fundamental part of the expansionary processes.

It is easy to see that the new model is able to account for the existence of governments, national defense, and other service institutions or to explain, for example, the maintenance of certain deficit operations such as, say, the Vienna Opera to promote a profitable Austrian tourist traffic. In Chapter 8 we give specific illustrations. In a similar way, *maximum expansion* can be placed under constraints such as "no pollution," "no poison production," "protection of the environment," etc. While this is hardly surprising, the point is that previous models could not include them. Rigorous existence theorems for such models are only established in this work on the firm basis of the open model.

Finally, we note that the rate of expansion of the open economy is partly determined by the government, i.e., by the drain the "unprofitable" activities exert on the profitable sector, and partly by the outside world via the world prices to which the economy has to adjust itself. It is highly satisfactory that this result emerges, because it is one that might be expected intuitively. However, once again, it must be stated that it is one thing to have an expectation of this sort, but to give a rigorous proof is quite another matter. We note that this result is obtained under the simplest possible circumstances: domestic expansion, presumably dependent on consumption and savings preferences and influenced via the same processes by the government, plus the price structure offered by a neutral "world." If we drop the neutrality and, instead, consider an economy that is faced with deliberately acting foreign open economies, the far more complicated situation mentioned earlier arises. The latter is the subject matter of Chapter 12 first for a two-country, then a three-country, and an *n*-country situation.

It is necessary to restate here some fundamentals concerning different types of economies and their relation to the process of expansion: In a centrally directed economy, decisions concerning the kinds and quantities of goods and services to be produced and their prices are made by a central planning committee. Therefore, indirectly, and sometimes even explicitly, the committee decides what the expansion rate of the economy shall be. The committee may make wrong decisions: If it sets the expansion rate too high, the program will be infeasible. If it sets the expansion rate too low, there is the failure to optimize. Whatever its decision, the committee requires vast amounts of very specific and highly accurate information to make a decision, and in order to make an optimal decision, it would have to carry out an enormous number of calculations. We will describe ways in which these calculations can be carried out.

In a free-exchange economy, no such committee exists. Therefore the corresponding decisions are made "somehow" by the economy itself. Classical and neoclassical economics are primarily concerned with the problem of how consumers' decisions or preferences make themselves felt via demand, and how they affect prices and production. But nowhere in this mechanism[i] is there an explanation of how consumer preferences ultimately determine or influence things such as the expansion rate or the interest rate in a multisector economy. There have been, of course, many attempts to explain change, e.g., via changes in tastes, technology, and income distribution, and there have been efforts to interpret change as expansion, e.g., by means of finding new markets, etc. But once more, there are no rigorous theorems. One of the purposes of the present work is to suggest an explanation for the phenomenon of consumers' influence via variable savings and consumption ratios. These, of course, are changes in

[i]In economics, or more generally in the social sciences, the word "mechanism" should be used *cum grano salis*, i.e., there is no parallelism with physical mechanics. The word is used here for want of a commonly accepted, more appropriate term. Game theory has shown that the structure of social theory is quite different from those classical ideas normally associated with mechanics. Consequently, adjustment processes also obey different rules and, if properly described, have different appearances.

The great physicist W. Nernst, who established fundamental laws of thermodynamics, showed a long time ago the difference between physical mechanisms and social processes by the following device: Assume a body to be in the position A upon which two forces 1 and 2 work as shown:

Then it is well known that the body will move along the dotted resultant toward A'. But, Nernst said, suppose the "body" is a dog and in (1) and (2) are two sausages, each exerting an influence on A. Clearly the dog will not walk to Point A' between (1) and (2)!

Nernst's profound observation, though put in a humorous form, is reported by H. Bernardelli [6]. We might add that besides "mechanism" also the free use of the term "system" is suspect. The same goes for the old "organic" analogy—more recently cast in biological terms (cf. e.g., Georgescu-Roegen). The economy *appears* to have mechanical and biological aspects and elements, but neither of them alone nor in conjunction can adequately describe what goes on in an economy whether changing or not. What is lacking is the fact that *decisions* are being made by individuals, committees, governments, etc. But that still does not necessarily give rise to a "system," taking this term at its proper meaning which involves a clear "inside and outside" and some hierarchical structure.

demand, but our theory treats them in an objective, nonideological manner.

Classical, and, in particular, neoclassical economics have also asserted the existence of subeconomies, i.e., partially self-sufficient segments of the economy that can operate as miniature economies by themselves. Some examples are individual households, firms, regions of a country, etc. Again, in a centrally directed economy, the central planning committee could decide that the economy should operate just one of its possible subeconomies if there were political, ideological, or military reasons for doing so. In a completely free-exchange economy, there is no way of taking any corresponding action. In a mixed economy, where there is a considerable amount of government intervention, certain price and quantity decisions can be enforced, particularly in times of stress. Nevertheless, even in a free-exchange economy we can observe that a "decision" has been made as to which particular subeconomies of the potential economy shall be used. It is once more the consumers who make these decisions via their individual consumption decisions. In addition, the government provides public goods according to public demand. Classical economics fails to provide an explanation of the "mechanism," or procedure, by which this is effected. What attempts there were have been based on production functions, not on ultimate consumers' preferences, although the latter are of primary importance. However, it would not be too difficult to show how such a mechanism might work in conformity with the results about subeconomies obtained in Chapter 5.

In a free-exchange economy the preferences of the consumers for private and public goods guide the entire course of the economy. If these preferences, together with technology and the supply of necessary inputs, warrant them, the economy will expand, presumably at the maximum rate consistent with the above preferences. The economy may even want to go to a zero expansion rate or, still worse, it may have a negative expansion rate.

If the government or some members of the economy desire a still higher or a still lower expansion rate, the preferences must be changed, either voluntarily or by intervention. Governments can control prices, consumption, exports and imports, and/or production. However, in doing so, the government may set up an infeasible program, which could be determined in advance by the proper computations. If a conflict exists between the consumers and the government, we have a true game situation which has to be treated as such. This aspect has as yet not been introduced, although it is of a very fundamental nature.

In the open model of Chapter 4 we take the first necessary step; we introduce specific *control variables*. These variables can be attached to any activities or groups of activities which the government or other agencies, control groups, etc., can influence or even exactly determine. The control can run the whole gamut from letting the "profit mechanism" work, to the making of individual consumption decisions (via changes in preferences), to submitting a program to parliamentary elections, to dictatorial planning. The basic structure of the economy is such that from some point on it cannot be changed, modified, or contorted without total collapse. More will be said about this in Chapters 9 and 10 where it will become clear that many controls are independent of the political organization of a country: the underlying economic reality alone sets limits beyond which an economy cannot be changed at will.

A further point worth making in this connection is that there can be, in economics, no sharp dividing line between macro- and micro-phenomena. The transition is gradual as, e.g., the difference between small and tall men. We can easily say when a man is small or tall, but we cannot give a precise dividing line.[j] We do not find it necessary to make such a distinction in this book since our models can be solved in their original differentiated form using the enormous power of contemporary computers.

3. Method of Analysis

It is now necessary to make some further brief remarks about the *method* of our analysis. Von Neumann's original paper used functional analysis; he also proved a generalization of Brouwer's fixed-point theorem. The KMT extension of the model applied two-person game theory as a powerful mathematical tool. This was possible because game theory rests on the minimax theorem, which is also basic in the original proof given in KMT. Being able to rely on matrix game theory brought about a vast simplification of the formal treatment of the extended problem. In what follows, we will on many occasions use linear programming techniques relying on the previously mentioned and by now well-known correspondence between a pair of linear programming problems and two-person zero-sum games. Since linear programming is applicable to our present problem, which contains the one von Neumann dealt with in 1932 as a special case, it follows that the latter can justifiably be viewed as one of the origins of linear programming methods.

Linear programming is now widely known, and thus the fact that we are able to transform the given problem into one of that kind may help to improve the accessibility of the profound thoughts contained in the original work. The ability to apply various linear programming techniques for actual calculations of very large scale multiperiod problems increases the

---

[j]This task, incidentally, transcends the power of present mathematical knowledge as von Neumann has remarked several times (before 1957) to Morgenstern. Since that time, nothing seems to have changed in this respect.

practical applicability of our subsequent results and gives new relevance to this new kind of economics, which should appropriately be called *mathematical programming economics*.

As mentioned earlier, we give theorems, together with elementary, constructive proofs, and provide examples. The role of the latter is frequently underestimated in the social sciences, or at least in economics, provided a theory exists. Examples bring out applications and lead away from possibly empty generalizations. Hence we give many examples, even of a homely nature dealing with eggs and chickens.[k] However simple this example is, the reader will note that it can only be studied with the aid of a joint production model such as those described in this book. Larger examples are computed in Chapter 8. Finally, *numbers* that are empirically relevant can be found: computations with these data leading to economic decisions are the real application.

We finally mention, or indeed emphasize, as we did already in KMT, that the application of game theory as a mathematical tool does not indicate that the situation described by the model is always in all respects truly a game situation. For this to be the case, deliberate actions of participants, who are sometimes opposed to each other and sometimes cooperate with each other, must occur. When we state, for example, that the government sets a certain rate of savings or consumption, this is to be understood as being done in a *neutral* sense. It is possible to transform the analysis so that there is a real struggle between private consumers, say, and the government as to the allocation of resources and the rate of expansion, thus giving a more realistic picture. Similarly, by using linear programming, we do not claim that the underlying situation is necessarily or correctly one in which a central authority decides in a deterministic way about the allocation of resources. If anything, this is far from reality and far from the substance of our discussion of the open economy. Linear programming in its initial formulation is in some ways *conceptually* a very limited matter: it replaces assumptions of continuous relationships by discontinuous ones and allows for inequalities.[1] This seemingly minor change makes linear programming far more realistic in applications because of the possibility of solving very large scale problems with it, provided the *basic* condition is met: there must exist a central authority on whose acts *alone* the outcome depends (of course, given objective, physical constraints). This must be due to the overriding fact that this authority (person, firm, government) has complete and unchallenged control over *all* variables. The influence of an indifferent nature that merely introduces a probabilistic uncertainty may be nullified by simple statistical procedures [106, p. 10, footnote 2]. Where there is not

---

[k] However, omitting the function of the cock as the reader will have to notice!

[1] Parametric linear programming, which also appears (cf. below and Chapter 4), is of course continuous.

complete, central control, i.e., when the outcome depends on several decision-makers as in game theory, linear programming does not give the complete answer. It can, however, provide answers *ceteris paribus*. We need not pursue this matter any further in the present context, but it will play a role in what follows.

In Chapter 11, a "world model" is presented which evolves naturally from our preceding analysis. This model too has a linear programming solution that depends parametrically on the various control variables, each set of which is controlled by the individual countries making up the "world."

4. Characteristics of Scientific Models

At this point it is opportune to state the proper view of a *model*. A model must fulfill the following requirements.

First, the model should be "similar" to reality. But reality must be perceived, possibly at first, in an intuitive manner. As far as modern economies are concerned, their description is clearly very difficult and complicated. But there can be no question of their expansion or growth in whatever manner this fact is perceived or recorded. Similarity can only be in terms of principal traits of the phenomenon to be mirrored in the model, which therefore is an abstraction from the full reality. Whether this abstraction is justifiable is partly determined by taste and partly by the success of the model itself.

Second, the model must be free of inner contradictions. This property will be determined by a correct use of the *axiomatic* method which we will use freely. The axioms themselves should be individually acceptable, preferably to common sense understanding and formulation. We shall endeavor to show this for each axiom used subsequently together with assuring their compatibility.

The axioms that will be used are stated in terms of variables subject to conditions, as is the case in any empirical science. Our axioms will be free from contradiction (the primary requirement). This is easily established by the fact that we can show simple economies whose solution exists, and this shows that freedom from contradiction is not always an interesting question. Categoricity need not be fulfilled, since there exist many different economies; and independence of the axioms is not an important question for us.[m]

The simplest proof of the usefulness of our axioms is shown by our ability to compute. Some solutions which might give zero prices, or nega-

---

[m] For a discussion of the role of axiomatization see the discussion in Chapter II of von Neumann-Morgenstern [106], which is applicable to the present case.

tive prices, are rejected on general grounds. Others are accepted even when they at first may run counter to intuition or expectations. Their acceptance is then the consequence of the axioms and of the theorems derived from them.

Third, the model must not be "too complicated" lest it cannot be handled, nor "too simple" lest it have no scientific interest or present not enough of a challenge. Clearly, the more similar to reality a model is, the more complicated it will be; ultimately it will be totally unmanageable, given the current state of our analytical instruments and devices. As far as these are concerned, there is frequent change over time: in part we are able to draw on a growing body of mathematical thought, in part the study of a model may require the creation of new mathematics itself. This was, for example, the case with Newton's creation of the differential calculus for the purpose of establishing a theory of mechanics. When adequate mathematics germane to the subject matter is not "available," one may have to fall back on the combinatoric roots of all mathematics until in the end the proper calculus is created or discovered. At Newton's time axiomatics would not have been very helpful; indeed, the development of the axiomatic method is a product of the 20th Century only. Here we can use the method already. The state of our general knowledge of economics and of game theory permits this procedure.

The final test is, of course, as mentioned, the ability to compute. The computations in the present work are a proof of the theory.

It follows from the above that the first concern regarding a proposed model is to prove that it is indeed *workable*, i.e., that meaningful theorems can be established and proved. Such theorems will then be as compatible with each other as the axioms of which they are implications. They illuminate reality further than the immediately given reality as described by—and accessible through—the axioms. As already stated, if these implications are not intuitively acceptable, they nevertheless must be accepted provided the proofs on which they rest are valid. This is standard in scientific development and in the following chapters we will find important examples for such occurrences. Gradually what at first appears to be an "uncommon" result becomes over time more familiar and will ultimately be embedded in the accepted part of the respective science.

This development points up another important aspect of using mathematics. We are concerned with a genuine use of mathematics; with the aid of mathematical tools, old and new, structures are laid bare which are not otherwise accessible. Without mathematics, their existence might at best have been suspected, but could not be proved. Thus in the present work, mathematics is used not as a mere "language," but as an essential instrument for discovery and analysis of structures. To consider mathematics merely to be another language would at any rate be wholly unjustified and contradict the findings of modern logic as is exemplified by the great work of Kurt Gödel.[n]

In general, in the first stages of the development of a new theory, one strives to obtain *existence proofs* for theorems. Such was the case, for example, in the original paper by von Neumann. These proofs are often difficult and at first frequently employ very advanced and uncommon mathematical tools as von Neumann did. In some cases, even new tools must be invented. (In his case, a generalization of a certain fixed point theorem was needed and achieved.) Then, with a gradual, better understanding of the results obtained, it sometimes becomes possible to invent, use and develop simpler tools and devices, and greater clarity of the description can be achieved, until finally even a great discovery can perhaps be communicated in simple form, sometimes even verbally.

During this process, it is desirable to make the important transition (seldom easy and not always possible) from existence proofs to *constructive proofs*. The latter are more desirable because they are usually more transparent, allow illustration by means of simple examples, and often give rise to new ideas. From there the next step is computation in the large, which requires powerful computers and the design of proper algorithms to implement the constructive proof procedures. In the long run, algorithmic efficiency also becomes an important issue. We note as an example of this transition the change from existence proofs for Walrasian systems to the computational methods given by the valuable work of H. Scarf [115].

Our own studies follow these steps. We emphasize, wherever possible, constructive proofs of our theorems and we make every effort to remain at as simple or elementary a mathematical level as possible without making any concession regarding rigor. Even where we enter really new areas, uncharted land, our proofs are elementary and constructive. We avoid mathematical bypaths such as generalized function spaces, etc., in order to stay with the given economic problem. In that sense we are moving in another direction from much of current mathematical economics, still concerned with the older ideas of Walras' type equilibria, where more and more outlying mathematical disciplines, for example, measure theory, nonstandard analysis, etc., are being employed and largely existence theorems are proved.

Though many single steps in what follows are elementary, the theory presented as a whole ceases to be so. Our examples, too, are simple and have a homely flavor and, we hope, appeal, dealing as many of them do, with chickens and eggs. We have made a considerable effort to make these examples accessible to the reader, hoping that thereby the theory itself will be illuminated. At the end of several chapters, we have appended exer-

[n] See Hao Wang [135]; see statements by Gödel there on pp. 8-11 and pp. 324-326. See also Morgenstern [85].

cises, some very elementary and others more difficult. The reader should use the simpler ones to test his immediate understanding of the models presented, but leave the more difficult ones for more intensive study. Finally, sophisticated algorithms are developed, capable of handling large numerical problems and applications speedily. The fact that it has been possible to go through these successive steps proves a certain maturity of the subject matter and of the analysis. While it is clearly possible to carry research further along this path, it will take a profoundly new thought to present a superior model fulfilling all the requirements listed earlier, especially a model that would be more similar to reality—as now perceived—than the present one. But, as will be seen, even the models developed in the following chapters allow us to interpret actual problems and situations to an often astonishing degree, going into the essentials rather than dealing with mere surface phenomena.

At this point, a word of caution regarding observation and measurement is in order. It is necessary to bear in mind what Albert Einstein said: "Most scientists naively think they know what they should observe and how they should measure it."[o] These words also sharply characterize the situation in economics: it is not at all clear which "economic" phenomena should be observed. Is it the production of physical goods, of services, or both in some admixture? Is it expectations, tastes, decisions, money flows, prices, or what? Clearly, not all facts can be observed and measured at once and equally well, since there are infinitely many facts and the choice is difficult. A successful theory depends on a "good" choice; which leads us back to what was said earlier about the similarity of models, intuitive acceptance, and the difficulty of an optimal decision in that respect.

As stated earlier, we attempt to describe fundamental *structures* of an economy. They are hard to discover by any mere description, no matter how rich, because institutional elements also prevail and have an important influence on the behavior of the economy. We refer, in particular, to the organization of the economy as either centrally directed or left alone, i.e., to individual decisions, a state of affairs usually, but not adequately, called "free competition." Though these two types of economies differ greatly, they also, in many important ways, have common characteristics: goods are produced from goods already produced (including labor); there are technological restrictions, i.e., feasibility conditions; there must be an accommodation of output either to the central plan or to the interacting individual preferences, and there must be an accounting or a price system. It is these features which are independent of organization—and obviously of ideologies—that our models will essentially lay bare and many of which are, of course, also found in von Neumann's model from which we start.

---

[o] This comment was made several times by Einstein to Oskar Morgenstern; it has not been possible so far to find a printed source.

Even these basic processes can be subjected to further influences: technological progress (exemplified by the gradual, but sometimes sudden availability of new processes and new commodities), cyclical variations of activity due to ceilings of various kinds, and changes in plans and tastes or goals of the society. These influences can be considered and when done, give rise to interesting variations. These factors produce, in some sense, uncertainty, but uncertainty is not an essential part of our studies. The systematic introduction of uncertainty in its various forms is a difficult task of its own. The analysis of a deterministic system must precede this step and is, as is evident, not only difficult but gives important and rewarding insights in the functioning of the economy.

The absence of uncertainty is also a consequence of the fact that *money* is not considered in the various models. Money is, of course, one of the prime factors causing uncertainty (of a certain type). Our model is linear and deterministic. Neither is there money in the ordinary input-output model except indirectly in that the coefficients used there are obtained from price sums, which, of course, will have been affected by preceding monetary policy and by any other influence upon prices due to the existence of true money.[p] Uncertainty of a different kind is, however, compatible with our model: Whenever a game appears in the model, there is uncertainty as to which coalition in an n-person game will form, which imputation out of a well-defined solution set will materialize, etc.

5. Contraction and Compression

This book is largely concerned with economic *expansion*, but it is well to recall that the title of von Neumann's paper merely indicates that it deals with "a system of economic equations" (more specifically, inequalities) though they describe an expansionary process. As will be seen later (Chapter 10), expansion is only one kind of activity the economy can exhibit. It is possible for it to contract, to run down (though one would not normally be interested in such an economy nor wish to establish one having this property), or to remain stationary (which among other things would probably, but not necessarily, mean the exclusion of some types of technological progress and innovation).[q] More important, it will be shown that by introducing control variables, first done by the authors in 1969, it is possible to modify the original model (as well as the KMT model and our open models) in such a manner that desired growth rates, as well as desired consumption and investment rates, can be chosen deliberately and, if necessary, be

---

[p] We return to this in Chapter 13.

[q] Even an expansion factor $\alpha = 1$ or $\alpha < 1$ would be consistent with technological progress, contrary to widespread beliefs and such theories as Schumpeter's.

changed from time to time according to political, social, or technological circumstances. Given this important extension, it is clearly relevant to study the properties of an expanding economy even in times when many of the world's economies may have to contract. The processes of one type are closely related to those of the other, and it is necessary first to become more familiar with the one that has held most attention of economists.

The use of control variables makes it possible to study at some depth a phenomenon of modern economies, so far little explored by economists, if at all: the *contraction*. A contraction as well as a *compression* [87] is to be distinguished from an ordinary cyclical downswing, which has been attributed variously to monetary policy, to overinvestment, etc. Rather, contraction is due to a basic change in the composition of demand, e.g., a profound shift from civilian to military goods, or a diversion from productive goods to luxury goods. More recently, attention has been drawn to shortages of materials and energy which cannot be overcome by price increases. The problem then arises as to how the economy can adapt itself to the new conditions such that "essential" functions are maintained and to determine what those functions are in the complex interdependent network of activities that makes up an economy. This notion also leads to an important change of the idea of "interdependence" which then is seen *not* to be *mutual* as far as *all* economic activities are concerned, but rather in some cases *sequential* or chainlike.

The distinction between "essential" and "inessential" activities must, of course, not be arbitrary, determined by ideology, etc. Rather the distinction is one whereby some activities can be omitted such that the given rate of expansion is not adversely affected. For example it is possible to abandon musical concerts entirely,[r] but not steel production (beyond a certain point). The energy and resources going into eliminated activities can sometimes be transferred to expand others which, at best, only need to be reduced. These transformations of the economy will be quite different from an ordinary contraction. It should be clear from this that the distinction between essential and inessential is free of value judgement but uses neutral criteria which depend on the technological development of the given economy.

Thus the models developed in the following chapters are of wide applicability in spite of their seeming simplicity and the severe constraints imposed upon them. Chapters 8 and 10 give specific examples of many interesting phenomena that can be analyzed with the aid of these models.

The power of these models is also not diminished by the fact that they are parametrically *linear* in equations and inequalities. Naturally, any linear theory is preferable to a nonlinear one because of its greater mathe-

---

[r] There is some parallel in this operation to the phenomenon of the "removable" set of players in certain *n*-person games. (Cf. von Neumann-Morgenstern [106] pp. 533-535.)

matical accessibility. Linearization is a widely practiced art in science, of course. In particular, the operations research literature contains many examples of the modeling of nonlinear situations using linear methods [15, 18, 28, 59]. We do not exclude the possibility that further work may show that some kinds of nonlinearities are so important that linearization will not work.

6. Controlled Changes of Expansion

The von Neumann expanding economy model with all our revisions, extensions, and generalizations so far mentioned would properly be called a *dynamic* model. It is indeed different from any strictly *static* model, where time after time exactly the same things happen. Yet the model is thus far not truly dynamic, because the economy is expanding at a *fixed* rate at which it is in equilibrium. In that sense, it too is "static." We distinguish it therefore from the new case which we introduce where, due to the previously mentioned availability of *control variables*, we can allow the rate of expansion to be changed deliberately from period to period according to some goals given to the economy.

An economy of this type is described by a model much richer than the other ones (cf. Chapter 9). It is possible for the economy to attach a *utility* to a specific expansion factor or to imports or exports. For example, an economy, for its own reasons, may wish to be an important factor in the world export market. In order to do so, it may have to reduce its expansion rate below its attainable maximum so as, instead, to maximize its exports and to provide a desired balance between essential and inessential goods. One could also include a cost factor for changing the control parameter or change the utility function, etc. All this will be considered in Chapter 9 after the necessary groundwork has been laid.

Although we have gone a long way from the original von Neumann model, we do not assert that other extensions may not be possible beyond those we have made ourselves. In fact, at various places in the text, we have indicated problems giving directions for further research. In Chapter 14, we discuss specifically both empirical and theoretical questions that are worthy of further study.

2

The KMT[a] Closed Model

1. Introduction

We consider a model of a closed economy that has a finite set of m processes and that produces a finite set of n different goods. Each process may produce one or more goods, and there may be alternative ways of producing any given good. Thus we do not make any mathematical assumption about the relationship between m and n. However, from an economic point of view, one usually has $m > n$ because, for most goods, there are several alternative production processes. These processes may represent manufacturing but they may also represent consumption, storage, services, and (as we show later) outside, or even foreign, demand. We assume constant returns to scale and at first—but only at first—the unlimited availability of the natural factors of production, such as labor and land. Our model will operate within a discrete time interval and is *closed* in the sense that the inputs needed for the processes at time t are the outputs produced by the economy during the preceding time $t - 1$, plus the natural factors of production. (In Chapter 4, we will consider an *open* economic model in which there is the additional possibility of exporting and/or importing goods to or from an "outside world.")

Each process operates at an *intensity* x, where x is a real non-negative number. In the present chapter we assume that these intensities are normalized so that the ith process operates at intensity x_i, where $0 \le x_i \le 1$ and $\sum_{i=1}^{m} x_i = 1$. Thus the (row) *intensity vector* $x = (x_1, \ldots, x_m)$ shall be viewed as an m-dimensional probability vector. It will be convenient to state this fact in vector form as

$$x \ge 0, \qquad xf = 1 \tag{1}$$

where f is an m-component column vector, all of whose entries are 1s. Even though normalized, the component x_i should be interpreted as still retaining its original units. Thus each component of the x-vector will have its own units.[b]

---

[a] KMT stands for the Kemeny, Morgenstern, Thompson model first published in the paper [48]. This chapter is almost exclusively based on that paper.

[b] Here and elsewhere we shall use the convention that if u and v are vectors, then $u \ge v$ means that the corresponding inequalities are true for the corresponding components of u and v. Also, we shall not distinguish between the number zero and the zero vector since the context will always be clear. The transpose of a vector or a matrix will be denoted by a prime; thus y' is the transpose of y, and A' is the transpose of A.

When the ith process is operating, it requires a_{ij} units of good j and produces b_{ik} units of good k ($j, k = 1, \ldots , n$). Thus we assume that a_{ij} and b_{ij} are non-negative numbers measured in appropriate technological units for all i and j. Symbolically, we can represent physical production change during one time period as follows:

$$\text{(time } t - 1) \qquad xA \rightarrow xB \qquad \text{(time } t)$$

where A and B are non-negative $m \times n$ matrices with entries a_{ij} and b_{ij}, respectively. The components of the vector xA give the inputs used up in production and the components of the vector xB give the outputs.

Each good is assigned a *price y*, where y is a real non-negative number. Prices are also normalized so that the jth good is assigned price y_j, where $0 \leq y_j \leq 1$ and $\Sigma_{y=1}^{m} y_j = 1$. Thus the (column) *price vector* $y = (y_1, \ldots , y_n)'$ is an n-dimensional probability vector satisfying

$$y \geq 0, \qquad ey = 1 \tag{2}$$

where e is an n-component row vector, all of whose entries are 1s. Because y_j is a normalized price, it is a pure number. Symbolically, we can represent value changes during one time period as follows:

$$\text{(time } t - 1) \qquad Ay \rightarrow By \qquad \text{(time } t)$$

The components of the vector Ay give the values of the inputs entering into the production processes and the components of By give the values of their outputs.

It is assumed in the model that there is an *interest rate b* (percent) from which we derive the *interest factor* $\beta = 1 + b/100$ for convenience in writing formulas. The purpose of the interest rate or interest factor is to enable us to compare the value of a bundle of goods during period $t - 1$ with the value of the same or another bundle of goods during period t. In this sense it can be considered a *technological* interest rate. It is also assumed that there is an expansion rate a (percent) from which we derive the *expansion factor* $\alpha = 1 + a/100$. The expansion rate or factor permits us to compare the volume of production during the period $t - 1$ with that during period t, as far as the input-output processes are concerned.

Because of the assumed unlimited supplies of "land and labor," i.e., the original means of production, expansion can continue indefinitely. What we want to do is discover conditions under which there is an *equilibrium* path, along which the economy can maintain balanced growth.

Labor, land, and other natural factors must be treated as free since they are not produced.[c] But there are simple means for entering the costs

---

[c] In the open model (Chapter 4) there may even be foreign finished goods received *free*, i.e., as foreign aid.

connected with these factors in the model. For instance, the cost of labor can be introduced in terms of the reproduction-consumption of the worker and his family. Using this approach, consumer goods become the inputs of every process. (We will go into this point in more detail in Chapter 6.)

2. Axioms for the Model

By an *equilibrium solution* to the model we shall mean vectors x and y and numbers α and β that satisfy the following five axioms. We use the word axiom here to indicate a precise description of an economic requirement, not in the sense of mathematical logic.

The *first axiom* states the conservation condition that the outputs of time $(t - 1)$, which are xB, limit the inputs at time t, namely $\alpha x A$. In inequality form, this is

Axiom (C1): $xB \geq \alpha x A$ or $x(B - \alpha A) \geq 0$

In other words, this axiom states that the inputs for one period can only be supplied from the outputs of the preceding period, i.e., the economy is *closed*.

The *second axiom* makes the economy profitless, that is, the value βy of the outputs should not be more than the discounted value $\beta A y$ of the inputs needed to make them. In inequality form, we have

Axiom (C2): $By \leq \beta A y$ or $(B - \beta A)y \leq 0$

Both these conditions will be relaxed in the open model of Chapter 4.

The *third axiom* requires that a zero price be charged for goods that are overproduced, that is, those goods for which the inequality in Axiom (C1) is strict; in other words,

Axiom (C3): $x(B - \alpha A)y = 0$

Observe that Axiom (C3) means that overproduced goods can be disposed of without cost. We shall occasionally refer to this as the *free disposal condition*.

The *fourth* axiom is

Axiom (C4): $x(B - \beta A)y = 0$

which requires inefficient processes, that is, those for which the inequality in Axiom (C2) is strict, to be used with zero intensity.

The *fifth* axiom is

Axiom (C5): $xBy > 0$

which requires that the total value of all goods produced, i.e., the sum of the products of outputs times prices, must be positive.

Example 2-1. In order to fix on these ideas, we consider a chicken farm as a simple economy.[d] There are two processes (laying eggs and hatching eggs) and two goods (chickens and eggs). Let us consider a one-month time period and assume that during this period a laying chicken will lay 12 eggs and a hatching chicken will hatch four chickens. The A and B matrices are as follows:

$$A = \begin{array}{c} \\ \text{Laying Eggs} \\ \\ \text{Hatching Eggs} \end{array} \begin{array}{cc} \text{Chicken} & \text{Egg} \\ \left(\begin{array}{cc} 1 & 0 \\ & \\ 1 & 4 \end{array} \right) \end{array}$$

$$B = \begin{array}{c} \\ \text{Laying Eggs} \\ \\ \text{Hatching Eggs} \end{array} \begin{array}{cc} \text{Chicken} & \text{Egg} \\ \left(\begin{array}{cc} 1 & 12 \\ & \\ 5 & 0 \end{array} \right) \end{array}$$

Thus for the laying process we need one chicken as input, and we get that chicken plus 12 eggs as output. And for the hatching process, we need one chicken plus four eggs as input and we get the original chicken plus four new ones as outputs. This means that *we are considering joint production from the outset;* we need only chickens to lay eggs, but we need both chickens and eggs to produce more chickens (we ignore the possibility of incubators).

We will eventually describe how to solve this model, but for now, note that the following quantities provide the solution:

$$x = (1/2, 1/2), \qquad y = \begin{pmatrix} 6/7 \\ \\ 1/7 \end{pmatrix}, \qquad \alpha = \beta = 3.$$

Thus if the farmer begins with two chickens and four eggs and runs both processes with equal intensity, he will have six chickens and 12 eggs after one time period, 18 chickens and 36 eggs after two time periods, etc. This input-output process is shown for three stages in Figure 2-1. He can continue this process (assuming no other limitations) in equilibrium indefinitely. From the equilibrium price vector y we see that the equilibrium prices make a chicken six times as valuable as an egg.

---

[d]This example is taken from [50], second edition, pp. 434-440.

	Time Period						
	1		*2*		*3*		
Laying	1		3		9		...
Hatching	1		3		9		...
Chickens		6		18		54	...
Eggs	4	12	12	36	36	108	...

Figure 2-1

3. The von Neumann Assumption

Without further assumptions about the matrices A and B, there may be no solution satisfying the above axioms. Consider the following example.

Example 2-2: For the economy with

$$A = \begin{pmatrix} 0 & 0 \\ 0 & 1 \end{pmatrix}, \quad B = \begin{pmatrix} 0 & 1 \\ 1 & 0 \end{pmatrix}$$

we have

$$B - \alpha A = \begin{pmatrix} 0 & 1 \\ 1 & -\alpha \end{pmatrix}$$

and from Axiom (C2),

$$(B - \alpha A)y = \begin{pmatrix} y_2 \\ y_1 - \alpha y_2 \end{pmatrix} \leq \begin{pmatrix} 0 \\ 0 \end{pmatrix}$$

Since $y_2 \geq 0$ from (2), it follows that $y_2 = 0$. From this it follows that $y_1 \leq 0$ and so $y_1 = 0$ also; but then we cannot satisfy $y_1 + y_2 = 1$. Since there are no equilibrium prices, we cannot satisfy Axioms (C2) through (C4). Hence the model does not have a solution.

In his original expanding economy model [105] von Neumann had the first four Axioms, but not Axiom (C5). Example 2-2 shows that further assumptions are needed for his model. Von Neumann made the following assumption:

Assumption (AO): $A + B > 0$

With this assumption he was able to prove that an equilibrium solution always exists to his model. [Note that Assumption (AO) is satisfied in Example 2-1 but is not satisfied in Example 2-2.]

If we write (AO) in component form, we get $a_{ij} + b_{ij} > 0$ for all i and j. The intuitive meaning of this assumption is that every process must either consume or produce a positive amount of every good. Von Neumann made this assumption to ensure the uniqueness of α and to prevent the economy from breaking up into subeconomies. This is clearly a very strong condition, we will remove it in the next section. Nevertheless, we will see later that when the model is highly aggregated or when there is outside demand, Assumption (AO) will be automatically satisfied.

Example 2-3:   Suppose that the chicken farmer of Example 2-1 also raises wheat to feed his chickens. The model now becomes

$$
\begin{array}{c}
\quad\quad\quad\quad\quad \text{Wheat}\ \ \text{Chicken}\ \ \text{Egg} \\
\begin{array}{l} \text{Wheat} \\ \text{Laying} \\ \text{Hatching} \end{array}
\quad A = \left(\begin{array}{ccc} 1 & 0 & 0 \\ 1 & 1 & 0 \\ 1 & 1 & 4 \end{array} \right),
\end{array}
$$

$$
\begin{array}{c}
\quad\quad\quad\quad\quad \text{Wheat}\ \ \text{Chicken}\ \ \text{Egg} \\
\begin{array}{l} \text{Wheat} \\ \text{Laying} \\ \text{Hatching} \end{array}
\quad B = \left(\begin{array}{ccc} 9 & 0 & 0 \\ 0 & 1 & 12 \\ 0 & 5 & 0 \end{array} \right)
\end{array}
$$

Note that we assume that planting one unit of wheat gives nine units back at the end of the period, and that each chicken needs one unit of wheat each period for food. Since $a_{13} + b_{13} = a_{23} + b_{23} = 0$, the example does not satisfy (AO). It can be shown, however, that there are two possible equilibrium solutions with different expansion rates:

$$\textit{Solution } 1:\ \alpha = \beta = 9, \quad\quad x = (1,0,0) \quad\quad y = \begin{pmatrix} 1 \\ 0 \\ 0 \end{pmatrix}$$

$$\textit{Solution } 2:\ \alpha = \beta = 3, \quad\quad x = \left(\frac{1}{3}, \frac{1}{3}, \frac{1}{3} \right), \quad\quad y = \begin{pmatrix} 0 \\ 6/7 \\ 1/7 \end{pmatrix}$$

In Solution 1, only wheat is produced and the expansion rate is nine. (Later, in Chapter 5, we will define the idea of a subeconomy, show that the wheat industry is one and explain how Solution 1 corresponds to running the wheat subeconomy only.) Solution 2 represents the case in which all three industries are operated and all three products are produced. Note, however, that here wheat has a zero equilibrium price, a defect that we will remove in Section 7. (Other ways of overcoming zero prices for over-produced goods will be discussed in Chapters 4 and 5.)

If we observe that the numbers a_{ij} and b_{ij} can be made extremely small, we can see that Assumption (AO) can be satisfied without changing the model very much. We will see later that there are many realistic situations in which (AO) is naturally satisfied, as in the following example.

Example 2-4: Suppose that the chicken farmer of Example 2-1 takes into account the labor needed to operate his chicken farm. The model now becomes:

$$
\begin{array}{c}
\\
\text{Laying} \\
\text{Hatching} \quad A = \\
\text{Labor}
\end{array}
\begin{array}{ccc}
\text{Chicken} & \text{Egg} & \text{Labor} \\
\left(\begin{array}{ccc}
1 & 0 & 1 \\
1 & 4 & 1 \\
4 & 8 & 0
\end{array} \right) ,
\end{array}
$$

$$
\begin{array}{c}
\\
\text{Laying} \\
\text{Hatching} \quad B = \\
\text{Labor}
\end{array}
\begin{array}{ccc}
\text{Chicken} & \text{Egg} & \text{Labor} \\
\left(\begin{array}{ccc}
1 & 12 & 0 \\
5 & 0 & 0 \\
0 & 0 & 2
\end{array} \right)
\end{array}
$$

Here the inputs to the labor industry serve merely to provide for the consumption of four chickens and eight eggs by the workers during each time period. The workers are needed for each of the laying and hatching industries as indicated. The reader can now verify that the following quantities satisfy the axioms.

$$
\alpha = \beta = 1, \qquad x = \left(\frac{1}{3}, \frac{1}{3}, \frac{1}{3} \right), \qquad y = \left(\begin{array}{c} 4/17 \\ 1/17 \\ 12/17 \end{array} \right)
$$

It should be observed that in the present example we have $A + B > 0$, so that the von Neumann's Assumption (AO) is satisfied. Thus by paying workers in real goods, the economy has been tied together and has a unique expansion rate. This is also an example of a stationary economy, i.e., one having zero expansion rate.

Observe that the following uninteresting economies satisfy Axioms (C1) through (C4) and Assumption (AO).

Example 2-5: Let A and B be matrices with $a_{ij} = 1$ and $b_{ij} = 0$ for all i and j; let $\alpha = \beta = 0$ and let x and y be arbitrary probability vectors. This is an economy that uses raw materials but produces nothing.

Example 2-6: Let $a_{ij} = 0$ and $b_{ij} = 1$ for all i and j; let $\alpha = \beta = \infty$ and let x and y be arbitrary probability vectors. This is an economy that produces outputs without any inputs! The model even satisfies Axiom (C5)!

Neither of these examples corresponds to economic reality; they do, however, fit into the original von Neumann model as special limiting cases. In the next section, we make different, economically plausible, assumptions that will rule them out.

4. The KMT Assumptions

Instead of using Assumption (AO), our principal assumptions will be the following two: *First*, every process uses some inputs, i.e., goods produced in the preceding time period. This can be stated as

Assumption (A1): Every row of A has at least one positive entry.

Second, every good can be produced in the economy, i.e., given a good, there is some process in the economy that can produce it. This can be stated as

Assumption (A2): Every column of B has at least one positive entry.

(*Note*: Examples 2-2 and 2-6 violate Assumption (A1) while Example 2-5 violates Assumption (A2).

Example 2-3 does not satisfy (AO) but does satisfy the new (KMT) conditions (A1) and (A2). Thus the two new conditions admit a much wider class of economic phenomena than the original condition.

These two conditions are clearly economically meaningful because there is no known physical process that produces physical outputs without any physical inputs. Also, if a certain good cannot be produced by any process in the economy, then there is no point in including it.[e]

5. Interpretation as a Game Theory Problem

The rest of the analysis in this chapter makes use of concepts and theorems from matrix game theory. In Appendix 1 there is a brief discussion of this concept, and references are given to more complete expositions. In the

---

[e] In Chapter 5 we shall see that, with these assumptions, the model can break up into a finite number of subeconomies, each with its own expansion rate. And there is a constructive algorithm for calculating all these expansion rates in Chapter 3.

next chapter we will give an alternate approach using linear programming ideas.

Game theory is here used as a mathematical tool in order to obtain mathematical results (of which only those having economic meaning are admitted). Game theory appears, therefore, as a mathematical technique, comparable to, say, the calculus of variations or group theory. This use of the theory does not preclude its application to a large stationary or expanding economy in a very different sense, i.e., as a model, for example, when the participants in the economy are viewed as playing a nonzero sum n-person game. In the latter case, results may be obtained that are different from those we find here, especially because of the possibility of the formation of coalitions among the players. The emergence of the theory of games as a strictly mathematical tool for the analysis of more conventional economic situations, besides its role as a model of economic reality, is a noteworthy phenomenon and gives it unusual significance for the economist.

We now restate conditions (A1) and (A2) in game-theoretical terms: We consider B and $-A$ as matrix games, where the maximizing player controls the rows and the minimizing player controls the columns. Let $v(B)$ and $v(-A)$ be the values of each of these games. Then, remembering that the entries of A and B are non-negative, it is easy to see (e.g., Exercises 6 and 7) that the conditions (A1) and (A2) are equivalent to the conditions

$$v(-A) < 0 \qquad\qquad\qquad \text{(A1)}$$

and

$$v(B) > 0 \qquad\qquad\qquad \text{(A2)}$$

If we have numbers α and β and vectors x and y that satisfy Axioms (C1) through (C5), then these quantities will provide solutions to the economic model that hold in *every time period*. We then say that the economy is in *equilibrium*.

We can now interpret the whole problem in game-theoretic terms. It will become clear that some parts of the problem which are of game-theoretic interest are not of economic interest. Therefore we need the following lemma.

LEMMA 2-1: If x, y, α, and β are solutions satisfying Axioms (C1) through (C5), then $\alpha = \beta = xBy/xAy$.

Proof: From (C5) we see that $xBy > 0$; hence from (C3) and (C4), $xBy = \alpha xAy = \beta xAy > 0$. From the last equation, we see that $xAy > 0$ so that $\alpha = \beta = xBy/xAy$.

Thus we only need to look for solutions in which $\alpha = \beta$; in other words, the model requires that the interest rate equal the expansion rate. Under this assumption, Axiom (C4) becomes the same as Axiom (C3). Making the abbreviation $M_\alpha = B - \alpha A$, the conditions of the model become

$$xM_\alpha \geq 0 \tag{3}$$

$$M_\alpha y \leq 0 \tag{4}$$

$$xBy > 0 \tag{5}$$

Observe that we have omitted expression (C3) [and its equivalent (C4)]. This is permissible since, if we have a solution to (3) and (4), then the solutions must satisfy Axiom (C3) as well. To see this, we multiply (3) by y, obtaining $xM_\alpha y \geq 0$; and we multiply (4) by x, obtaining $xM_\alpha y \leq 0$. These two expressions imply that $xM_\alpha y = 0$, which is (C3).

If we interpret M_α as a matrix game where the maximizing player controls the rows and the minimizing player controls the columns, we see that (3) and (4) imply that $v(M_\alpha) = 0$. Moreover, (3) and (4) show that the solutions x and y to the economic problem are optimal strategies in the game M_α. We now restate our problem in game-theoretic terms.

Problem: Given non-negative $m \times n$ matrices A and B such that $v(-A) < 0$ and $v(B) > 0$, we set $M_\alpha = B + \alpha(-A)$ and find an α such that $v(M_\alpha) = 0$. Then we find a pair of probability vectors (x,y) such that $xBy > 0$ and such that x is optimal for the maximizing player and y is optimal for the minimizing player in the game M_α.

We shall call an α such that $v(M_\alpha) = 0$ an *allowable* α. Even if we can find an allowable α we will have to distinguish between two types of pairs of optimal strategies in the game M_α. If (x,y) is a pair of optimal strategies for M_α such that $xBy > 0$, we call these *economic solutions* to the game M_α; on the other hand, if (x',y') is a pair of optimal strategies for M_α such that $x'By' = 0$, we call them *noneconomic* solutions to the game M_α. It turns out that if the expansion rate is not unique (and perhaps even if it is unique, see Exercises 10, 11), then there always exist noneconomic solutions to the game. Since we are not interested in finding noneconomic solutions, we do not emphasize them, and in this sense our problem becomes more economic than game-theoretic.

6. Existence of Economic Solutions

The purpose of this section is to discuss, under Assumptions (A1) and (A2), the existence of economic solutions to Axioms (C1), (C2), and (C3).

Let S_m be the set of all m-dimensional probability vectors and let S_n be the set of all n-dimensional probability vectors. In what follows we shall use $x \, \varepsilon \, S_n$ to denote a strategy for the maximizing player in M_α and $y \, \varepsilon \, S_n$ to denote a strategy for the minimizing player in M_α.

Lemma 2-2: If α' and $\alpha''\,(<_{\alpha'})$ are two distinct allowable values of α (that is, $v(M_{\alpha'}) = v(M_{\alpha''}) = 0$), then $v(M_\alpha) = 0$ for α in the interval $_{\alpha'} \geq \alpha \geq _{\alpha''}$. Moreover, if x' is optimal in $M_{\alpha'}$ and y'' is optimal in $M_{\alpha''}$, then the pair (x', y'') is optimal in M_α for all α in the same interval.

Proof: Let x' be an optimal strategy for the maximizing player in the game $M_{\alpha'}$; then $x'M_{\alpha'} \geq 0$. If α is any number less than α', we have

$$x'M_\alpha = x'(B - \alpha A) = x'(B - \alpha'A) + x'(\alpha' - \alpha)A \geq 0.$$

Hence $v(M_\alpha) \geq 0$.

Similarly, let y'' be optimal for the minimizing player in $M_{\alpha''}$; then $M_{\alpha''}y'' \leq 0$. If α is any number greater than α'', we have

$$M_\alpha y'' = (B - \alpha A)y'' = (B - \alpha''A)y'' + (\alpha'' - \alpha)Ay'' \leq 0.$$

Hence $v(M_\alpha) \leq 0$.

The inequalities obtained at the conclusion of each of the two paragraphs above show that $v(M_\alpha) = 0$ and also show that (x', y'') are optimal strategies in the game M_α for $\alpha' \geq \alpha \geq \alpha''$. This concludes the proof of the lemma.

Corollary: If (AO) holds, then there is at most one allowable α.

Proof: Suppose there were two such, α and α', with $\alpha > \alpha'$. Then let (x,y) and (x',y') be two economic solutions corresponding to these allowable α's. By the lemma, the pair (x, y') is optimal at α and α' so that

$$xM_\alpha y' = xBy' - \alpha xAy' = 0$$

and

$$xM_{\alpha'}y' = xBy' - \alpha'xAy' = 0.$$

Subtracting these two equations, we have

$$(\alpha' - \alpha)xAy' = 0$$

and subtracting α times the second from α' times the first we get

$$(\alpha' - \alpha)xBy' = 0.$$

Hence we see that $xAy' = xBy' = 0$. Since x and y' are probability vectors, we can choose indices i and j such that $x_i y'_j > 0$; then necessarily

$$x_i a_{ij} y'_j = x_i b_{ij} y'_j = 0$$

so that $a_{ij} = b_{ij} = 0$ which contradicts condition (AO).

Theorem 2-1: There are at most $\min(m,n)$ allowable α's for which economic solutions to M_α exist.

Proof: For each such α there is a pair (x,y) so that $xBy > 0$; hence for each such α we can choose components (x_i, y_j) so that $x_i b_{ij} y_j > 0$; hence $xB^{(j)} > 0$. Then (C1) and (C3) imply that $xA^{(j)} > 0$. (A *single* superscript j on a matrix indicates the jth column of that matrix.) We next show that the indices of the components so chosen are different for different such allowable α's. Let γ and δ be two such allowable α's with $\gamma > \delta$, and let the corresponding component pairs (x_i, y_j) and (x_h, y_k) be such that

$$x_i b_{ij} y_j > 0 \quad \text{and} \quad x_h b_{hk} y_k > 0$$

We must show that $i \neq h$ and $j \neq k$. We will show that $j \neq k$ and the proof of the other assertion is similar. Suppose, on the contrary, that $j = k$. By Lemma 2-2 there is a strategy x (corresponding to $\alpha = \gamma$) for the maximizing player which is optimal in M_α for $\delta \leq \alpha \leq \gamma$. Then, letting $M_\alpha^{(j)}$ be the jth column of M_α, we have

$$xM_\gamma^{(j)} \geq 0 \quad \text{and} \quad xM_\delta^{(j)} \geq 0$$

However, since

$$xM_\delta^j = (xB^j - \gamma xA^j) + (\gamma - \delta)xA^j = xM_\gamma^j + (\gamma - \delta)xA^j$$

we see that

$$xM_\delta^j = xM_\delta^k > 0$$

By condition (C3), this implies that $y_k = 0$ which, in turn, implies that $x_h b_{hk} y_k = 0$, contrary to the way in which y_k was chosen.

Since to each allowable α for which there are economic solutions there corresponds an entry $b_{ij} > 0$ in the matrix B, and since the indices of two such entries are pairwise distinct, we see that the maximum number of such allowable α's is equal to the longest diagonal which can be chosen in B. Because B is an $m \times n$ matrix, the longest such diagonal is $\min(m,n)$. This completes the proof of the theorem.

Theorem 2-2 *(Existence Theorem):*

(a) If Assumptions (A1) and (A2) hold, then there is at least one and at most a finite number of allowable α's for which the game M_α has economic solutions.

(b) *(von Neumann).* If Assumption (AO) holds, then there is a unique allowable α.

(c) If Assumptions (AO), (A1), and (A2) hold, then there is a unique allowable α; moreover, for that α the game M_α has economic solutions.

Proof:

(a) A nonconstructive proof of this theorem is given in the proof of Theorem 3-5 of Section 5, Chapter 3. Also given at the end of Chapter 5 is a short historical discussion of the various alternative proofs devised for the theorem since it was first proved in 1955. A constructive method for finding all solutions to the KMT model is provided by the algorithm of Section 6 of Chapter 3.

(b) This theorem was first proved by von Neumann (see Appendix 3). It is interesting to note that under Assumption (AO) alone, one cannot prove the existence of solutions which satisfy Axiom (C5). Example 2-5 has no solution satisfying (C5).

(c) This theorem follows from (a) and the Corollary to Lemma 2-1.

Example 2-2 does not satisfy either (AO) or (A1) and does not have an economic solution. Examples 2-1 and 2-4 satisfy (AO) and hence have a unique expansion rate. Example 2-3 satisfies (A1) and (A2), but not (AO). As indicated, it has two economic expansion factors, $\alpha = 9$ and $\alpha = 3$.

Theorem 2-1 states that there are at most a finite number of allowable α's. Observe that for each allowable α there is at least one, but there may be an infinite number of strategy pairs (x, y), which give economic solutions (see Appendix 1).

Also observe that we can prove nothing concerning the magnitudes of the α's except that they are positive and less than infinity. Obviously, an α greater than 1 (as in Example 2-1) corresponds to an expanding economy (*expansion rate* and *interest rate* positive); an α equal to 1 (as in Example 2-4) corresponds to a stationary economy (*expansion rate* and *interest rate* zero); and an α less than 1 (see Section 4, Chapter 10) corresponds to a contracting economy (*expansion rate* and *interest rate* negative). Other examples are given in Exercise 12.

7. Relaxation of the Free Goods and Inefficient Processes Restrictions

Let us make the ideas of free goods and inefficient processes more precise.

Definition: Let $\alpha = \beta$ be an allowable expansion factor which has economic solutions, and let (x, y) be a pair of economic solutions corresponding to this α.

Good j is free relative to the solution (x,y) if and only if in this solution $x(B^{(j)} - \alpha A^{(j)}) > 0$ so that to satisfy condition (C3), $y_j = 0$. ($A^{(j)}$ and $B^{(j)}$ indicate the jth columns of these matrices.)

Process i is inefficient relative to the solution (x, y) if and only if in this solution $(B_{(i)} - \beta A_{(i)})y < 0$ so that to satisfy condition (C4), $x_i = 0$. ($A_{(i)}$ and $B_{(i)}$ indicate the ith rows of these matrices.)

Note that for a given expansion rate α and an economic solution (x,y), the good j may be free, while for another expansion rate α' (or perhaps even for the same expansion rate) and another solution (x',y') it could happen that good j would not be free. On the other hand, there might well be goods that are free in every economic solution. (See the definition of the set J^* in Chapter 5.) Completely analogous remarks can be made about inefficient processes.

If we are considering a deterministic model, conditions (C3) and (C4) are not unreasonable. If, on the other hand, we consider that the entries in the matrices A and B are technological coefficients and hence subject to possible error, it seems unreasonable that small changes in the entries of the matrices A and B should change free goods or inefficient processes into efficient processes and vice versa. Nevertheless, this can happen as shown by the following examples.

Example 2-7: Consider the following matrices:

$$
A = A' = \begin{pmatrix} 1 & \varepsilon \\ \varepsilon & 1 \end{pmatrix}, \quad B = \begin{pmatrix} 1 & 2\varepsilon \\ \varepsilon & 1 + \varepsilon \end{pmatrix}, \quad B' = \begin{pmatrix} 1 + \varepsilon & \varepsilon \\ 2\varepsilon & 1 \end{pmatrix}
$$

where $\varepsilon > 0$, and consider the two models $M_\alpha = B - \alpha A$ and $M'_\alpha = B' - \alpha'A'$. The unique expansion rates for each of these models is $\alpha = \alpha' = 1$. Thus we have

$$
M_1 = \begin{pmatrix} 0 & \varepsilon \\ 0 & \varepsilon \end{pmatrix} \quad \text{and} \quad M'_1 = \begin{pmatrix} \varepsilon & 0 \\ \varepsilon & 0 \end{pmatrix}
$$

so that good one has unit price in the first model but is free in the second, while good two is free in the first model but has unit price in the second. Observe that

$$
B' - B = \begin{pmatrix} \varepsilon & -\varepsilon \\ \varepsilon & -\varepsilon \end{pmatrix}
$$

so that each entry in the matrix B' differs from the corresponding entry in the matrix B by at most ε so that a small change in the technological coefficients can radically change the price structure.

Example 2-8: Consider the following matrices:

$$A = A' = \begin{pmatrix} 1 & 2\varepsilon \\ 2\varepsilon & 1 \end{pmatrix}, \quad B = \begin{pmatrix} 1 - \varepsilon & \varepsilon \\ 2\varepsilon & 1 \end{pmatrix}, \quad B' = \begin{pmatrix} 1 & 2\varepsilon \\ \varepsilon & 1 - \varepsilon \end{pmatrix}$$

where $\varepsilon > 0$, and consider the two models $M_\alpha = B - \alpha A$ and $M'_\alpha = B' - \alpha'A'$. The unique expansion rates for each of these models is $\alpha = \alpha' = 1$. Thus we have

$$M_1 = \begin{pmatrix} -\varepsilon & -\varepsilon \\ 0 & 0 \end{pmatrix} \quad \text{and} \quad M'_1 + \begin{pmatrix} 0 & 0 \\ -\varepsilon & -\varepsilon \end{pmatrix}$$

so that process one is inefficient and process two is used with unit intensity in the first model, while process one is used with unit intensity in the second model and process two is inefficient. Again a small change in coefficients can radically change the intensity structure.

These examples are extreme and are partly the result of using a linear model, but they do illustrate the possible economic unreality of conditions (C3) and (C4). Suppose now that we had a solution which satisfies conditions (C1), (C2), and (C5), but not necessarily conditions (C3) and (C4). In order for (C2) and (C5) to be satisfied, we must have $xAy > 0$. Hence we can define the following ratios:

$r = xM_\alpha y/xAy =$ the ratio of the value of overproduced goods to the value of inputs;

$s = xM_\beta y/xAy =$ the ratio of the value of inefficient processes to the value of inputs.

Clearly condition (C3) is equivalent to the condition $r = 0$ and condition (C4) is equivalent to $s = 0$. If we are only looking for solutions to (C1), (C2), and (C5), then the most we can say is that $r \geq 0$ and $s \leq 0$, which follow easily from (C1) and (C2).

Theorem 2-3: If (AO) or (A1) and (A2) hold, then there always exist numbers α and β and probability vectors (x, y) satisfying conditions (C1), (C2), and (C5); moreover, for each such solution, $\beta - \alpha = r - s \geq 0$ so that $\beta \geq \alpha$ always.

Proof: Let r be any nonnegative number; let s be any nonpositive number; and consider the following expressions:

$$xM_{\alpha+r} \geq 0 \qquad \qquad \text{(6)}$$

$$M_{\beta+s}y \leq 0 \qquad \qquad \text{(7)}$$

$$xM_{\alpha+r}y = 0 \qquad \qquad \text{(8)}$$

$$xM_{\beta+s}\,y = 0 \qquad \qquad \text{(9)}$$

$$xBy > 0 \qquad \qquad \text{(10)}$$

These expressions are the same as expressions (C1) through (C5) of Section 2 if we replace α by $\alpha + r$ and β by $\beta + s$. It is easy to check that if (6) is satisfied, then so is (C1), and if (7) is satisfied, then so is (C2). Hence, if we can find a solution to (6) through (9) and (C5), it will furnish us automatically with a solution to (C1), (C2), and (C5). However, if (A1) or (A2) is satisfied, then our existence theorem (Theorem 2-2) immediately gives a solution to (6) through (9) and (C5) and shows that $\alpha + r = \beta + s$, completing the proof of the theorem.

Since r can be any nonnegative number and s can be any nonpositive number, there is a continuum of such solutions. It is economically reasonable to require that r and s be made small enough in absolute value so that α and β are positive, since negative expansion or interest *factors* do not have economic meaning. The paradox raised in the two examples discussed above can now be resolved by letting r and s take on nonzero values.

Examples 2-7 and 2-8 are reconsidered in the light of these results in Exercises 14 and 15.

A final remark can be made for the case when $r = 0$. A plausible assumption is that r, the ratio of the value of the overproduced goods to the total value of the inputs, should be very small compared to one, that is, $r \ll 1$. From the results of the above theorem, we than see that

$$0 < \beta - \alpha = r \ll 1$$

In other words, if we replace condition (3) by the assumption that the value of the overproduced goods is very small compared to the value of the inputs, then solutions to the economy exist with the expansion rate only slightly lower than the interest rate. Analogous remarks can be made about the ratio s when $r = 0$ and when both r and s are close to zero.

Still another way of handling the free goods and inefficient processes conditions can be obtained by adding *constraints* to the game. For example, by putting constraints to prevent overproduction of a given (formerly free) good, we can find solutions in which that good has a positive price. (See Exercise 16.) We shall make use of this device further in Chapters 5 and 11.

8. The Introduction of Demand Into the KMT Model

We now add to the KMT model the requirement that at each time period the economy should supply to an outside consumer a vector d of goods already being produced by the economy. Hence d is a $1 \times n$ row vector. We assume that d is always a constant fraction of the output at any given time, i.e., that the outside additional demand is expanding at the same rate as the economy.

The introduction of outside demand into the model opens up several new avenues of approach, some of which shall be studied or at least mentioned. The outside demand may be physically outside the economy, such as foreign aid to another country, but it may also represent additional consumption by the workers within the economy. If viewed in the latter sense, we have removed the objection (noted earlier) to the original assumption that the model requires the restriction of the consumption by workers to the level of subsistence. As we shall see, the rates of expansion and the size of the outside demand can be closely connected. The result demonstrated below that decreasing the outside demand will allow a faster growth of the economy is economically very plausible and, indeed, corroborated from observations pertaining to economic development and the role of savings.[f] This phenomenon has consequently been treated in business cycle analysis.

To simplify our equations we assume that this external demand at time t is supplied out of the production of time $t - 1$. This assumption is consistent with the interpretation of the outside demand as added consumption, i.e., as the economy expands, the percentage of the total production going to the consumers will remain constant. Our expressions now become

$$x(B - \alpha A) \geq \alpha d \tag{11}$$

$$(B - \beta A)y \leq \beta f(dy) \tag{12}$$

$$x(B - \alpha A)y = \alpha dy \tag{13}$$

$$x(B - BA)y = \beta dy \tag{14}$$

$$xBy > 0 \tag{15}$$

In expression (12), the vector f is an $m \times 1$ (column) vector, each of whose entries is one. These expressions may be more briefly stated if we make greater use of the vector f. Observe that fd is an $m \times n$ matrix, each of whose rows is the vector d. Then we can write the above expressions as

---

[f] The possibility of introducing cyclical components into the outside demand and hence into the behavior of the entire system easily suggests itself, but we chose not to proceed in that direction at the present occasion.

$$x[B - \alpha(A + fd)] \geq 0 \qquad (11')$$

$$[B - \beta(A + fd)]y \leq 0 \qquad (12')$$

$$x[B - \alpha(A + fd)]y = 0 \qquad (13')$$

$$x[B - \beta(A + fd)]y = 0 \qquad (14')$$

$$xBy > 0 \qquad (15')$$

Observe that these expressions correspond to (C1) through (C5) in Section 2 if we substitute the matrix $A' = A + fd$ for A. Hence all of the preceding work holds, and the existence theorem ensures that at least one economic solution exists.

Theorem 2-8: The introduction of outside demand into the economic model has the following effect. Consider a subeconomy of the economy having a unique expansion factor:

1. If the outside demand includes any good (produced by the subeconomy) which has a positive price, then the expansion factor of the (sub-) economy must be decreased in order to supply the outside demand.
2. If the outside demand for goods (produced by the subeconomy) having a positive price is decreased, then the expansion factor can be increased correspondingly.

Proof: 1. Let A and B be the matrices of the subeconomy. Let α, (x, y) and α^*, (x^*, y^*) be solutions to Axioms (C1) through (C5) of Section 2 and (11') through (15') of this section, respectively. Suppose that $\alpha^* \geq \alpha$. Then $x^*[B - \alpha^*(A + fd)] \geq 0$ implies that $x^*[B - \alpha A] \geq 0$; and also $[B - \alpha A]y \leq 0$ implies that $[B - \alpha^*(A + fd)]y \leq 0$. Hence the pair (x^*, y) is a game-theoretic (possibly noneconomic) solution to both problems. Then we have the following two equations:

$$x^*By - \alpha^*x^*Ay - \alpha^*dy = 0$$

$$x^*By - \alpha x^*Ay = 0$$

Subtracting the second equation from the first, we find that

$$(\alpha - \alpha^*) x^*Ay - \alpha^*dy = 0$$

Now if $dy > 0$, that is, if the outside demand includes nonfree goods, then this equation implies that $x^*Ay < 0$, which is impossible. Hence $\alpha^* < \alpha$, completing the proof.

The proof of (2) is similar to the proof of (1).

Exercises

1. Show that $\alpha = \beta = 3$, $x = (1/2, 1/2)$ and $y = (6/7, 1/7)$, solve the chicken farm economy of Example 2-1.

2. Verify the numbers shown in Figure 2-1.

3. In Example 2-3, verify that the two solutions shown are correct.

4. In Example 2-4, verify that the solution given solves the model.

5. Show that Examples 2-2 and 2-5 do not satisfy Assumption (A1) and that Example 2-6 does not satisfy Assumption (A2).

6. Show that Assumption (A1) implies that $v(-A) < 0$. [*Hint*: Use strategy y with $y_j = 1/n$ for all j for column player.]

7. Show that Assumption (A2) implies that $v(B) > 0$. [*Hint*: Use strategy x with $x_i = 1/m$ for all i for the row player.]

8. Assume $\alpha = \beta$. Then show that condition (C1) and expression (3) are the same. Also show that condition (C2) and expression (4) are the same.

9. Show that if $\alpha = \beta$, then solutions to expression (3) and (4) automatically satisfy Axioms (C3) and (C4).

10. Consider the economy with input-output matrices:

$$A = \begin{pmatrix} 1 & 0 \\ 0 & 1 \end{pmatrix} \quad \text{and} \quad B = \begin{pmatrix} 1 & 0 \\ 0 & 1 \end{pmatrix}$$

(a) Show that Assumptions (A1) and (A2) but not (AO) are satisfied.

(b) Show that $\alpha = \beta = 1$ is the unique expansion rate satisfying the axioms.

(c) Show that $x = (1,0)$, $y = (1,0)'$ and $x = (0,1)$, $y = (0,1)'$ are each pairs of economic solutions to the corresponding matrix game M_1.

(d) Show that $x = (1,0)$, $y = (0,1)'$ and $x = (0,1)$, $y = (1,0)'$ are each pairs of noneconomic solutions to the matrix game M_1.

11. Consider the economy with input-output matrices:

$$A = \begin{pmatrix} 1 & 0 \\ 1 & 1 \end{pmatrix}, \quad B = \begin{pmatrix} 3 & 0 \\ 0 & 2 \end{pmatrix}$$

(a) Show that $\alpha = 3$, $x = (1,0)$, $y = (1,0)'$ is an economic solution to M_3.

(b) Show that $\alpha = 2$, $x = (1/2,1/2)$, $y = (0,1)'$ is an economic solution to M_2.

(c) Show that $x = (1,0)$, $y = (0,1)'$ is a noneconomic solution to M_3.

12. Consider the chicken, eggs, and labor economic model whose input-output matrices are

$$A = \begin{pmatrix} 1 & 0 & 1 \\ 1 & 4 & 1 \\ 4 & 8 & 0 \end{pmatrix}, \qquad B = \begin{pmatrix} 1 & 12 & 0 \\ 5 & 0 & 0 \\ 0 & 0 & c \end{pmatrix}$$

where c is a parameter related to the per capita consumption of labor.

(a) Show that the expansion coefficient is always unique for the model.

(b) If $c = 2$, show that there is a solution to the economic model with $\alpha = 1$. [*Hint*: See Example 2-4.] This is a stationary economy.

(c) If $c = 4$, show that the solution is given by $\alpha = 1.303$, $x = (.377, .377, .246)$ and $y = (.318, .074, .608)'$. This is an expanding economy.

(d) If $c = 1$, show that the solution is given by $\alpha = .75$, $x = (.286, .286, .428)$ and $y = (.170, .046, .784)'$. This is a contracting economy.

(e) Give reasons for the various expansion rates in (b), (c), and (d) in terms of per capita consumption of labor.

13. Show that the solutions described in Examples 2-7 and 2-8 are correct for the models given.

14. In Example 2-7, show that the following quantities solve M_α, M'_α, M_β, and M'_β (in the sense of Theorem 2-3):

$$x = (1/2, 1/2), \quad y = (1/2, 1/2)', \quad \alpha = 1/(1 + \epsilon)$$

$$r = 2\epsilon/(1 + \epsilon), \quad \beta = (1 + 2\epsilon)/(1 + \epsilon), \quad s = 0$$

15. In Example 2-8, show that the following quantities solve M_α, $M_{\alpha'}$, M_β, and M'_β:

$$x = (1/2, 1/2), \quad y = (1/2, 1/2)', \quad \alpha = (1 + \epsilon)/(1 + 2\epsilon)$$

$$r = 0, \quad \beta = (1 + 3\epsilon)/(1 + 2\epsilon), \quad s = -\epsilon/(1 + 2\epsilon)$$

16. By adding the constraint $2x_2 \geq x_1$ to the game M_α of the model in Exercise 11, show that now an economic solution is

$$\alpha = 2, \quad x = (2/3, 1/3), \quad y = (1/2, 1/2)'$$

and now good 1 is not free.

3

A Constructive Solution
Method for the KMT Model

1. Introduction

We discuss in this chapter some of the technical problems connected with the existence and computation of solutions to the KMT model. A reader who is willing to accept the fact that such solutions and computer programs for finding them in a finite number of steps exist can skip the present chapter entirely without losing the continuity of the development of the models that appear in later chapters. Only the computational discussions of Chapter 11 will require knowledge of the present chapter.

In Sections 2, 3, and 4, we briefly present three different linear programming problem formulations that can be used to find the optimal strategies for a matrix game having zero value. The formulation of Section 4 is then used to derive the constructive solution techniques in Sections 5 and 6 for the KMT model recently developed by Thompson [119].

2. The First Method for Solving Fair Games

An $m \times n$ matrix game G with zero value, that is, $v(G) = 0$, is called a *fair game*. If x and y are optimal strategies for such a game, then they satisfy

$$xG \geq 0, \quad x \geq 0, \quad xf = 1 \tag{1}$$

$$Gy \leq 0, \quad y \geq 0, \quad ey = 1 \tag{2}$$

where x is $1 \times m$, y is $n \times 1$, f is the $m \times 1$ column vector of all ones, and e is the $1 \times n$ row vector of all ones.

There are several ways of finding x and y that solve (1) and (2), all involving linear programming. The first method which involves *goal programming* (see Appendix 2) will be discussed in the present section. Two other methods shall subsequently be discussed in the following sections.

To describe the goal programming approach we replace (1) and (2) by

$$x^*G \geq 0, \quad x^* \geq 0, \quad x^* \leq f' \tag{3}$$

$$Gy^* \leq 0, \quad y^* \geq 0, \quad y^* \leq e' \tag{4}$$

where x^* is $1 \times m$ and y^* is $n \times 1$; f' is the transpose of f and e' is the transpose of e.

By direct substitution, we can show that $x^* = 0$, $y^* = 0$ solves (3) and (4). We call $x^* = 0$, $y^* = 0$ the *trivial* solution to (3) and (4). Solutions with $x^* \neq 0$ and $y^* \neq 0$ are called *nontrivial*.

Finally, we say that a solution x^* to (3) such that $x_i^* = 1$ for some i is a *tight solution*. Similarly, a solution y^* to (4) such that $y_j^* = 1$ for some j is a *tight solution*. Obviously, tight solutions are nontrivial.

We now want to show that there is a one-to-one correspondence between solutions to (1) and (2) and tight solutions to (3) and (4). Let x satisfy (1) and define the number s by

$$s = \operatorname*{Max}_{1 \leq i \leq m} x_i \tag{5}$$

Then define

$$x^* = \left(\frac{1}{s}\right) x \tag{6}$$

It follows from (5) that $x^* \leq f'$ and x^* is a tight solution to (3), since $x_i \leq s$ for all i and $x_i = s$ for at least one i. A similar transformation shows that a solution y to (2) corresponds to a solution y^* to (4) (see Exercise 1). Similarly, let x^* be a tight solution to (3) and define the number t by

$$t = x^* f' \tag{7}$$

Then since x^* is tight, $t > 0$, so that we can define

$$x = \left(\frac{1}{t}\right) x^* \tag{8}$$

A straightforward calculation shows that $xf = (1/t) x^* f = (1/t) t = 1$ so that x is a solution to (1). A similar transformation shows that a tight solution y^* to (4) corresponds to a solution y of (2) (see Exercise 2).

The above remarks constitute a proof of the following theorem.

Theorem 3-1: Equations (6) and (8) define a one-to-one correspondence between solutions of (1) and (2) and tight solutions of (3) and (4).

In essence, what this theorem says is that we can choose to normalize the solutions to the KMT model in either the manner prescribed by (1) and (2) or (3) and (4). We will find that sometimes one and sometimes the other is more convenient. In the next chapter, we will show that the formulation of (3) and (4) leads directly to the open model.

Now we want to use a goal programming model to solve (3) and (4). The reader is advised to read Appendix 2 for information on linear goal programming models if necessary.

Consider the following pair of dual linear goal programming programs:

$$\text{Minimize} \quad w^i e'$$

Subject to

$$xG - w^e + w^i = 0$$
$$-x \geq -f'$$
$$x \geq 0 \qquad\qquad (9)$$

$$w^e, w^i \geq 0$$

$$\text{Maximize} \quad -f'z^p$$

Subject to

$$Gy - z^p + z^n = 0$$
$$-y \leq 0$$
$$y \leq e' \qquad\qquad (10)$$

$$z^p, z^n \geq 0$$

Here the variable vectors w^e and w^i are each $1 \times n$ and the vectors z^p and z^n are each $m \times 1$. (The superscripts on these variables were chosen to relate this model to the open model of Chapter 4, where they will describe specific economic quantities.)

Since $(x, w^e, w^i) = (0,0,0)$ and $(y, z^p, z^n) = (0,0,0)$ are feasible solutions, it is clear that these problems have the trivial identically zero solutions which, in fact, are optimal. This also implies that $w^i = 0$ and that $z^p = 0$ for *every* optimal solution. We are interested in nontrivial optimal solutions.

We say that solutions (x, w^e, w^i) and (y, z^p, z^n) of (9) and (10) are *nontrivial* if $x \neq 0$ and $y \neq 0$. And we say they are *basic* if they are basic in the ordinary linear programming sense (see Appendix 2).

Theorem 3-2: Any convex combination of basic nontrivial solutions to (9) and (10) gives a tight solution to (1) and (2).

Proof: We first show that a nontrivial basic solution to (9) and (10) is a tight solution to (3) and (4). Let (x^*, w^e, w^i) be a basic nontrivial solution to (9). Since $w^i = 0$, we have $x^*G - w^e = 0$ and $w^e \geq 0$ shows that $x^*G \geq 0$. If x^* is not a tight solution to (9), then there is a number $k > 1$ such that (kx^*, kw^e, kw^i) is still optimal for (9). But then (x^*, w^e, w^i) is a convex combination of (kx^*, kw^e, kw^i) and $(0,0,0)$ and hence is not basic. We now use (8) to derive from x^* a solution x to (1). The argument for y is similar.

It is easy to show that a convex combination of tight solutions corresponds to a tight solution (see Exercises 3 and 4). This completes the proof.

From Theorems 3-1 and 3-2, we see that a solution technique for finding every solution to (1) and (2) is to first find all the basic solutions to (9) and (10); then to take any convex combination of the nontrivial ones, we find the corresponding tight solution and then use (7) and (8) and the results of Exercise 2 to get a solution to (1) and (2).

The condensed tableau for Problems (9) and (10) is shown in Figure 3-1. Note that given an $m \times n$ fair matrix game G, the tableau of Figure 3-1 is $(m + 2n) \times (2m + n)$. Thus the goal programming method described here leads to a relatively large tableau. Methods leading to smaller tableaus appear in the next two sections.

Example 3-1. Consider the fair matrix game shown in Figure 3-2. It was constructed from the chicken and eggs example described in Example 2-1 with $\alpha = 3$. That is the 2×2 matrix in the upper left-hand corner of Figure 3-2. The last row and column were added to extend the example to a 3×3 game.

The condensed tableau for the linear program of (9) and (10) is shown in Figure 3-3. Dotted lines were added to the tableau to show the same

	y	z^p	z^n	
x	G	$-I$	I	$= 0$
w^e	$-I$	0	0	≤ 0
w^i	I	0	0	$\leq e'$
	$= 0$	$\geq -f$	≥ 0	

Figure 3-1

$$G = \begin{bmatrix} -2 & 12 & -1 \\ 2 & -12 & 3 \\ -1 & 2 & 1 \end{bmatrix}$$

Figure 3-2

	y_1	y_2	y_3	z_1^p	z_2^p	z_3^p	z_1^n	z_2^n	z_3^n	
x_1	-2	12	-1	-1	0	0	1	0	0	$=0$
x_2	2	-12	3	0	-1	0	0	1	0	$=0$
x_3	-1	2	1	0	0	-1	0	0	1	$=0$
w_1^e	-1	0	0	0	0	0	0	0	0	≤ 0
w_2^e	0	-1	0	0	0	0	0	0	0	≤ 0
w_3^e	0	0	-1	0	0	0	0	0	0	≤ 0
w_1^i	1	0	0	0	0	0	0	0	0	≤ 1
w_2^i	0	1	0	0	0	0	0	0	0	≤ 1
w_3^i	0	0	1	0	0	0	0	0	0	≤ 1
	$=0$	$=0$	$=0$	≥ -1	≥ -1	≥ -1	≥ 0	≥ 0	≥ 0	

Figure 3-3

partitioning that is indicated in Figure 3-1.

The reader should now show that the following quantities give an optimal solution to the linear programming problem whose tableau is in Figure 3-3:

$$x = (1, 1, 0), \qquad w^e = (0, 0, 2), \qquad w^i = (0, 0, 0)$$

$$y = \begin{pmatrix} 1 \\ 1/6 \\ 0 \end{pmatrix}, \qquad z^p = \begin{pmatrix} 0 \\ 0 \\ 0 \end{pmatrix}, \qquad z^n = \begin{pmatrix} 0 \\ 0 \\ 2/3 \end{pmatrix}$$

From this solution we can use (8) to derive the optimal solution for the matrix game G as

$$x = \left(\frac{1}{2}, \frac{1}{2}, 0 \right) \qquad \text{and} \qquad y = \begin{pmatrix} 6/7 \\ 1/7 \\ 0 \end{pmatrix}$$

Although this may seem like an unnecessarily clumsy way of solving a simple problem, we will see that it leads directly to the open model of Chapter 4 and will turn out to be of particular interest.

46

3. The Second Method for Solving Fair Games

We now briefly discuss another method for solving (1) and (2) which has a smaller tableau than the previous method. Although we will not make use of this new method for computations, we mention it because it makes use of a linear programming formulation that is a direct restatement of (1) and (2).

Consider the following pair of dual linear programming problems:

$$
\left.
\begin{aligned}
\text{Minimize} \quad &-u \\
\text{Subject to} \quad & \\
xG - ue &\geq 0 \\
x(-f) &= -1 \\
x &\geq 0
\end{aligned}
\right\} \tag{11}
$$

$$
\left.
\begin{aligned}
\text{Maximize} \quad &-v \\
\text{Subject to} \quad & \\
Gy - vf &\leq 0 \\
(-e)y &= -1 \\
y &\geq 0
\end{aligned}
\right\} \tag{12}
$$

Here the quantities x, y, e, and f are as previously defined, and u and v are unconstrained variables.

In Exercise 5 the reader is asked to show that both problems have feasible solutions. From this and the duality theorem of linear programming (Appendix 2), it follows that both have optimal solutions, and, at the optimum, the objective functions are equal, that is, $u = v$. The value of the matrix game G is this common value.

In our case $u = v = 0$ so that the optimal solutions to (11) and (12) yield the solutions $xG \geq 0$, $xf = 1$ and $Gy \leq 0$, $ey = 1$ as required.

The initial condensed tableau for the problems (11) and (12) is shown in Figure 3-4. Note that it is $(m + 1) \times (n + 1)$, which is considerably smaller than the tableau of the method described in the previous section.

Example 3-1 (continued): The corresponding initial tableau for the matrix game G of Figure 3-2 is shown in Figure 3-5. Again, dotted lines have been added to make the partitioning of Figure 3-5 correspond to that in Figure 3-4.

The reader should show that the following quantities provide the optimum solution to the dual linear programs of Figure 3-5:

$$
\begin{array}{c}
\begin{array}{cc} y & v \end{array} \\
\begin{array}{c} x \\ u \end{array}
\left[
\begin{array}{c|c}
G & -f \\
\hline
-e & 0
\end{array}
\right]
\begin{array}{c} \leq 0 \\ = -1 \end{array} \\
\begin{array}{cc} \geq 0 & \;\; = -1 \end{array}
\end{array}
$$

Figure 3-4

$$
\begin{array}{c}
\begin{array}{cccc} y_1 & y_2 & y_3 & v \end{array} \\
\begin{array}{c} x_1 \\ x_2 \\ x_3 \\ u \end{array}
\left[
\begin{array}{ccc|c}
-2 & 12 & -1 & -1 \\
2 & -12 & 3 & -1 \\
-1 & 2 & 1 & -1 \\
\hline
-1 & -1 & -1 & 0
\end{array}
\right]
\begin{array}{c} \leq 0 \\ \leq 0 \\ \leq 0 \\ = -1 \end{array} \\
\begin{array}{cccc} \geq 0 & \geq 0 & \geq 0 & = -1 \end{array}
\end{array}
$$

Figure 3-5

$$
x = \left(\frac{1}{2}, \frac{1}{2}, 0\right), \quad u = 0, \quad y = \begin{pmatrix} 6/7 \\ 1/7 \\ 0 \end{pmatrix}, \quad v = 0
$$

4. The Third Method for Solving Fair Games

We describe next a method for solving an $m \times n$ fair game G that requires that we solve an $m \times n$ linear programming problem. This method will be used in the remainder of the chapter to develop the constructive algorithm for finding all expansion factors for the KMT closed model.

We begin by considering, for any matrix game G (fair or not), the following pair of dual linear programming problems:

$$
\left.
\begin{array}{ll}
\text{Minimize} \quad wf & \qquad \text{Maximize} \quad eu \\
\text{Subject to} & \qquad \text{Subject to} \\
\quad w(G + kE) \geq e & \qquad\qquad (G + kE)u \leq f \\
\quad w \qquad\qquad \geq 0 & \qquad\qquad\qquad u \geq 0
\end{array}
\right\} \quad (13)
$$

where E is an $m \times n$ matrix of all ones. Assume that k is chosen so large that $v(G + kE) > 0$. In Exercise 6, the reader will be asked to show that the minimizing problem has a feasible solution and is bounded from below, so that it has an optimal solution. By the dual theorem, both problems have optimal solutions w^0, u^0 and share a common value

$$c = w^0 f = e u^0 \tag{14}$$

We use c to compute the following quantities:

$$x = (1/c)w^0, \qquad y = (1/c)u^0 \tag{15}$$

Theorem 3-3: Let G be any $m \times n$ matrix game and let k be any number so large that the value of $G + kE$ is positive. Then the solutions of the dual programs give x and y in (15), which are optimal strategies for the game G; moreover

$$v(G) = (1/c) - k \tag{16}$$

Proof: By hypothesis, we have

$$w^0(G + kE) = w^0 G + k c e \geq e$$

Dividing this equation through by c and using (15) gives us

$$\frac{1}{c} w^0 G + ke \geq \frac{1}{c} e \qquad \text{or} \qquad xG \geq \left(\frac{1}{c} - k \right) e$$

Hence setting $v = (1/c) - k$, we have

$$xG \geq ve \tag{17}$$

Also, because of (14) and (15), we have

$$xf = \left(\frac{1}{c} \right) w^0 f = \left(\frac{1}{c} \right) = 1 \tag{18}$$

so that since $w^0 \geq 0$ implies $x \geq 0$ we see that x is a feasible row player strategy for the game G.

    In Exercise 7 the reader will be asked to show that the y defined by (15) satisfies

$$Gy \leq ve, \quad y \geq 0, \quad ey = 1 \tag{19}$$

so that y is a feasible column player strategy.

    We can now see from (17) and (19) that v is the value of the game and that x and y are optimal strategies for G, completing the proof.

    We now specialize Theorem 3-3 by assuming that G is a fair game. We set $k = 1$ and state the following pair of dual linear programs:

$$\left. \begin{array}{l} \text{Minimize} \quad xf \\ \text{Subject to} \\ \qquad x(G + E) \ \geq \ e \\ \qquad x \qquad\quad \geq 0 \end{array} \right\} \qquad \left. \begin{array}{l} \text{Maximize} \quad ey \\ \text{Subject to} \\ \qquad (G + E)y \leq f \\ \qquad\qquad y \geq 0 \end{array} \right\} \qquad (20)$$

Theorem 3-4: If G is a fair game, then the common value of the dual linear programming problems (20) is 1 and their solutions x and y are optimal strategies for G.

Proof: If we set $k = 1$ and use the fact that $v(G) = 0$, then from (16) we get $c = 1$, so that in (15) $x = w^0$ and $y = u^0$ are optimal strategies for G, completing the proof.

Theorem 3-4 permits us to give the initial condensed tableaus for the linear programming problems in (20) and shown in Figure 3-6. Clearly this tableau is the most economical of the three ways of solving G.

Example 3-1 (continued): For the fair matrix game that appears in Figure 3-2, this initial tableau corresponding to Figure 3-6 is given in Figure 3-7.

$$\begin{array}{c} \qquad\quad y \\ x \quad \boxed{G + E} \quad \leq f \\ \qquad\quad \geq e \end{array}$$

Figure 3-6

	y_1	y_2	y_3	
x_1	-1	13	0	≤ 1
x_2	3	-11	4	≤ 1
x_3	0	3	2	≤ 1
	≥ 1	≥ 1	≥ 1	

Figure 3-7

The reader should show that the vectors

$$x = \left(\frac{1}{2}, \frac{1}{2}, 0\right) \qquad \text{and} \qquad y = \begin{pmatrix} 6/7 \\ 1/7 \\ 0 \end{pmatrix}$$

are optimal for the linear program in Figure 3-7 and also that the objective value of this linear programming problem is 1. We know from our previous work that they are also optimal strategies for the fair game G.

5. Basic Results

In this section we prove some results first given in [118] and [119] that will provide the theoretical justification for the constructive algorithm to be presented in the next section.

Lemma 3-1: If $v(M_{\alpha^*}) = 0$, x^* and y^* are associated central optimal strategies, and $x^* B y^* = 0$, then there exist positive numbers μ_1 and μ_2 [defined in (23) and (24) below] such that x^* and y^* are optimal and $v(M_\alpha) = 0$ for all α in the interval

$$\alpha^* - \mu_2 \leq \alpha \leq \alpha^* + \mu_1 \tag{21}$$

Proof: Since $x^* B y^* = 0$ and $\alpha^* > 0$, it follows that $x^* A y^* = 0$ also so that the rows and columns of M_{α^*} can be rearranged as shown in Figure 3-8. Considered as matrix games, we must have $v(M_{\alpha^*}^{(1)}) > 0$ and $v(M_{\alpha^*}^{(2)}) < 0$, which can be seen as follows.

Consider the case in which $v(M_{\alpha^*}^{(1)}) > 0$ and $v(M_{\alpha^*}^{(2)}) = 0$. Then there is a strategy

$$x' = a(x^{*(1)}, 0) + (1 - a)(0, x'^{(2)})$$

where $x^{*(1)}$ is a central strategy for $M_{\alpha^*}^{(1)}$, $x'^{(2)}$ is any optimal strategy for $M_{\alpha^*}^{(2)}$, and a is selected so that

$$a x^{*(1)} M_{\alpha^*}^{(1)} + (1 - a) x'^{(2)} Q_{\alpha^*} \geq 0. \tag{22}$$

Because $v(M_{\alpha^*}^{(1)}) > 0$, it is possible to choose an a satisfying $0 < a < 1$ with the inequality in (22) holding, but the new strategy x' is optimal for M_{α^*} and has positive components where x^* has zero components, contradicting the fact that x^* was a central solution.

The argument for the case where $v(M_{\alpha^*}^{(1)}) = 0$ and $v(M_{\alpha^*}^{(2)}) < 0$ is similar.

Finally, consider the case $v(M_{\alpha^*}^{(1)}) = 0$ and $v(M_{\alpha^*}^{(2)}) = 0$. Let $\bar{Q}_{\alpha^*}$ be the matrix game Q_{α^*} in which the row player is restricted to the use of

	$y^{*(1)} = 0$	$y^{*(2)} > 0$
$x^{*(1)} > 0$	$M_{\alpha*}^{(i)}$	0
$x^{*(2)} = 0$	$Q_{\alpha*}$	$M_{\alpha*}^{(2)}$

Figure 3-8

strategies $x'^{(2)}$ that are optimal in $M_{\alpha*}^{(2)}$ and the column player is restricted to the use of strategies $y'^{(1)}$ that are optimal in $M_{\alpha*}^{(1)}$. If the value of $\bar{Q}_{\alpha*}$ is nonnegative, then a construction like the one above shows that x^* is not a central solution, which is a contradiction. And if the value of $\bar{Q}_{\alpha*}$ is nonpositive, a similar construction shows that y^* is not central, and is also a contradiction.

Since $v(M_{\alpha*}^{(2)}) > 0$, the set $S = \{\mu \,|\, x^{*(1)} M_{\alpha+\mu}^{(1)} \geq 0, \ \mu \geq 0\}$ contains a positive μ and 0; hence it contains a positive interval. Define

$$\mu_1 = \underset{\mu \epsilon S}{\text{Maximum }} \mu. \tag{23}$$

Similarly, $v(M_{\alpha*}^{(2)}) < 0$ shows that the set $T = \{\mu \,|\, M_{\alpha-\mu} y^{*(2)} \leq 0, \ \mu \geq 0\}$ contains a positive interval. Define

$$\mu_1 = \underset{\mu \epsilon T}{\text{Maximum }} \mu. \tag{24}$$

Because S and T contain intervals, $\mu_1 > 0$ and $\mu_2 > 0$. Then Lemma 2-2 and (23) and (24) show that x^* and y^* remain optimal (but not necessarily central) in the entire interval given in Equation (21), completing the proof of the lemma.

We now use the result of this lemma to prove Theorem 2-2(a) which we restate as follows:

Theorem 3-5: If A and B are $m \times n$ matrices satisfying Assumptions (A1) and (A2) and $M_\alpha = B - \alpha A$, then there is at least one and at most a finite number of allowable α's for which the game M_α has economic solutions.

Proof: By assumption (A2), $v(M_0) = v(B) > 0$. By assumption (A2) for α sufficiently large (see Exercise 8), $v(M_\alpha) < 0$. Since $v(B - \alpha A)$ is a continuous function of α (see Appendix 2), the set

$$S = \{\alpha \,|\, v(M_\alpha) = 0, \ \alpha \geq 0\}$$

is nonempty, closed, bounded, and contains only positive elements. Let

α^* be the maximum element of S, which exists by a well known theorem of topology. We will show that α^* has economic solutions.

Suppose, on the contrary, that $x^*By^* = 0$ for all optimal pairs (x^*,y^*) to M_{α^*}; then the same is true if (x^*,y^*) are central strategies. But then by Lemma 3-1, just proved, (x^*,y^*) continue to be optimal for M_α with α in the interval $\alpha^* \leq \alpha \leq \alpha^* + \mu_1$, where $\mu_1 > 0$. Since $x^*By^* = x^*Ay^* = 0$, it follows that $v(M_\alpha) = 0$ in the same interval, which contradicts the maximality of α^*. This contradiction shows that $x^*By^* > 0$ for some optimal pair (x^*,y^*) which shows that α^* is an economic solution.

If we let α^{**} be the minimum element of S, the same kind of proof shows that α^{**} is also an allowable α that has economic solutions.

We have just shown that there is at least one allowable α having economic solutions. Theorem 2-1 proved that there were at most a finite number of such solutions. This completes the proof of Theorem 3-5.

Lemma 3-2: For all α' in the open interval,

$$\alpha^* - \mu_2 < \alpha' < \alpha^* + \mu_1 \tag{25}$$

Let x' and y' be the corresponding central solutions; then $x'By' = 0$.

Proof: Let α' be in the interval (25); say $\alpha^* - \mu_2 < \alpha' < \alpha^*$. (The proof for the other case when $\alpha^* < \alpha' < \alpha^* + \mu_1$ is similar.) Suppose that $x'By' > 0$. Then since x' is optimal in M_{α^*} and y^* is a central solution, we have $x'By^* > 0$. Hence there is some component, say the ith component, such that $x'_i > 0$, $(M_{\alpha'}y^*)_i \geq 0$ and $x^*_i = 0$, $(M_{\alpha'}y^*)_i < 0$. If we now choose $\alpha'' = \frac{1}{2}$ $\alpha' + \frac{1}{2}(\alpha^* - \mu_2)$, then $\alpha^* - \mu_2 < \alpha'' < \alpha^*$ and we have $(M_{\alpha''}y^*)_i > 0$, which contradicts the definition of the set T used in the definition of μ_2 in (24). This contradiction completes the proof.

Definition: Strategies x^* and x' are said to *agree* if $x^*_i > 0$ implies that $x'_i > 0$ and conversely. Similarly, y^* and y' agree if $y^*_j > 0$ implies that $y'_j > 0$ and conversely.

Lemma 3-3: Let (α^*,x^*,y^*) and (α',x',y') be triples with $\alpha^* < \alpha'$, x^*,y^*,x',y' central and satisfying $x^*By^* = x'By' = 0$; then

(a) x^* and x' agree if and only if y^* and y' agree.
(b) x^* and x' agree if and only if x^* and x and y^* and y agree for all α in $\alpha^* \leq \alpha \leq \alpha'$, where (α,x,y) is also a central economic triple.

Proof: (a) Assume that x^* and x' agree but there is a component j such that $y'_j > 0$ and $y^*_j = 0$. Then $[x^*(B - \alpha^*A)]_j > 0$ and $[x'(B - \alpha'A)]_j = 0$. Since A and B are nonnegative, this implies that $[x^*B]_j > 0$, and since x^*

and x' agree, $[x'B]_j > 0$ also. But then $x'By' \geq [x'B]_j y_j > 0$, contradicting the assumption that $x'By' = 0$.

(b) If α satisfies $\alpha^* \leq \alpha \leq \alpha'$ and x^* and x did not agree then because $\alpha^* \leq \alpha$ and Lemma 2-2 there is an i such that $x_i^* = 0$ and $x_i > 0$. However, since $\alpha \leq \alpha'$ and x' is central, we have $x_i' > 0$ also so that x^* and x' cannot agree, which is a contradiction. The argument for y^* and y' is similar.

Theorem 3-6: If (α^*, x^*, y^*) is a triple with x^* and y^* central, $\alpha_i < \alpha^* < \alpha_{i+1}$ and $x^*By^* = 0$, then

(a) $\alpha_i \leq \alpha^* - \mu_2$ and $\alpha^* + \mu_1 \leq \alpha_{i+1}$, where μ_2 and μ_1 are given in (23) and (24).

(b) For $\alpha_i \leq \alpha \leq \alpha_{i+1}$ and (α, x, y) being a central triple, $x^{(i)}$ and x agree.

(c) For $\alpha_i < \alpha \leq \alpha_{i+1}$ and (α, x, y) being a central triple, y and $y^{(i+1)}$ agree.

(d) $\alpha_1, \ldots, \alpha_i$ are the natural expansion factors for the submodel $M_\alpha^{(1)}$ given by the decomposition of Figure 3-8.

(e) $\alpha_{i+1}, \ldots, \alpha_r$ are natural expansion factors for the model $M_\alpha^{(2)}$ given by the decomposition of Figure 3-8.

Proof: Assertion (a) follows from Lemma 3-2. Assertions (b) and (c) follow from Lemma 2-2 and Lemma 3-3. Assertions (d) and (e) follow from the facts that $v(M_\alpha^{(1)}) > 0$, $v(M_\alpha^{(2)}) < 0$ and the monotone nature of $v(M_\alpha)$, $v(M_\alpha^{(1)})$, and $v(M_\alpha^{(2)})$.

6. The Algorithm for Finding the Natural Factors

In the algorithm to be presented, two lists are maintained. List P contains problems to be solved with each problem indicated by a quadruple $(L, x^{(L)}, R, y^{(R)})$, where L is the left-most trial expansion factor and $x^{(L)}$ is its central row strategy, R is the right-most trial expansion factor, and $y^{(R)}$ is its central column strategy. List E consists of central economic triples and is initially empty.

Algorithm: For finding all natural expansion factors of $M_\alpha = B - \alpha A$ to within the accuracy $\epsilon > 0$.

(0) Let $E = \phi$. Choose L so that $v(M_L) > 0$ and R so that $v(M_R) < 0$. Calculate μ_1 and μ_2. Store problem $[L+\mu_1, x^{(L)}, R-\mu_2, y^{(R)}]$ in list P.

(1) If $P = \phi$, then E contains all the natural factors, stop. Otherwise select and remove a problem $[L, x^{(L)}, R, y^{(R)}]$ from P.

(2) Let $\alpha = (R+L)/2$. If $|R - L| < \epsilon$, put $(\alpha, x^{(R)}, y^{(L)})$ into E and go to (1). Otherwise go to (3).

(3) Find the central triple (α,x,y) and μ_1 and μ_2 for M_α.

(4) If $v(M_\alpha) < 0$ put $[L,x^{(L)},\alpha-\mu_2,y]$ into P. Go to (1).

(5) If $v(M_\alpha) > 0$ put $[\alpha + \mu_1,x,R,y^{(R)}]$ into P. Go to (1).

(6) If $v(M_\alpha) = 0$ and $xBy > 0$, add (α,x,y) to E.

    (a) If $\mu_2 > 0$ put $[L,x^{(L)},\alpha-\mu_2,y]$ into P.

    (b) If $\mu_1 > 0$ put $[\alpha + \mu_1,x,R,y^{(R)}]$ into P. Go to (1).

(7) If $v(M_\alpha) = 0$ and $xBy = 0$, then

    (a) If x and $x^{(R)}$ agree put $(\alpha + \mu_1,x,R,y^{(R)})$ into P. [Here the interval (L,α) has no natural factors.] Go to (1).

    (b) If y and $y^{(L)}$ agree, put $(L,x^{(L)},\alpha - \mu_2,y)$ into P. [Here the interval (α,R) has no natural factors.] Go to (1).

    (c) If neither (a) nor (b) holds, put problems $(L,x^{(L)},\alpha - \mu_2,y)$ and $[\alpha + \mu_1,x,R,y^{(R)}]$ into P. Go to (1).

The proofs of the validity of each of these steps were given in the preceding section. Convergence is ensured because in step (2) we are repeatedly bisecting the problem interval and hence eventually arrive at intervals with length less than ϵ. Of course, if the problem has natural factors closer together than ϵ, the algorithm cannot separate them. The ϵ chosen should be related to the accuracy of the computing machine being used.

7. Solution of an Example

Consider the example with the following data:

$$
B = \begin{pmatrix} 4 & 0 & 0 & 0 \\ 2 & 3 & 0 & 0 \\ 0 & 2 & 2 & 0 \\ 2 & 0 & 6 & 1 \end{pmatrix}, \quad A = \begin{pmatrix} 1 & 0 & 0 & 0 \\ 6 & 1 & 0 & 0 \\ 0 & 1 & 1 & 0 \\ 0 & 1 & 1 & 1 \end{pmatrix}
$$

so that

$$
M_\alpha = \begin{pmatrix} 4-\alpha & 0 & 0 & 0 \\ 2-6\alpha & 3-\alpha & 0 & 0 \\ 0 & 2-\alpha & 2-\alpha & 0 \\ 2 & -\alpha & 6-\alpha & 1-\alpha \end{pmatrix}
$$

It is not hard to see that the natural expansion factors are 4,3,2, and 1. We carry out the steps of the algorithm to show that it will find them.

(0) $E = \phi$, $L = 0$, $v(M_0) = 3/4$, $R = 5$, $v(M_5) = -5/8$, $\mu_1 = 3/8$, $\mu_2 = 1$, $P = \{[3/8, (0,1/4,0,3/4), 4, (2/3,1/3,0,0)']\}$, $\epsilon = .001$.

(1) Select the only problem in P.

(2) $\alpha = 35/16$.

(3) We find the central triple
$[35/16, (5/6,1/6,0,0), (0,0,2/5,3/5)']$ and $\mu_1 = 13/16$, $\mu_2 = 3/16$.

(7) (c) Put $[3/8, (0,1/4,0,3/4), 2, (0,0,2/5,3/5)']$ and $[3, (16/17,1/17,0,0), 4, (0,0,2/5,3/5)']$ into P.

(1) Select $[3/8, (0,1/4,0,3/4), 2, (0,0,2/5,3/5)']$ from P.

(2) Let $\alpha = 19/16$.

(3) We find the central triple
$[19/16, (5/7,1/7,1/7,0), (0,0,0,1)']$ and $\mu_1 = 13/16$, $\mu_2 = 3/16$.

(7) (c) Put $[3/8, (0,1/4,0,3/4), 1, (0,0,0,1)']$ and $[2, (5/7,1/7,1/7,0), 2, (0,0, 1/5,4/5)']$ into P.

(1) Select $[2, (5/7,1/7,1/7,0), 2, (0,0,1/5,4/5)']$ from P.

(2) $\alpha = 2$ and $|R - L| < \epsilon$, so put
$[2, (5/7,1/7,1/7,0), (0,0,1/5,4/5)']$ into E.

(1) Select $[3, (16/17,1/17,0), 4, (2/3,1/3,0,0)']$ from P.

(2) $\alpha = 7/2$.

(3) We find the central triple
$[7/2, (1,0,0,0), (0,1/3,1/3,1/3)']$ and $\mu_1 = \frac{1}{2}$, $\mu_2 = \frac{1}{2}$.

(7) (a) Since x and x^R agree and since $\alpha + \mu_1 = R$, we put $[4, (1,0,0,0), (2/3,1/3,0,0)']$ into E. [This includes steps (1) and (2).]

(7) (b) Since y and y^L agree and since $\alpha - \mu_2 = L$, we put $[3, (16/17, 1/17,0,0), (0,1/3,1/3,1/3)']$ into E. [This includes steps (1) and (2).]

(1) We select the only remaining element of P, $(3/8, (0,1/4,0,3/4), 1, (0, 0,0,1)']$.

(2) $\alpha = 11/16$, etc.

The remaining steps of the algorithm make α converge from the left to 1 and culminate by putting

$$[1, (1/4,1/4,1/4,1/4), (0,0,0,1)']$$

into E.

8. Historical Remarks Concerning Computational Methods and Proofs

A binary search method for finding the maximum and minimum economic expansion factors for the KMT model was found in the early 1960s by Hamburger and Thompson, was later extended and elaborated with Weil, and was finally published in [36] in 1967. These same authors carried out some computations and reported on them in [37]. Weil used the method for computing examples in [139]; Truchon [129] used the same method to recompute the Japanese example of Tsukui [130]; and in [17] Cremeans used the same method in computing his models for pollution abatement.

The proof of Theorem 3-6 is essentially that of Thompson in [118] which was the first published existence proof for the KMT model. A contemporaneous proof was constructed by Kemeny but not published. We include his proof as Appendix 4. Many later existence proofs (all non-constructive) for the KMT model have appeared. Some are listed here: Howe, et. al, [43], 1960; Los, [62], 1971; Gale, [27], 1974.

Weil discussed a way of finding all economic solutions to the KMT model in [140] but his method depends on a very cumbersome method of decomposing the model. The algorithm for finding all economic solutions to the KMT model given in Section 6 provides the desired decomposition of the model as a by-product (see Chapter 5).

Exercises

1. Let y satisfy (2) and define u by

$$u = \underset{1 \le j \le n}{\text{Max}} \ y_j$$

   Then define $y^* = (1/u)y$.
   (a) Show that $y^* \le e'$.
   (b) Show that y^* is a nontrivial tight solution to (4).
2. Let y^* be a tight solution to (4) and define v by $v = ey^*$.
   (a) Use the fact that y^* is tight to show that $v > 0$.
   (b) Define $y = (1/v)y^*$ and show that y solves (2).
3. Let z^* and z^{**} be two tight solutions to (3) and consider $x^* = az^* + (1 - a)z^{**}$, where $0 < a < 1$.
   (a) Show that x^* is nontrivial.
   (b) Use (7) and (8) to derive a solution x to (1).
4. Let v^* and v^{**} be two tight solutions to (4) and consider $y^* = ay^* + (1 - a)y^{**}$ where $0 < a < 1$.
   (21) Show that y^* is nontrivial.
   (b) Use the results of Exercise 2 to derive a solution y to (2).

5. (a) Consider the minimizing problem in (11).

Let x be any probability vector; show that u can be chosen large enough, say $(u = U)$, that the constraints of (11) are satisfied, show that the set of feasible x vectors and u vectors is bounded if we add the constraint $u \leq U$; then show that the minimum problem in (11) has a solution.

(b) Use reasoning similar to that in (a) to show that (12) has a solution.

6. For the minimizing problem in (13):

(a) Show that k can be chosen so large that $G + kE$ is a positive matrix.

(b) For the value of k found in (a), show that the components of the vector w can be chosen large enough so that the constraints of the minimum problem are feasible.

(c) Show that the objective is bounded below.

(d) Now show that the problem has an optimal solution.

7. Show that the y vector in (15) satisfies the constraints of (19).

8. Let A and B satisfy the assumptions of Theorem 3-5. Let y be a column probability vector.

(a) Let $k = -v(-A)$. Show $k > 0$.

(b) Define h as follows:

$$h = \underset{\substack{i=1,\ldots,m \\ \text{all feasible } y}}{\text{Max}} \sum_{j=1}^{n} b_{ij} y_j.$$

Show that $h > 0$.

(c) Define $\bar{\alpha} = 2h/k$. Now show that $v(M_\alpha) < 0$ for any $\alpha \geq \bar{\alpha}$. [*Hint*: Try using an optimal strategy y for the column player in the game $-A$.]

9. If you have a computer available to solve small linear programming problems, verify the steps of the solution of the example shown in Section 7.

4

The Open Expanding
Economy Model

1. Axioms and Assumptions

In Chapters 2 and 3 we discussed closed models, that is, models of expanding economies for which the inputs of a given time period must be the outputs of the previous period. Now we wish to permit the economy to be in contact with an "outside world" and to be able, within certain prescribed rules, to import and export goods. Here the sole effect of the outside world economy shall be to provide the possibility of exporting and importing various goods at stated export and import prices. We treat the export and import prices as exogenous variables and assume that the open economy is small relative to the outside world economy so that exports and imports by the open economy do not influence world prices. For the case in which world prices are so influenced, see Chapter 11.

The meanings of the quantities $A, B, \alpha, \beta, x, y, e$, and f are as defined in Chapter 2. In addition, we define the new quantities shown in Table 4-1.

We define the following matrices:

$$M_\alpha = B - \alpha A \qquad (1)$$

$$M_\beta = B - \beta A \qquad (2)$$

and we can now state the axioms of the open expanding economy model.

The first axiom is a conservation condition that states that the outputs of time $(t - 1)$, which are xB, together with the imports w^i, are sufficient for the exports from time $(t - 1)$, w^e and the inputs αxA needed for period t. See Figure 4-1 for a diagram of the physical flow of goods. In equation form, this is

$$xB + w^i - w^e = \alpha xA$$

Rewriting, we obtain

Axiom (O1): $xM_\alpha = w^e - w^i$.

(Outputs + imports = inputs + exports.)

This chapter is based on our papers [91] and [92]. In this chapter we adopt the notation of the latter.

Table 4-1

	Dimension	Name	Interpretation
	1×1	α	Expansion factor
	1×1	β	Interest factor
	$m \times n$	A	Input matrix
	$m \times n$	B	Output matrix
	$1 \times m$	x	Activity vector
	$n \times 1$	y	Price vector
Goods	$1 \times n$	w^e	Vector of exports
	$1 \times n$	w^i	Vector of imports
	$n \times 1$	p^e	Vector of export prices
	$n \times 1$	p^i	Vector of import prices
Activities	$m \times 1$	z^p	Vector of profits
	$m \times 1$	z^n	Vector of negative profits
	$1 \times m$	t^p	Vector of upper bounds
	$1 \times m$	t^n	Vector of lower bounds

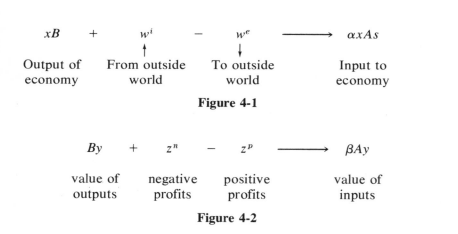

$$xB \quad + \quad w^i \quad - \quad w^e \quad \longrightarrow \quad \alpha xAs$$

| Output of economy | From outside world | To outside world | Input to economy |

Figure 4-1

$$By \quad + \quad z^n \quad - \quad z^p \quad \longrightarrow \quad \beta Ay$$

| value of outputs | negative profits | positive profits | value of inputs |

Figure 4-2

The second axiom is an accounting condition that requires that the value of the outputs of time $(t - 1)$, which are By, together with the negative profits z^n, be equal to the profits z^p from time $(t - 1)$ and the value βAy of the inputs needed for time t_0. See Figure 4-2 for a diagram of these accounting values. In equation form, this condition is

$$By + z^n - z^p = \beta Ay$$

Rewriting gives:

Axiom (O2): $M_\beta y = z^p - z^n$

(Value of outputs + negative profits = value of inputs + positive profits.)

The next condition is the balance of payments condition, which is well known in economics.

Axiom (O3): $w^e p^e = w^i p^i$

(External value of exports = internal value of imports.)

This axiom states that in order to achieve stable long-run economic growth, the value of exports must equal the value of imports when evaluated in terms of the *external* world prices.

However, the next condition, which is a balance of profits condition, is not a standard economic construct. It is

Axiom (O4): $t^p z^p = t^n z^n$

(Profits of profitable industries = losses of unprofitable industries.)

This axiom says that for stable long-run growth, the losses of the unprofitable industries must equal the profits of the profitable industries when *internal* prices are used and the industries are evaluated at their upper and lower bounds of activity level. The reason for this is that the government can then tax the excess profits of profitable industries and use the tax money to sustain the unprofitable industries as well as finance its own activities or services.

We wish to emphasize here that the term "unprofitable industry" does not have a derogatory connotation. It merely designates an industry for which the value of its outputs is less than the value of its inputs. The economy may find it desirable to operate such industries, such as the defense industry, the entertainment industry, or various service industries for reasons other than that of making a profit. Axiom (O4) merely requires that the financial support for such actions be forthcoming. Instead of speaking of "profitable" and "unprofitable" industries, we could have called them "supporting" and "supported" industries but unfortunately neither set of terms is free from possible derogatory attributes. We hope it is clear that such value judgements are not intended.

The fifth condition is exactly the same as Axiom (C5) in Chapter 2, namely,

Axiom (O5): $xBy > 0$

(Something of value is produced by the economy.)

To state the next axiom, we must consider the vectors t^p and t^n whose components set upper and lower bounds to the intensities with which the various industries are to be run. This requirement is given by

Axiom (O6): $t^n \leq x \leq t^p$

(Activities are within desired bounds.)

We want to emphasize the fact that the components of t^n and t^p are basically *control variables* of the economy. That is, they are selected by a combination of decisions by government agents, businesspeople, and consumers. The exact way in which they are determined depends on the political system and will vary from economy to economy. (In Chapter 9 they will also appear in an economy-wide long-range planning model whose principal purpose is to determine the correct setting of these variables to achieve certain objectives.) A final remark is that, since the t variables are controlled by the economy, they may be set so that the expanding economy is one that permits capital accumulation by those processes that produce goods desired by the economy.

The last axiom indicates the way in which the world prices affect the economy. It is

Axiom (O7): $p^e \leq y \leq p^i$

(Internal prices are between export and import prices.)

This axiom states the economically reasonable condition that the internal price of each commodity must be more than its export world price and less than its import world price.

Definition 1:   Given the data A, B, t^n, t^p, p^e, and p^i, a set of non-negative vectors, x, w, y, z, and factors α and β that satisfy Axioms (O1) through (O7) are said to be a solution to the open model.

As in previous chapters, solutions to these axioms need not exist without making certain assumptions. Thus we make the following assumptions:

(A1) Every process must have at least one positive input, i.e., A has no zero rows.

(A2) Every good can be produced in the economy, i.e., B has no zero columns.

(A3) $0 \leq p^e \leq p^i$.

(A4) $0 \leq t^n \leq t^p$.

Observe that (A1) and (A2) are exactly the same as in Chapter 2. Also, Assumptions (A3) and (A4) are clearly necessary, for, without them, we could not possibly find vectors x and y satisfying Axioms (O6) and (O7).

We will see shortly that the solutions to the closed models in the previous chapter are also solutions to the open model and that the open model permits other solutions. We distinguish between these solutions in the next definition.

Definition 2: A solution to the open model yields an *open economy* if the value of exports (evaluated at the export prices) is positive, that is,

$$w^e p^e > 0.$$

A solution with $w^e p^e = 0$ gives a *closed economy*.

Theorem 4-1: If $t^n = 0$ and $p^e = 0$ in Axioms (O1) through (O7), then there are solutions to the closed model in Chapter 2 that give a closed economy.

Proof: In Axioms (O1) through (O7), set $t^n = 0$, $p^e = 0$, $w^i = 0$, $z^p = 0$, and $\alpha = \beta$. Then it is easy to check that Axioms (O3) and (O4) are automatically satisfied. If we interpret t^p and p^i as the upper bounds on x and y, respectively, and are chosen so that x and y are probability vectors, we see that Axioms (O1), (O2), (O5), (O6), and (O7) are the same as those appearing in Chapter 2. Finally, since $p^e = 0$ we have $w^e p^e = 0$, so the solutions found in that chapter yield a closed economy.

This theorem shows that the open model contains the closed KMT model as a special case.

We now change the chicken-and-eggs example of Chapter 2 so that its solution yields an open economy.

Example 4-1: In the chicken-and-egg example of Chapter 2, we had

$$M_\alpha = \begin{pmatrix} 1 - \alpha & 12 \\ 5 - \alpha & -4\alpha \end{pmatrix}$$

Suppose we require that x and y satisfy the following constraints corresponding to Axioms (O6) and (O7):

$$t_1^n = 2 \leq x_1 \leq 3 = t_1^p \tag{3}$$

$$t_2^n = 0 \leq x_2 \leq 1 = t_2^p \tag{4}$$

$$p_1^e = 5 \leq y_1 \leq 6 = p_1^i \tag{5}$$

$$p_2^e = 2 \leq y_2 \leq 3 = p_2^i \tag{6}$$

Here (3) means that the laying industry is constrained and is operated at an intensity between 2 and 3, while (4) says that the hatching industry is operated with a nonnegative intensity of at most 1. Similarly, (5) says that the internal price, y_1, for chickens must lie between the chicken export price 5 and the import price 6. Finally, (6) says that the internal price, y_2, for eggs is between the egg export price 2 and the import price 3.

Note that the outside world has priced eggs to chickens relatively more highly than did the internal prices of the closed economy. Hence we would expect that our open economy will want to export eggs and, if necessary, import chickens. For this reason it is plausible to try to find a solution with $y_1 = 6$ and $y_2 = 2$. Because our economy wants to export eggs, we try a solution with $x_1 = 3$, that is, we run the laying industry at its maximum permitted intensity. We also look for solutions where $\alpha = \beta$. Hence we have two variables to determine, x_2 and α.

We will describe how to determine the solution in Section 2. Here we merely note that it is given by $x_2 = 0$ and $\alpha = 5$. Hence we can summarize the solution as follows:

$$x = (3,0), \quad w^e = (0,36), \quad w^i = (12,0)$$

$$y = \begin{pmatrix} 6 \\ 2 \end{pmatrix}, \quad z^p = \begin{pmatrix} 0 \\ 0 \end{pmatrix}, \quad z^n = \begin{pmatrix} 0 \\ 40 \end{pmatrix}$$

If the reader will substitute these quantities into the expressions given in each axiom, he will find that each one is fulfilled. Note that the existence of an outside world and the control variables have produced an entirely different solution than that found in Chapter 2 for the chicken and eggs economy.

Let us assume that the farmer starts with three chickens and utilizes this solution over time. The resulting production, imports, and exports take place as indicated in Figure 4-3. As in Chapter 2 we have divided each period into two parts representing the status at the beginning and at the end of the period.

Time Period

Activity	1		2		3		
Laying	3	3	15	15	75	75	...
Import chickens		12		60		300	...
Export eggs		36		180		900	...

Figure 4-3

Since

$$w^e p^e = (0,36) \begin{pmatrix} 5 \\ 2 \end{pmatrix} = 72 > 0$$

we have an open economy.

Note that in this solution we have shut down the hatching industry completely. Suppose that our economy, for some reason, does not want to eliminate the hatching industry. To prevent this, a policy change in t_2^n must be made which will have the consequences shown in the next example.

Example 4-2: Suppose that the economy makes $t_2^n = 1$, that is, decides to keep the hatching industry active. All other data are the same as in Example 4-1. The solution now becomes $\alpha = 15/4$ and

$$x = (3,1) \quad w^e = (0,21), \quad w^i = (7,0)$$

$$y = \begin{pmatrix} 6 \\ 2 \end{pmatrix}, \quad z^p = \begin{pmatrix} 15/2 \\ 0 \end{pmatrix}, \quad z^n = \begin{pmatrix} 0 \\ 45/2 \end{pmatrix}$$

The reader may again check from the axioms that these quantities provide a solution to an open economy.

We illustrate the economy over time in Figure 4-4, where we have assumed that the farmer started with 64 chickens and 64 eggs, $t_1^p = 48$, $t_2^n = 16$, $x = (48, 16)$, $w^e = (0, 336)$, and $w^i = (112, 0)$.

Example 4-3. In order to evaluate the consequences of the policy decision over time to keep the hatching industry active, let us rework Example 4-1

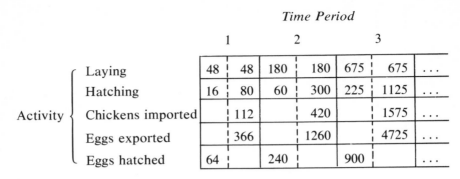

Time Period

Activity		1		2		3		
Laying		48	48	180	180	675	675	...
Hatching		16	80	60	300	225	1125	...
Chickens imported			112		420		1575	...
Eggs exported			366		1260		4725	...
Eggs hatched		64		240		900		...

Figure 4-4

Time Period

Activity	1		2		3		
Laying	28	28	140	140	700	700	...
Import chickens		112		560		2800	...
Export eggs		336		1680		8400	...

Figure 4-5

by having the farmer start with 28 chickens and $t_1^p = 28$. Figure 4-5 shows the solution for this case over time.

If we now compare the exportation of eggs in Figures 4-4 and 4-5, we see that at the first time period both economies export exactly the same number of eggs (336), even though the economy of Example 4-3 has less than half the number of chickens (28 compared to 64). However, in period 2 the Example 4-3 economy exports 33% more eggs and in period 3 the Example 4-3 economy exports 78% more eggs than that of Example 4-2. These differences show more clearly in the graph of Figure 4-6.

These simple numerical examples illustrate the great differences over time, which are the consequences of choosing one rather than another expansion policy. The existence of control variables is thus very important for the economy. (This point will be examined in greater detail in Chapter 9.)

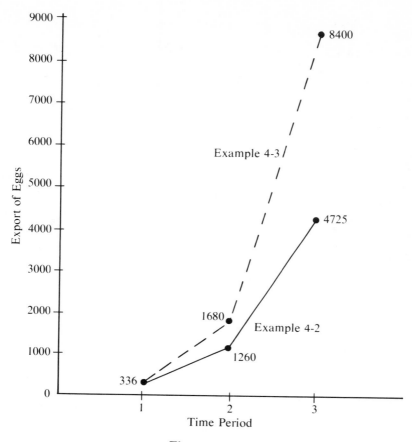

Figure 4-6

2. Existence of Solutions

As in Chapter 2, the existence of solutions implies immediately that the expansion and interest factor (and rates) are firmly related to each other.

Lemma 4-1: If there are solutions to Axioms (O1) through (O7), then

$$\alpha \leq \frac{xBy}{xAy} \leq \beta$$

Proof: Assume that we have vectors x, y, w^e, w^i, z^p, and z^n satisfying these axioms. Then by multiplying the expression in (O1) by y and using (O3) and (O7), we have

$$xM_\alpha y = w^e y - w^i y \geq w^e p^e - w^i p^i = 0$$

Similarly, multiplying the expression in (O2) by x and using (O4) and (O6) yields

$$xM_\beta y = xz^p - xz^n \leq t^p z^p - t^n z^n = 0$$

Using Equations (1) and (2) and Axiom (O5), we then have

$$\alpha \leq \frac{xBy}{xAy} \leq \beta$$

Throughout the rest of this section we show that solutions exist with $\alpha = \beta = xBy/xAy$. In Section 5 we give an example that has a solution with $\alpha < \beta$.

As previously remarked, we use the theory of linear programming to provide solutions to the model. Consider the following linear programming problem:

$$\text{Minimize} \quad -w^e p^e + w^i p^i \tag{7}$$

$$xM_\alpha \quad -w^e + w^i = 0 \tag{8}$$

$$-x \quad \geq -t^p \tag{9}$$

$$x \quad \geq t^n \tag{10}$$

$$w^e, w^i \quad \geq 0 \tag{11}$$

The derivation of this problem from the axioms is as follows: (8) is Axiom (O1); constraints (9) and (10) are formally equivalent to Axiom (O6); the term $-w^e p^e$ has been put in the objective function (7) to maximize the value of exports; and the term $w^i p^i$ has been put into (7) to minimize the value of imports.

The dual problem to this one is derived in a purely formal way using the rules described in Appendix 2. We assign dual variables y to (8), z^p to (9), and z^n to (10). Then the dual problem is:

$$\text{Maximize} \quad -t^p z^p + t^n z^n \tag{12}$$

$$M_\alpha y \quad -z^p + z^n = 0 \tag{13}$$

$$-y \quad \leq -p^e \tag{14}$$

$$y \quad \leq p^i \tag{15}$$

$$z^p, z^n \quad \geq 0 \tag{16}$$

Again note that (14) and (15) are formally equivalent to Axiom (O7), and (13) is Axiom (O2).

We now prove that this pair of dual linear programming problems has an optimal solution for every $\alpha \geq 0$.

Lemma 4-2: If assumptions (A3) and (A4) hold, then both problems (7) through (11) and (12) through (16) have optimal solutions for every $\alpha \geq 0$.

Proof: By the duality theorem of linear programming, one of the problems has an optimal solution if, and only if, the other one does. We show first that both problems have feasible solutions for every $\alpha \geq 0$. Choose such an α, and consider the maximizing problem. By using assumption (A3), we can find a y satisfying (14) and (15). Select any such y. Now choose z^p and z^n as follows: Let $(M_\alpha y)_i$ be the ith component of $M_\alpha y$. Then

$$\text{if} \quad (M_\alpha y)_i \geq 0, \quad \text{then let } z^p = (M_\alpha y)_i \quad \text{and} \quad z^n = 0$$

$$\text{if} \quad (M_\alpha y)_i < 0, \quad \text{then let } z^p = 0 \quad \text{and} \quad z^n = -(M_\alpha y)_i$$

The resulting y, z^p, and z^n clearly satisfy constraints (13) through (16) and provide a feasible solution to the maximizing problem. In an entirely analogous way, one can display a feasible solution to the minimizing problem constraints (8) through (11). Since both problems have feasible solutions, it is well known (see Appendix 2) that they both also have optimal solutions, completing the proof.

Actually, the duality theorem of linear programming also provides further properties that connect these two solutions, and we proceed now to exploit these properties.

Suppose now that, with α fixed, we have solutions x, y, w^e, w^i, z^p, and z^n to these dual problems. By the duality theorem, the optimal values of the pair of problems are equal, that is,

$$-w^e p^e + w^i p^i = -t^p z^p + t^n z^n \tag{17}$$

Also, when multiplying (8) by y, we have

$$x M_\alpha y - w^e y + w^i y = 0 \tag{18}$$

Similarly, multiplying (13) by x gives

$$x M_\alpha y - x z^p + x z^n = 0 \tag{19}$$

Now using, successively, (18), (14), (15), (17), (9), (10), and (19), we obtain the following string of inequalities:

$$-x M_\alpha y = -w^e y + w^i y$$
$$\leq -w^e p^e + w^i p^i$$
$$= -t^p z^p + t^n z^n \tag{20}$$
$$\leq -x z^p + x z^n$$
$$= -x M_\alpha y$$

Since the first and last terms are identical, every inequality in the string is actually an equality. Using the second equality in (20), we obtain

$$w^e(p^e - y) = w^i(p^i - y) \tag{21}$$

Since by (11) w^e and w^i are non-negative, and by (14) and (15) both $p^e - y \leq 0$ and $p^i - y \geq 0$, we conclude that

$$w^e(p^e - y) = 0 \tag{22}$$
$$w^i(p^i - y) = 0 \tag{23}$$

These results follow because the quantity on the left of (21) is non-positive while the quantity on the right of (21) is non-negative.

By similar analysis, using the fourth equality in (20), one can show that

$$(t^n - x) z^n = 0 \tag{24}$$
$$(t^p - x) z^p = 0 \tag{25}$$

As we saw in Theorem 4-1, in some cases there are closed economy solutions to the seven axioms. We now want to consider situations in which there are open economy solutions.

In order to be certain that there will be an open economy solution, there must be some requirement that forces the economy to export and import goods with the outside world. There are many possible such conditions that will do this. Here[a] we concentrate on the following condition:

$$t^n A p^e > 0 \tag{26}$$

The economic meaning of this condition is: *When the economy evaluates its goods at the lowest possible prices, namely at the export prices p^e, then even when operating at its minimum intensities the economy must have a positive demand to input at least one good which has a positive export price.* This assumption prevents the possibility of operating industries at high intensities that require only inputs that are free (because they have a zero export price) and producing goods that have positive value. Stated in this way the condition is economically meaningful. Observe that the verifi-

---

[a] This condition was used by us in our paper [91]. Since then, other authors have succeeded in weakening this condition, see [74, 80]. However, we prefer to retain (26) for our present purpose because of its simplicity.

cation of condition (26) involves world export prices and the lower bounds on intensities with which local industries are to be operated. Hence (26) can rather easily be checked in any specific case.

There are still three axioms to be satisfied, (O3), (O4), and (O5). (We leave the discussion of (O5) until later.) In order to satisfy (O3) and (O4) we must make a special choice of α. Note that on the right side of Equation (17) we have the difference between the profits of the unprofitable and the profitable industries and on the left side we have the difference between the value of the imports and the value of the exports. We now show that if (26) holds, we can select an α so as to make these two quantities satisfy Axioms (O3) and (O4)) simultaneously.

Lemma 4-3: If (26) holds, then there exists at least one non-negative expansion factor α such that

$$-w^e p^e + w^i p^i = -t^p z^p + t^n z^n = 0 \tag{27}$$

That is, the balance of profits and the balance of payments conditions are both satisfied.

Proof: Equation (17) gives the common value of the two linear programming problems. We can show that this value is non-positive for small α and positive for large α. Then, since the objective function value of this linear programming problem is a continuous function[b] of the parameters in its constraints, there is an intermediate value of α yielding (27).

We first show that the optimal value of (27) is negative when $\alpha = 0$. Then (8) becomes

$$xB - w^e + w^i = 0 \tag{28}$$

Since $B \geq 0$, we have $w^i = 0$ since, by linear independence of basic solutions,[c] $w_k^e w_k^i = 0$ for $k = 1, \ldots, n$, and

$$- w^e p^e = -xBp^e \leq - t^n Bp^e \leq 0 \tag{29}$$

where the last inequality follows from $t^n \geq 0$ and $p^e \geq 0$. Hence the objective value (27) of the optimal solution, when $\alpha = 0$, yields a nonpositive balance of trade (= balance of profits).

Because the conditions $w_k^e w_k^i = 0$ for $k = 1, \ldots, n$ and $z_k^n z_k^p = 0$ for $k = 1, \ldots, m$ always hold for *basic* solutions to (7) through (11) and (12) through (16), Moeschlin and Rahut in [82] suggest adding the following two axioms to the open model: $w^e w^{i'} = 0$ and $z^n z^{p'} = 0$. Moeschlin adopted this proposal in his excellent book [80] on von Neumann growth models. We do

---

[b] For a proof that this function is a continuous function of α, see Appendix 1.

[c] For further discussion of this result, see Appendix 2. See also Exercise 7.

not quarrel with the logical or mathematical correctness of these two additional axioms. However, we have not adopted them here because we do not wish to rule out either the economically observable possibility of the same country both exporting and importing the same good (such as automobiles, beer, specialty goods, etc.) or the equally observable possibility of a profitable industry being subsidized (such as farm production in the United States, the Lockheed Corporation, etc.). An additional mathematical objection to using the Moeschlin-Rahut axioms is that with them the set of optimal solutions to the open model is not convex. In any case the addition or subtraction of these axioms to the model causes no computational or conceptual difficulties.

Next we show that the optimum value of (27) is positive when α is very large. Equation (13) becomes

$$(B - \alpha A)y - z^p + z^n = 0 \tag{30}$$

Since $0 \le p^e \le y \le p^i$, we have

$$-z^p + z^n = -(B - \alpha A)y \ge -Bp^i + \alpha Ap^e \tag{31}$$

Multiplying on the left by x yields

$$-xz^p + xz^n \ge -xBp^i + \alpha xAp^e \tag{32}$$

Since $t^n \le x \le t^p$, we can set $x = t^n$ and deduce the inequality

$$-t^n z^p + t^n z^n \ge -t^n Bp^i + \alpha(t^n Ap^e) \tag{33}$$

Now (26) says $t^n Ap^e > 0$ so that we can make this quantity arbitrarily large by making α large. The objective function of the dual linear programs is $-t^p z^p + t^n z^n$ which differs by the term $-(t^p - t^n)z^p$ from (33). Because the left-hand side of (30) decreases with α, z^p cannot increase with α, and we see that the objective function of the dual programs must also become arbitrarily large as α becomes large. This completes the proof.

Lemma 4-3 shows that with condition (26) there is at least one nonnegative expansion factor α for which Axioms (O3) and (O4) are satisfied. The next lemma shows that α must be positive.

Lemma 4-4: There is no open economy with $\alpha = 0$.

Proof: If $\alpha = 0$, then, as in the proof of Lemma 4-3, it follows that $w^i = 0$ so that $w^i p^i = 0$. However, $w^e p^e > 0$ is the requirement for an open economy, so that the balance of payments condition cannot be satisfied when $\alpha = 0$.

All the previous developments permit us now to state the following existence theorem.

Theorem 4-2: If Assumptions (A1) through (A4) hold, then there exists at least one $\alpha > 0$ such that there are solutions x, y, w^e, w^i, w^p, and z^n satisfying Axioms (O1) through (O7), and $\beta = \alpha$. If Equation (26) holds, then there is a solution which is an open economy.

Proof: For any α, let $v(\alpha)$ be the common value of the dual linear programming problems (7) through (11) and (12) through (16). If $v(0) = 0$, then we have a necessarily closed economy (by Lemma 4-4) for which all the axioms, including (O5), will be satisfied as shown in Chapters 2 and 3. Suppose that $v(0) < 0$. Then, because of (A1), $v(\alpha)$ will be positive for large α. Hence by continuity of $v(\alpha)$ there is an intermediate $\alpha > 0$ such that $v(\alpha) = 0$, so that Axioms (O3) and (O4) are satisfied. Let x and y be the corresponding solution vectors. Since $\alpha = xBy/xAy$, we see that $xBy > 0$ so that Axiom (O5) is satisfied. A simple check whether $w^e p^e > 0$ or $w^e p^e = 0$ tells whether the solution to the economy is open or closed. Finally, if (26) holds, Lemmas 4-3 and 4-4 show that the resulting economy must be open.

The question now arises as to whether or not solutions to the dual linear programming problems are the only possible solutions to the open economic model characterized by Axioms (O1) through (O7). The answer to this question is positive, as demonstrated by the Theorem 4-3.

Theorem 4-3: Every solution to Axioms (O1) through (O7) with $\alpha = \beta$ provides a pair of solutions to the dual linear programming problems (7) through (11) and (12) through (16).

Proof: Let x, y, w^e, w^i, z^p, and z^n be non-negative vectors satisfying Axioms (O1) through (O7). By Axioms (O1), (O2), (O6), and (O7) these vectors are feasible for the dual linear programming problems, that is, they satisfy constraints (8) through (11) and (13) through (16). By Axioms (O3) and (O4) the objective functions of the two dual problems are both zero and hence are equal. It follows, therefore, that the above vectors are optimal for the dual programs.

3. Properties of Solutions

Having proved the existence of solutions to the open model, given certain economically plausible assumptions and having shown that these solutions are identical to those of a pair of dual linear programs, we now proceed to characterize and interpret such solutions. We shall be especially interested in economic interpretations.

Theorem 4-4: In any solution to the model with $\alpha = \beta$, the following conditions hold:

$$w^e y = w^i y \tag{34}$$

$$xz^p = xz^n \tag{35}$$

That is, there is a balance of payments and a balance of profits with respect to internal prices and activities.

Proof: Equation (19) holds for every set of feasible solutions. At the optimum, we also have $xM_\alpha y = 0$, and hence (19) implies (34) and (35).

Our next results are obvious consequences of Equations (22) through (25). These results correspond to the "theorem of the alternative," or the "complementary slackness conditions" in game theory and linear programming, respectively. (See Appendices 1 and 2.)

Theorem 4-5: If $\alpha, x, y, w^e, w^i, z^p$, and z^n are solutions to the open model with $\alpha = \beta$, then the following results hold:

(a) $\qquad\qquad\qquad w^e_j > 0 \quad$ implies that $\quad y_j = p^e_j$

$\qquad\qquad\qquad\quad\; y_j > p^e_j \quad$ implies that $\quad w_j = 0$

(Good j can be exported if, and only if, its internal price equals its export price.)

(b) $\qquad\qquad\qquad w^i_j > 0 \quad$ implies that $\quad y_j = p^i_j$

$\qquad\qquad\qquad\quad\; y_j < p^i_j \quad$ implies that $\quad w_j = 0$

(Good j can be imported if, and only if, its internal price equals its import price.)

(c) $\qquad\qquad\qquad z^p_i > 0 \quad$ implies that $\quad x_i = t^p_i$

$\qquad\qquad\qquad\quad\; x_i < t^p_i \quad$ implies that $\quad z^p_i = 0$

(The ith process can be profitable if, and only if, it is run at maximum intensity.)

(d) $\qquad\qquad\qquad z^n_i > 0 \quad$ implies that $\quad x_i = t^n_i$

$\qquad\qquad\qquad\quad\; x_i > t^n_i \quad$ implies that $\quad z^n_i = 0$

(The ith process can be unprofitable if, and only if, it is run at minimum intensity.)

The proofs of these results follow immediately from the non-negativity conditions and Equations (22) through (25).

We now turn to the interpretations of the effects of the parameters p^e, p^i,

t^p, and t^n on the resulting expansion rate. Clearly the α produced by the solution depends on these parameters, that is,

$$\alpha = \alpha(t^p, t^n, p^e, p^i) \tag{36}$$

The exact form of this functional dependence is, of course, very complicated; however, the following facts are evident:

Theorem 4-6:

(a) If t^n or p^i are increased or if t^p or p^e are decreased, then α goes down or stays the same.

(b) If t^n or p^i are decreased or if t^p or p^e are increased, then α goes up or stays the same.

The proofs of these assertions are obvious consequences of the maximizing and minimizing problems and the effects on them of the right-hand sides of their constraints (See Exercises 8 and 9.)

We characterize next the range of possible α's. Since p^i and p^e are given exogenously, we cannot control them and therefore assume that they are fixed. We can, however, vary both t^n and t^p continuously within the ranges determined by Assumptions (A3) and (A4), see page 63. Hence we will see that the resulting value of α can vary *continuously* in an interval. This is in distinct contrast to the closed KMT model of Chapters 2 and 3 for which there was only a discrete set of feasible expansion rates.

Theorem 4-7: For the open model there exist maximum and minimum expansion factors α_M and α_m for which there are feasible solutions. Moreover, every α satisfying $\alpha_m \leq \alpha \leq \alpha_M$ is also a feasible expansion factor for the model.

We will only sketch the proof of this theorem. As in the proof of Lemma 4-3, if we consider larger and larger α, a point is reached at which there are no longer *any* profitable industries. Hence α_M is at most as large as the smallest α for which there are only unprofitable or profitless industries. Similarly, if we consider smaller and smaller $\alpha > 0$, there is some sufficiently small value at which *every* industry is profitable. Thus α_m is at least as large as the largest α for which there are only profitable or profitless industries.

Now let t_m^p, t_m^n, t_M^p, and t_M^n be the control variables that cause the model to achieve expansion rates α_m and α_M. Consider the model with the control variables:

$$t_k^p = kt_m^p + (1-k)t_M^p$$

$$t_k^n = kt_m^n + (1-k)t_M^n$$

If we consider the dual linear programming problems (7) through (11) and (12) through (16) for these t's, we see that the parameters of these problems vary continuously with k. Hence the value of α required to make the values of both programs equal to zero also varies continuously with k. Also, when $k = 1$, we have $\alpha = \alpha_m$, and when $k = 0$ we have $\alpha = \alpha_M$. Hence intermediate α's can be achieved.

It is interesting to note that the maximum expansion factor in the open model is characterized by the largest α at which there is a profitless *industry* and no profitable industries, whereas the maximum expansion factor in the closed model was the largest α at which there was a profitless *subeconomy* and no profitable subeconomies. It follows, therefore, that the maximum expansion factor in the open model can be larger than that of the corresponding closed model. As example of this is given next.

Example 4-4: Consider the model with input-output matrices:

$$B = \begin{pmatrix} 4 & 0 \\ 0 & 3 \end{pmatrix}, \quad A = \begin{pmatrix} 1 & 2 \\ 1 & 0 \end{pmatrix}$$

If we solve it as a closed model with constraints,

$$0 \le x_1 \le 1 \qquad 0 \le y_1 \le .5$$
$$0 \le x_2 \le 1 \qquad 0 \le y_2 \le .5$$

we find the solution

$$\alpha = 1.81, \quad x = (.828, 1), \quad y = \begin{pmatrix} .303 \\ .5 \end{pmatrix}$$

Next we make it into an open model with constraints:

$$t_1^n = .5 \le x_1 \le 1 \qquad .5 \le y_1 \le .5$$
$$.5 \le x_1 \le 1 \qquad .5 \le y_2 \le .5$$

We have indicated $t_1^n = .5$ since we will change it later. (Note that we have assumed that export and import prices for both goods are equal to .5 to make calculations easy.) Now the solution to the open economy is

$$\alpha = 2, \quad x = (.5, 1), \quad w^e = (0, 1), \quad w^i = (1, 0)$$

$$y = \begin{pmatrix} .5 \\ .5 \end{pmatrix}, \quad z^p = \begin{pmatrix} 0 \\ .5 \end{pmatrix}, \quad z^n = \begin{pmatrix} 1 \\ 0 \end{pmatrix}$$

We see that the open economy makes both goods but exports good 2 and imports good 1. Industry 2, which produces only good 2, is profitable while industry 1, which produces only good 1, is unprofitable.

Observe that the expansion factor of the open economy is larger than that of the closed economy. It could be made still larger by decreasing t_1^n. Let us solve the problem with $t_1^n = 0$. The solution is

$$\alpha = 3, \quad x = (0,1), \quad w^e = (0,3), \quad w^i = (3,0)$$

$$y = \begin{pmatrix} .5 \\ .5 \end{pmatrix}, \quad z^p = \begin{pmatrix} 0 \\ 0 \end{pmatrix}, \quad z^n = \begin{pmatrix} 2 \\ 0 \end{pmatrix}$$

Since t_1^n cannot be reduced below 0, it is impossible to increase the expansion factor any further. This is also clear from the fact that when $\alpha = 3$, industry 2 is profitless and industry 1 is unprofitable, so that the balance of profits condition cannot be satisfied for larger expansion factors.

In general, the maximum expansion rate in the open model can be obtained by finding the most profitable industry and changing the control variables so that α increases until the most profitable industry becomes just profitless. However, it is doubtful that any real economy would actually try to use its largest expansion factor because it would correspond to a very low "quality of life."

Our final result gives a *necessary* condition such that the solution gives an open economy and a *sufficient* condition such that it gives a closed economy.

Theorem 4-8: (a) A necessary condition that the solution to the expanding economy model be open is

$$xBp^e > 0 \tag{37}$$

(b) A sufficient condition that the solution be closed is

$$p_i^e > 0 \quad \text{implies that} \quad y_i > p_i^e \tag{38}$$

Proof: (a) If

$$xBp^e = 0 \tag{39}$$

then multiplying the expression in Axiom (O1) by p^e, we have

$$xM_\alpha p^e = -\alpha xAp^e = w^e p^e - w^i p^e \leq 0 \tag{40}$$

Using (A3), we obtain

$$w^e p^e \leq w^i p^e \leq w^i p^i \tag{41}$$

Axiom (O3) shows that the inequalities in (41) are equalities. However,

(39) says that nothing is produced that has positive export price, so (41) gives

$$w^e p^e = w^i p^i = 0 \qquad (42)$$

and the solution yields a closed economy.

(b) If (38) holds, then the economy values all goods with internal prices higher than export prices so that it will export nothing. But because the balance of payments condition must hold, it will import either nothing or only free goods, and hence the economy is closed.

It is impossible to sharpen either of the statements in Theorem 4-8 because counter examples can be constructed that show that (37) is not a sufficient condition and (38) not a necessary condition. See Examples 4-7 and 4-8, discussed in the next section.

4. Further Examples

Example 4-5: We consider the closed example discussed in [91] and [92] in which there are two goods, labeled essentials and inessentials, and two industries, one for producing each good. The matrices are:

Essentials industry

Inessentials industry

$$A = \begin{pmatrix} \text{E} & \text{I} \\ 1 & 0 \\ 1 & 1 \end{pmatrix}, \qquad B = \begin{pmatrix} \text{E} & \text{I} \\ 4 & 0 \\ 0 & 2 \end{pmatrix}$$

Thus if we run just the essentials industry, we can expand with $\alpha = 4$, but if both industries are operated, the expansion factor drops to 2.

We make it into an open model by adding the following constraints:

$$t_1^n \leq x_1 \leq 1$$

$$0 < t_2^n \leq x_2 \leq t_2^p$$

$$0 < p_1^e \leq y_1 \leq p_1^i$$

$$p_1^e \leq y_2 \leq 1.$$

Note that we assume that $t_1^p = 1$, and $t_2^n > 0$, that is, we assume that the economy desires to produce some inessentials. We also assumed, for simplicity, that $p_2^e = 1$ and $p_1^i > p_1^e$. With these assumptions, the optimal strategies are

$$x = (1, t_2^n) \quad \text{and} \quad y = \begin{pmatrix} p_1^e \\ 1 \end{pmatrix}$$

From this it follows (see Exercise 11) that the expansion rate is

$$\alpha = \frac{4p_1^e + 2t_2^n}{p_1^e + p_1^e t_2^n + t_2^n} = \frac{4(p_1^e/t_2^n) + 2}{(p_1^e/t_2^n) + p_1^e + 1}$$

Clearly, the smaller t_2^n is, the larger α is, and conversely. It is also clear that in this case we have $2 < \alpha < 4$; that is, the open economy expansion factor lies between the two closed economy expansion factors. For instance, when $p_1^e = 1/4 = t_2^n$, we have $\alpha = 8/3$.

Example 4-6: As a slightly more complicated version of this example, we consider the problem with

$$B = \begin{pmatrix} 4 & 0 & 0 \\ 0 & 3 & 0 \\ 0 & 0 & 2 \end{pmatrix}, \qquad A = \begin{pmatrix} 1 & 0 & 0 \\ 1 & 1 & 0 \\ 1 & 1 & 1 \end{pmatrix}.$$

The closed economy has expansion factors 2, 3, and 4. Suppose we add the following constraints:

$$0.1 \le y_1 \le 1 \qquad 0.3 \le x_1 \le 0.9$$
$$0.2 \le y_2 \le 0.9 \qquad 0.2 \le x_2 \le 0.8$$
$$0.3 \le y_3 \le 0.8 \qquad 0.1 \le x_2 \le 0.7$$

It can then be shown by use of a computer that the expansion factor is $\alpha = 2.38$ and the solution vectors are

$$x = (0.9, 0.39, 0.1)$$
$$w^e = (0.3, 0, 0)$$
$$w^i = (0, 0, 0.04)$$

$$y = \begin{pmatrix} 0.1 \\ 0.39 \\ 0.8 \end{pmatrix}, \quad z^p = \begin{pmatrix} 0.162 \\ 0 \\ 0 \end{pmatrix}, \quad z^n = \begin{pmatrix} 0 \\ 0 \\ 1.46 \end{pmatrix}.$$

Note that x_2 and y_2 lie in between their respective bounds.

The next two examples are related to Theorem 4-8.

Example 4-7: To show that (37) is not a *sufficient* condition that the solution gives an open economy, consider the following example:

$$B = \begin{pmatrix} 4 & 0 \\ 0 & 2 \end{pmatrix}, \qquad A = \begin{pmatrix} 1 & 0 \\ 0 & 1 \end{pmatrix}$$

$$0 \le x_1 \le 1 \qquad .5 \le y_1 \le 1$$
$$0 \le x_2 \le 1 \qquad 0 \le y_2 \le 1$$

Then one solution is

$$\alpha = 4, \quad x = (1, 0), \quad w^e = (0, 0), \quad w^i = (0, 0)$$

and

$$y = \begin{pmatrix} 1 \\ 0 \end{pmatrix}, \quad z^p = \begin{pmatrix} 0 \\ 0 \end{pmatrix}, \quad z^n = \begin{pmatrix} 0 \\ 0 \end{pmatrix}$$

which is a closed economy. However, we can calculate that

$$xBp^e = (1, 0) \begin{pmatrix} 4 & 0 \\ 0 & 2 \end{pmatrix} \begin{pmatrix} .5 \\ 0 \end{pmatrix} = 2 > 0$$

so that (37) is satisfied. Thus (37) gives a necessary, but not sufficient, condition that a solution to the model be an open economy.

Example 4-8: To show that (38) is not a *necessary* condition, we modify the previous example slightly as follows:

$$B = \begin{pmatrix} 4 & 0 \\ 0 & 2 \end{pmatrix}, \quad A = \begin{pmatrix} 1 & 0 \\ 0 & 1 \end{pmatrix}$$

$$0 \le x_1 \le 1 \qquad 0 \le y_1 \le 1$$
$$0 \le x_2 \le 1 \qquad .5 \le y_2 \le 1$$

Then a solution is given by

$$\alpha = 2, \quad x = (0, 1), \quad w^e = (0, 0), \quad w^i = (0, 0)$$

and

$$y = \begin{pmatrix} 0 \\ 1 \end{pmatrix}, \quad z^p = \begin{pmatrix} 0 \\ 0 \end{pmatrix}, \quad z^n = \begin{pmatrix} 0 \\ 0 \end{pmatrix}$$

so that we have a closed economy ($w^e p^e = 0$), satisfying (38).

5. Unequal Expansion and Interest Factors

Lemma 4-1 proves that in any open solution to the model $\alpha \le \beta$. It is of interest to investigate conditions under which $\alpha < \beta$ is possible.

We begin by presenting an example in which the strict inequality holds. The example is the same as that given in section 4, with

$$B = \begin{pmatrix} 4 & 0 & 0 \\ 0 & 3 & 0 \\ 0 & 0 & 2 \end{pmatrix}, \qquad A = \begin{pmatrix} 1 & 0 & 0 \\ 1 & 1 & 0 \\ 1 & 1 & 1 \end{pmatrix}$$

and

$$t^p = (0.9,\ 0.8,\ 0.7)$$
$$t^n = (0.3,\ 0.2,\ 0.1)$$

and

$$p^e = \begin{pmatrix} 0.1 \\ 0.2 \\ 0.3 \end{pmatrix}, \qquad p^i = \begin{pmatrix} 0.1 \\ 0.9 \\ 0.8 \end{pmatrix}$$

Next we set $\beta = 2.38$ (as we did in the section 4) so that

$$y = \begin{pmatrix} 0.1 \\ 0.384 \\ 0.8 \end{pmatrix}, \quad z^p = \begin{pmatrix} 0.162 \\ 0 \\ 0 \end{pmatrix}, \quad z^i = \begin{pmatrix} 0 \\ 0 \\ 1.46 \end{pmatrix}$$

as before. However, we choose $\alpha = 2.31$, that is, we deliberately reduce the expansion rate of the economy below the 2.38, which is economically feasible. The vectors

$$x = (0.73,\ 0.33,\ 0.1)$$
$$w^e = (0.2404,\ 0,\ 0)$$
$$w^i = (0,\ 0,\ 0.031)$$

provide the rest of the solution. The reader may check that Axioms (O1) through (O7) are now satisfied.

The solution for $\alpha = 2.38$ was given in Example 4-5 as follows:

$$x = (0.9,\ 0.384,\ 0.1)$$
$$w^e = (0.3,\ 0,\ 0)$$
$$w^i = (0,\ 0,\ 0.04)$$

Hence the new solution ($\alpha = 2.31$) can be achieved by reducing x_1 to 0.73 and x_2 to 0.33. Our purpose is not to discuss why an economy would arbitrarily limit the production rate of particular industries, although there might well be reasons such as pollution control, labor difficulties, etc., that would cause such a limitation. Here we merely demonstrate by means of an example that solutions with $\alpha < \beta$ are, in fact, mathematically possible and often economically meaningful within the model.

In order to detect when an open economy has a solution with $\alpha < \beta$, we define two indices, r and s, measuring the internal balances of payments and profits.

Definition 3: Let x, y, α, and β be open solutions to the model. Define

$$r = xM_\alpha y = w^e y - w^i y$$

to be the *internal balance of payments index*, and

$$s = xM_\beta y = xz^p - xz^n$$

to be the *internal balance of profits index*. (*Note*: In the numerical example, $r = 0$ and $s = -0.028$.)

Lemma 4-5: For any open solutions,

$$s \leqq 0 \leqq r$$

Proof: Applying Definition 3, Axiom (O7), and Axiom (O3) successively, we have

$$r = w^e y - w^i y \geqq w^e p^e - w^i p^i = 0$$

Similarly, applying Definition 3, Axiom (O6), and Axiom (O4), we have

$$s = xz^p - xz^n \leqq t^p z^p - t^n z^n = 0$$

Theorem 4-9: The equation

$$\alpha = \beta$$

holds if, and only if, $r = 0 = s$.

Proof: From Axioms (O1) and (O2) and Definition 3, we have

$$\alpha = \frac{xBy - r}{xAy} \leqq \frac{xBy - s}{xAy} = \beta$$

Substituting $r = 0 = s$, we get $\alpha = \beta$; and substituting $\alpha = \beta$, we get $r = s$.

Note that this result is just a restatement of Theorem 4-4.

It is clear that, economically, the most interesting solutions are those with $r = s = 0$. For if $r > 0$, then the solution is not efficient (see M. Truchon [128]) in the sense that production is not being maximized over time. By using variants of Truchon's arguments, one can also show that if $s < 0$, the corresponding solution is not efficient. Hence even though $\alpha < \beta$ is mathematically possible, it seems to be economically uninteresting, at least for a one country economy.

Exercises

1. Verify that the solution to Example 4-1 satisfies all the axioms. Verify the numbers in Figure 4-3.
2. Verify that the solution to Example 4-2 satisfies all the axioms. Verify the numbers in Figure 4-4.
3. Verify the numbers in Figure 4-5.
4. Verify and comment on the graphs in Figure 4-6.
5. Show that the linear programming tableau corresponding to the dual linear programming problems in (7) through (11) and (12) through (16) is

	y	z^p	z^n	
x	M_α	$-I$	I	$= 0$
w^e	$-I$			$\leq -p^e$
w^i	I			$\leq p^i$
	$= 0$	$\geq -t^p$	$\geq t^n$	

(The blank areas in the tableau represent zeroes.)

6. Show that a linear programming problem equivalent to that of Exercise 5 is given by the problem whose tableau is

	y	z^p	z^n	v	v'	
x	M_α	$-I$	I			$= 0$
w^e	$-I$			p^e		≤ 0
w^i	I			$-p^i$		≤ 0
u		t^p	$-t^n$		1	$= 0$
u'				1		≤ 1
	$= 0$	≥ 0	≥ 0	$= 0$	≥ 1	

where v, v', u, and u' are scalar variables.

(a) Show that any solution to the problem in Exercise 5 is also a solution to the present problem if we set $u = v = 1$ and $u' = v' = 0$.

(b) Discuss how a solution to the present problem gives a solution to the problem in Exercise 5.

7. (a) Show that for a basic solution to the linear program of Exercise 5 (or 6) we must have $w_k^e w_k^i = 0$ for $k = 1, \ldots, n$.

   (b) If there is more than one basic solution to the linear program of Exercise 5 (or 6), show that by taking a positive convex combination of two or more of them we can obtain a solution in which $w_k^e w_k^i > 0$ for some values of k.

   (c) Interpret the result in (b) as a simultaneous import and export of the same good (e.g., wine, beer, automobiles) and comment on the economic reality of this possibility.

8. Prove Theorem 4-6(a).

9. Prove Theorem 4-6(b).

10. Verify that the solutions to the various problems given in Example 4-4 are correct.

11. In Example 4-5:

   (a) Show that the proposed solutions for x and y satisfy the constraints.

   (b) Verify that the choice of α is correct.

   (c) Show that all the axioms are satisfied.

   (d) Show that if $p_1^e = 1/4 = t_2^n$, then $\alpha = 8/3$. Find the numerical values of all solution vectors for this case.

12. Verify that Example 4-7 shows that (37) is not a sufficient condition that the solution to the open model be open.

13. Verify that Example 4-8 shows that (37) is not a necessary condition that the solution to the open model be open.

5

Subeconomies and Aggregation

1. Subeconomies in the Closed Model

In this section we return to the closed KMT model of Chapter 2 and require that Assumptions (A1) and (A2) hold. Then the existence theorem of that chapter (which was proved in Chapter 3) assures us that there are a finite number of allowable α's for which economic solutions (x,y) to M_α exist. We show here that for any allowable α for which there are economic solutions there is a self-sufficient part of the economy, in other words, a sub-economy, which can expand independently, in equilibrium, with the expansion coefficient α.

Consider one such allowable α; then $v(M_\alpha) = 0$. The minimax theorem of the theory of games ensures that there exist one or more optimal strategies for each player. The set of all optimal strategies for a player in a matrix game is convex and is spanned by a finite number of extreme points. These extreme points of the convex set of optimal strategies for a player are called *basic* optimal strategies for that player. Then for each allowable α there are a finite number of basic optimal strategies for each player. Let us call a pair of basic optimal strategies (x, y) which furnish an economic solution to M_α *basic economic solutions*. We call the x_i and y_j that occur in *basic* economic solutions the x- and y-components of basic economic solutions.

Suppose now that there are a finite number (say $r > 1$) of allowable α's for which economic solutions exist, and suppose that they are arranged in order of decreasing magnitude as follows:

$$\alpha_1 > \alpha_2 > \alpha_3 > \ldots > \alpha_r$$

An algorithm for finding all of these α's is given in Chapter 3. To simplify notation, let us indicate the game for $\alpha = \alpha_i$ simply by M_i for $i = 1, \ldots, r$.

Let I_1 be the set of all indices of rows i of M_1 for which there is an x-component of an economic solution to M_1 with $x_i > 0$; then let I_2 be the set of indices of rows i of M_2 which are *not* already contained in I_1 and for which there is an x-component of a basic economic solution to M_2 with $x_i > 0$. Let I_3 be the set of indices of rows i of M_3 which are *not* already contained in $I_1 \cup I_2$ and for which there is an x-component of a basic economic solution to M_3

The first three sections of this chapter are largely based on Section 9 of our paper with Kemeny [48]. The results of Section 4 of this chapter are new.

with $x_i > 0$; etc. Let I_r be the set of indices of rows of M_r which are *not* already contained in the set $I_1 \cup I_2 \cup I_3 \cup \ldots \cup I_{r-1}$ and for which there is an x-component of a basic economic solution to M_r with $x_i > 0$. And, finally, let I^* be the set of indices of all rows of M_α which are *not* contained in the set $I_1 \cup I_2 \cup \ldots \cup I_r$.

Let J_1 be the set of all indices of columns j of M_1 for which there is a y-component of an economic solution to M_1 with $y_j > 0$. Then let J_2 be the set of indices of columns j of M_2 which are not already contained in J_1 and for which there is a y-component of a basic economic solution to M_2 with $y_j > 0$. Let J_3 be the set of indices of columns j of M_3 which are not already contained in $J_1 \cup J_2$ and for which there is a y-component of a basic economic solution to M_3 with $y_j > 0$; etc. Let J_r be the set of indices of columns j of M_r which are not already contained in the set $J_1 \cup J_2 \cup \ldots \cup J_{r-1}$ and for which there is a y-component of a basic economic solution to M_r with $y_j > 0$. Finally, let J^* be the set of indices of all columns of M_α which are not contained in the set $J_1 \cup J_2 \cup \ldots \cup J_r$.

Now permute the rows and columns of the matrix M_α until it assumes the form shown in Figure 5-1. A specific instance of this decomposition is given in the wheat-chickens-eggs model of Example 2-3. In the decomposition of Figure 5-1, the entries M_α^{ij} are the submatrices of M_α which have their row indices belonging to I_i and their column indices belonging to J_j. The reader will observe that we have put zeros for the matrices M_α^{ij} when $i < j$, and this, of course, needs justification which is given in Lemma 5-1. The submatrices L_α^k have their row indices in I^* and their column indices in J_k, and the submatrices N_α^k have their column indices in J^* and their row indices in I_k. The matrix Q_α has its row indices in I^* and its column indices in J^*.

The processes which have their indices in I^* are those which are never used in any economic solution, that is, they are always inefficient processes. The goods which have their indices in J^* are those which have zero price in every economic solution; hence if they are ever produced in positive quantities, they are free goods. We shall be able to prove certain results about the submatrices L, M, and N but the submatrix Q can be completely arbitrary.

Lemma 5-1 If $i < j$, then $M_\alpha^{ij} \equiv 0$ for all α, that is, $A^{ij} = B^{ij} = 0$. (Here A^{ij} and B^{ij} indicate submatrices having row indices in I_i and column indices in J_j.)

Proof: Let x^0 be a central optimal strategy for α_i and let y^0 be a central optimal strategy for α_j. Then Lemma 2-2 shows that x^0 is optimal for α_j and y^0 is optimal for α_i. Therefore the following equations must be satisfied:

	J_1	J_2	J_3	$\cdots$	J_r	J^*
I_1	M_α^{11}	0	0	$\cdots$	0	N_α^1
I_2	M_α^{21}	M_α^{22}	0	$\cdots$	0	N_α^2
I_3	M_α^{31}	M_α^{32}	M_α^{33}	$\cdots$	0	N_α^3
$\vdots$	$\vdots$	$\vdots$	$\vdots$	$\cdots$	$\vdots$	$\vdots$
I_r	M_α^{r1}	M_α^{r2}	M_α^{r3}	$\cdots$	M_α^{rr}	N_α^r
I^*	L_α^1	L_α^2	L_α^3	$\cdots$	L_α^r	Q_α

Figure 5-1 —

$$x^0 B y^0 - \alpha_i x^0 A y^0 = 0$$

and

$$x^0 B y^0 - \alpha_j x^0 A y^0 = 0$$

Since $\alpha_i \neq \alpha_j$ these equations can be satisfied simultaneously if, and only if, $x^0 A y^0 = x^0 B y^0 = 0$. Since x^0 and y^0 are positive on I_i and J_j, respectively, this can happen only if $A^{ij} = 0$ and $B^{ij} = 0$, which in turn implies that $M_\alpha^{ij} \equiv 0$.

Definition: Let α' be an allowable expansion factor for M_α and let (x,y) be an economic solution corresponding to this α'. Let I be the set[a] of indices of processes which are used, i.e., those i such that $x_i > 0$. Let J be the set of indices of goods j which either have positive price or are free relative to the solution (x,y). And, finally, let M_α^{IJ} be the submatrix of M_α which has its row indices in I and its column indices in J. Then we call M_α^{IJ} a subeconomy of M_α. Considered as an economy itself, M_α^{IJ} can expand with the coefficient α', and (x,y) are economic solutions for the subeconomy for this α.

Thus a subeconomy is a subset (J) of the goods and a subset (I) of the processes of the original economy which has the same solution and same expansion coefficient as the original economy.

Theorem 5-1:   Let M_α be a KMT economy and let $\alpha_1, \alpha_2, \ldots, \alpha_r$ be the allowable expansion rates for which there are economic solutions. Then for each α_k there is at least one subeconomy, M_α^{IJ} with

[a] The reader is warned not to confuse the sets I and J with the sets I_k, I^*, J_k and J^* as previously defined.

$$I \subset I_1 \cup I_2 \cup \ldots \cup I_k \qquad (1)$$

and

$$J \subset J_1 \cup J_2 \cup \ldots \cup J_k \cup J^* \qquad (2)$$

which can expand at the rate α_k.

Proof: We prove this theorem by using mathematical induction on k. Our method of proof also provides an efficient calculation process for obtaining solutions to subeconomies once the decomposition of Figure 5-1 has been achieved.

When $k = 1$, we consider M_α^{11} shown in Figure 5-1. Let $(x^{(1)}, y^{(1)})$ be any pair of economic solutions for this economy considered by itself; such a pair of solutions must exist by the decomposition process that produced Figure 5-1. Let I be the subset of I_1 on which $x^{(1)}$ has positive components, and let J be the subset of J_1 on which $y^{(2)}$ has positive components, together with the indices in J^* of goods produced by the processes in I. Then M_α^{IJ} is a subeconomy which can expand at rate α_1.

Now assume that M_α^{IJ} has been constructed, satisfying (1) and (2) with k replaced by $k - 1$, which can expand at rate α_{k-1}. Let $(x^{(k-1)}, y^{(k-1)})$ be the corresponding solution pair. We must now show how to construct a subeconomy satisfying (1) and (2) that can expand at rate α_k. Consider M_α^{kk} shown on the main diagonal of Figure 5-1. Let (x, y) be a solution pair for M_α^{kk} and extend these strategies by adding zero components on $I - I_k$ and $J - J_k$. Call this new pair of strategies (x^0, y^0). Now add to the set I all row indices on which x^0 is positive. Also add to the set J all column indices on which y^0 is positive, together with the indices in J^* of goods produced by the process in I. Then we let

$$x^{(k)} = ax^{(k-1)} + (1 - a)x^{(k)}$$

and choose a large enough, but keep $a < 1$, so that $x^{(k)}M_{\alpha_k} \geq 0$. It is always possible to do this because all goods produced by the $(k-1)$st subeconomy will be overproduced when the whole economy is run at expansion rate $\alpha_k < \alpha_{k-1}$. Similarly, we let

$$y^{(k)} = by^{(k-1)} + (1 - b)y^0$$

and choose b large enough so that $M_{\alpha_k}y^{(k)} \leq 0$. The latter can always be done, if necessary, by setting $b = 1$ (which would mean that all goods in $J_1 \cup \ldots \cup J_{k-1}$ are free). Then M_α^{IJ} is a subeconomy that can expand at rate α_k.

Corollary: The subeconomy of Theorem 5-1 can always be chosen so that $I = I_1 \cup \ldots \cup I_k$ and $J \supseteq J_1 \cup \ldots \cup J_k$.

Proof: In the construction process of the proof of Theorem 5-1, use central strategies at each step (see Exercise 2).

As noted in the proof of Theorem 5-1, when operating the kth subeconomy, there usually will be overproduction of goods produced by the $(k-1)$st subeconomy so that these goods will be free. We can get around this by limiting the production of the industries in the $(k-1)$st subeconomy so that there is no overproduction and then by putting lower bounds on the prices of these goods. This leads to a model of the form

$$B = \begin{pmatrix} B^* & 0 \\ W & 0 \end{pmatrix}, \qquad A = \begin{pmatrix} A^* & Z \\ 0 & 0 \end{pmatrix}$$

B^* and A^* are the previous input and output matrices where the Z is a matrix that reflects the production constraints and W is a matrix that reflects the price constraints. Note that Z and W may have entries that are positive, negative, or zero, in contrast to the nonnegative requirements put on A^* and B^*. In two excellent papers, Los [65] and Mardon [74] have studied extended models with this structure and have shown that most of the results of the original models carry over to the extended case.

It is interesting to note that if new processes are developed, due to technological change or changes in taste, they must be added to the economy. This can be done by adding new rows to A and B and hence to M_α. Therefore the decomposition as described above may change. For example, if a new process is more efficient than an old one, then the new row of M_α will majorize an old row, and the index of the old row will be relegated to the limbo of I^*. Analogously, if a new good is added to the economy, which can be done by adding new columns to A and B and hence to M_α, then again the decomposition may change. The addition of the new good might make an old good, in comparison, always a free good, so that the index of the column of the old good would be shifted to J^*. Other more complicated changes can also occur. For instance, in Section 3 of Chapter 8 we discuss a rural economy that is gradually supplanted by an "agribusiness," representing a new technology. The latter occurs only gradually, however, as the control variables of the new process are slowly increased as the new technology comes "on stream."

Next we give a characterization of two of the allowable expansion rates. This characterization is essentially the same as that given by von Neumann for the unique expansion rate which he obtains. The difference is that here we must deal with more than one expansion rate.

Theorem 5-2: Let α^0 be the largest α such that there exists a vector x such that $xM_\alpha \geq 0$. Then α^0 is equal to the maximum allowable expansion factor for which economic solutions to the KMT model exist. In other words, the greatest (technically possible) expansion factor of the whole economy, neglecting prices, is equal to the maximum allowable α provided by Theorem 2-2.

Similarly, let β_0 be the smallest β such that there exists a vector y such that $M_\beta y \leq 0$. Then β_0 is equal to the minimum allowable interest factor for which economic solutions exist. In other words, the lowest interest factor β, at which a profitless system of prices is possible, is the minimum $\alpha = \beta$ provided by Theorem 2-2.

Proof: This theorem is simply a restatement of the fact that the maximum and minimum α such that $v(M_\alpha) = 0$ are also allowable α's for which economic solutions exist, which was proved in Chapters 2 and 3.

2. Disconnected Subeconomies in the Closed Model

Von Neumann made his Assumption (AO) because "it must be imposed in order to assure the uniqueness of α, β as otherwise W (the economy) might break up into disconnected parts." As we saw in the last section, if α is not unique, then it could be shown that many of the entries in the matrix M_α were zeros, and there were subeconomies which could function in a self-sufficient manner. However, these subeconomies were not always completely disconnected. Intuitively, one would say that two economies are disconnected if they have different expansion rates,[b] if they use different processes with positive weight, if they put positive prices on different sets of goods, and if they can be aggregated separately. The precise definition follows.

Definition: Let α and $\alpha'(\neq \alpha)$ be two allowable values of α for which there are economic solutions. Let M_α^{IJ} and $M_\alpha^{I'J'}$ be two subeconomies which can expand at the rates α and α' respectively and such that I and I' are disjoint and $J \cap J' \subseteq J^*$ and $M_\alpha^{I'J} = M_\alpha^{IJ'} = 0$. Under these assumptions we call M_α^{IJ} and $M_\alpha^{I'J'}$ *disconnected subeconomies* of M_α.

Economies that are not disconnected are characterized by the fact that the decomposition of Figure 5-1 has some nonzero entries below the M_α^{ij} entries. As we shall see in the next section, if one aggregates subeconomies that are *not* disconnected, then it is impossible, at least without further assumptions, to predict what effect such aggregation will have on the expansion factors. The case in which one can say something is the totally disconnected one which we proceed to define.

[b] This condition might also be dropped, but we prefer not to do so here. In Exercise 3 we go into the question in more detail.

Definition: An economy M_α is *totally disconnected* if, and only if, every pair of subeconomies having different expansion rates is disconnected.

An equivalent definition is that M_α is totally disconnected if, and only if, in the decomposition of Figure 5-1 we have $M_\alpha^{ij} = 0$ for $i > j$. Some examples of totally disconnected subeconomies are given in Exercise 4.

3. The Introduction of Aggregation into the Closed Model

By aggregation of processes or goods in the model we simply mean the adding together of weighted combinations of rows or columns of the matrices A and B. Such operations can be most conveniently done by pre- and post-multiplying with suitable matrices.

Definition: A *process aggregating matrix* P is a $p \times m$ matrix (where $1 \leq p \leq m$) having the following properties: each column of P has exactly one positive entry, each row of P has at least one positive entry, and all other entries in the matrix are zeros. If $p = m$, then P is essentially a diagonal matrix and there is no aggregation, while if $p = 1$, then P is a row vector having all entries positive and we call this *total process aggregation.*

A *goods aggregating matrix* Q is an $n \times q$ matrix (where $1 \leq q \leq n$) having the following properties: each row of Q has exactly one positive entry, each column of Q has at least one positive entry, and all other entries in Q are zeros. If $q = n$, then Q is essentially a diagonal matrix and there is no aggregation, while if $q = 1$, then Q is a column vector having all entries positive and we call this *total goods aggregation.*

It is obvious that if we start with an economy satisfying (A1) and (A2) and aggregate both goods and processes totally we will arrive at 1×1 matrices, A and B, which satisfy the (A0) condition. Even by partial aggregation we might arrive at a point where the aggregated matrices satisfy (AO) and hence we would obtain a unique expansion factor.

Theorem 5-3: Aggregating either processes or goods leaves the number of possible expansion factors for the economy decreased or unchanged. Moreover, if only processes are aggregated, then the magnitudes of the possible expansion factors, if anything, *decrease,* while if only goods are aggregated, then the magnitudes of the possible expansion factors, if anything, *increase.*

Proof: The first statement is obvious since aggregation can only increase the connectedness of the economy. Let us suppose that only processes are aggregated; then the game which we must solve is PM_α. The set of strategies for the minimizing player is unchanged. Hence, it is clear that if α is such that $v(M_\alpha)$ 0, then $v(PM_\alpha) \leq 0$. From this it follows that the magnitudes of the allowable α's for which there are economic solutions must, if anything, decrease. The proof of the other statement is similar.

Theorem 5-3 is economically meaningful on an intuitive basis: when the number of processes is decreased, the choices of methods of producing the given variety of goods become more restricted; when the number of goods is decreased, which is equivalent to obliterating distinctions among goods, the converse is the case.

The following example shows that if both goods and processes of a nontotally disconnected economy are aggregated, then the expansion rate may either go up or go down by any amount.

Example 5-1: Let A and B be the following matrices:

$$A = \begin{pmatrix} 1 & 0 \\ a & 1 \end{pmatrix}, \qquad B = \begin{pmatrix} 2 & 0 \\ b & 1 \end{pmatrix}$$

where a and b are parameters. Before aggregation the two natural expansion factors $\alpha = 1$ and $\alpha = 2$. Suppose now that we perform total aggregation of both goods and processes by letting $P = (1, 1)$ and $Q = (1, 1)'$. Then a simple computation (see Exercise 5) shows that the resulting unique expansion factor α' is given by the formula $\alpha' = (3 + b)/(2 + a)$ which can be made equal to any positive number by suitable choices of a and b.

This example shows that the computation of expansion factors should not be done without an examination of the degree and kind of aggregation that has been performed on the data used. Since economic data are necessarily presented in a highly aggregated form, the determination of expansion factors can, at best, be regarded as approximate even if the data are of the highest quality, which seldom is, in fact, the case. One obvious warning that should be made is that an artificial increase in expansion factors can be made by aggregating free goods with nonfree goods (see Exercise 6). It is evident that this does not correspond to economic reality and therefore should be avoided.

Thus without further assumptions or restrictions on what can happen below the diagonal of the matrix, it is impossible to predict what will happen to the expansion rate when aggregation takes place. The reader is invited to speculate on the meaning and value of computing expansion rates for economies by using a totally aggregated number such as the GNP, see [89].

With the assumption of a completely disconnected economy, one can prove a strong and economically meaningful result, which we proceed to derive. Let M_α be the totally disconnected economy whose decomposition is given in Figure 5-2. Since the entries below the diagonal are zero, it is not necessary to use double subscripts on the entries on the diagonal. Clearly, M_α^1, M_α^2, ..., M_α^r are disconnected subeconomies. Let p and q be total aggregation vectors. Consider the following numbers:

$$a_k = \sum_{\substack{i \in I_k \\ j \in J_k}} p_i q_j a_{ij}$$

$$b_k = \sum_{\substack{i \in I_k \\ j \in J_k}} p_i q_j b_{ij}$$

It is easy to see that if we totally aggregate the subeconomy M_α^k, then its expansion rate α_k' after aggregation is given by

$$\alpha_k' = b_k/a_k \quad \text{for } k = 1, 2, \ldots, r$$

If we totally aggregate the economy M_α, then its expansion rate α' after aggregation is

$$\alpha' = \frac{b_1 + b_2 + \ldots + b_r}{a_1 + a_2 + \ldots + a_r}$$

It can be shown (see Exercise 7) that α' lies between the smallest and the largest of the α_k'.

We summarize our results in the following theorem.

Theorem 5-4: Let M_α be a totally disconnected economy with subeconomies M_α^k for $k = 1, \ldots, r$. If α' is the unique expansion factor for M_α after total aggregation and α_k' is the unique expansion factor of M_α^k after total aggregation, then

$$\min_k \alpha_k' \leq \alpha \leq \max_k \alpha_k'$$

I_1	M_α^1	0	0	$\ldots$	0	N_α^1
I_2	0	M_α^2	0	$\ldots$	0	N_α^2
I_3	0	0	M_α^3	$\ldots$	0	N_α^3
$\vdots$	$\vdots$	$\vdots$	$\vdots$	$\ldots$	$\vdots$	$\vdots$
I_r	0	0	0	$\ldots$	M_α^r	N_α^r
I^*	L_α^1	L_α^2	L_α^3	$\ldots$	L_α^r	Q_α

Figure 5-2

Example 5-2: Let A and B be the following matrices:

$$A = \begin{pmatrix} 1 & 0 \\ 0 & 1 \end{pmatrix}, \qquad B = \begin{pmatrix} 2 & 0 \\ 0 & 1 \end{pmatrix}$$

The two natural expansion factors are, as before, $\alpha = 1$ and $\alpha = 2$. If we perform the same total aggregation as in Example 5-1 with $P = (1, 1)$ and $Q = (1, 1)'$, then the unique resulting expansion factor is $\alpha' = 3/2$, which lies half way between the maximum and minimum natural expansion factors.

4. Subeconomies in the Open Model

In Section 1 we defined a subeconomy of the closed model as a subset of goods and activities of the original economy that has the same solution and expansion factors as the original closed economy. Thus a closed sub-economy is entirely contained within the given economy and it is techno-logical in nature.

These same closed subeconomies exist in the open model, but there are many others. For, as we noted in Section 4-3, any sufficiently profitable industry of the open model can be run as a subeconomy by selecting the expansion factor so that some of the outputs of the industry can be exported and sold on the world market and the returns used to pay for whatever imports are needed by the industry. In the same way, any subset of industries—some profitable, and some profitless or unprofitable—can be run as a subeconomy by a suitable adjustment of control variables and expansion factors. Thus the creation of a subeconomy in the open model is the consequence of conscious decisions which fix the corresponding con-trol variables in order to select and operate the subeconomy.

We illustrate these concepts by returning to the farming example of Chapter 2 in which the farmer has three activities, wheat farming, laying eggs, and hatching chickens. The input and output matrices are:

		W	C	E			W	C	E
Wheat		1	0	0			9	0	0
Laying	$A =$	1	1	0	,	$B =$	0	1	12
Hatching		1	1	4			0	5	0

Let us assume that the constraints of the open model are

$$0 \leq x_1 \leq t_1^p \qquad p_1^e = 3 \leq y_1 \leq 5 = p_1^i$$

$$0 \leq x_2 \leq t_2^p \qquad p_2^e = 5 \leq y_2 \leq 6 = p_2^i$$

$$0 \leq x_3 \leq t_3^p \qquad p_3^e = 2 \leq y_3 \leq 3 = p_3^i$$

Clearly, if $\alpha \leq 9$ the first industry is always profitable, but the other two industries are profitable only when α is sufficiently small. We will discuss the following seven subeconomies as examples or exercises.

(a) The wheat industry only.

(b) The laying industry only.

(c) The hatching industry only.

(d) Wheat and laying industries.

(e) Wheat and hatching.

(f) Laying and hatching.

(g) All three industries.

Example 5-3: For subeconomy (a) we set $t_1^p = 1$, $t_2^p = t_3^p = 0$, and $\alpha = 9$. This subeconomy is closed since it neither exports nor imports. The solution vectors are:

$$x = (1,0,0) , \qquad y = (y_1, \, 6, \, 3)'$$

where y_1 is any number satisfying $3 \leq y_1 \leq 5$. The prices of chickens and eggs are irrelevant because this economy does not produce them and has no foreign exchange with which to import them. A variant of this example in which there is excess consumption is given in Exercise 9.

Example 5-4: For subeconomy (b), we set $t_1^p = t_3^p = 0$ and $t_2^p = 1$. This economy exports wheat and eggs and imports chickens; hence $y = (3,6,2)'$. To find α we must solve

$$(-\alpha, \, 1 - \alpha, \, 12) \begin{pmatrix} 3 \\ 6 \\ 2 \end{pmatrix} = -3\alpha + 6(1 - \alpha) + 24 = -9\alpha + 30 = 0$$

which gives $\alpha = 10/3$.

Subeconomies (c) and (d) are treated in Exercises 10 and 11.

Example 5-5: For subeconomy (e), let us set $t_1^p = 1$, $t_2^p = 0$, and $t_3^p = t_3^n = t$, which we want to determine. Clearly, $y = (3,5,3)'$. We must solve

$$(1,t) \begin{pmatrix} 9 - \alpha & 0 & 0 \\ -\alpha & 5 - \alpha & -4\alpha \end{pmatrix} \begin{pmatrix} 3 \\ 5 \\ 3 \end{pmatrix} = 0$$

which gives

$$3(9 - \alpha) - 3\alpha t + 5\, t(5 - \alpha) - 12\alpha t = 0$$

Upon solving this for α, we get

$$\alpha = \frac{25t + 27}{20t + 3}$$

When $t = 0$, $\alpha = 9$ as expected since we then return to subeconomy (a). As t increases, α decreases (see Exercise 12). Hence the economy selects its expansion rate by deciding the extent to which the hatching industry is to be run.

Subeconomy (f) is treated in Exercise 13.

Example 5-6: For subeconomy (g), we set $t_1^p = 1$, $t_2^p = t_2^n = u$, $t_3^p = t_3^n = v$. Then, if we assume that the subeconomy exports wheat and imports chickens and eggs, we have $y = (3,6,3)'$. Thus to find α we must solve

$$(1,u,v) \begin{pmatrix} 9 - \alpha & 0 & 0 \\ -\alpha & 1 - \alpha & 12 \\ -\alpha & 5 - \alpha & -4\alpha \end{pmatrix} \begin{pmatrix} 3 \\ 6 \\ 3 \end{pmatrix} = 0$$

The solution is

$$\alpha = \frac{27 + 42u + 30v}{3 + 9u + 21v}$$

One possible open-economy solution which satisfies all of the above conditions is $u = v = 1/2$, $\alpha = 3.5$. Further discussion of this example is given in Exercise 14.

In Chapter 11 we will discuss briefly the idea of *international subeconomies* that are made up of several different activities belonging to various countries. These are similar to, but not identical with, closed subeconomies, since each activity used in the subeconomy must also participate in the balance of payments problem of the country in which it is located, as well as contribute to the technological subeconomy.

Exercises

1. Show that the wheat-chicken-eggs example discussed in Example 2-3 is already in the decomposed form of Figure 5-1. Identify the various sets I_R, J_R and matrices M_α^{ij}. Show that there are two subeconomies.

2. Give the details of the proof of the Corollary to Theorem 5-1.

3. Consider the 2×2 model with

$$A = B = \begin{pmatrix} 1 & 0 \\ 0 & 1 \end{pmatrix}$$

Show that this model satisfies all the conditions for totally disconnected subeconomies except for the difference in expansion rates. Discuss.

4. Show that the following economies are totally disconnected and find all expansion factors for each.

$$M_\alpha = \begin{pmatrix} 6 - \alpha & 0 & 0 \\ 0 & 3 - \alpha & 0 \\ 0 & 0 & 1 - \alpha \end{pmatrix}$$

$$M_\alpha = \begin{pmatrix} \dfrac{3}{2} - \alpha & 0 & 0 \\ 0 & 5 - \alpha & 0 \\ 0 & 0 & \dfrac{1}{2} - \alpha \end{pmatrix}$$

5. Calculating

$$(1,1) \begin{pmatrix} 2 - \alpha & 0 \\ b - \alpha a & 1 - \alpha \end{pmatrix} \begin{pmatrix} 1 \\ 1 \end{pmatrix} = 0$$

show that the unique expansion factor of Example 5-1 after aggregation is $\alpha' = (3 + b)/(2 + a)$. Show how to obtain any positive expansion factor by suitably choosing a and b.

6. Consider the economy whose input-output matrices are:

$$A = \begin{pmatrix} 1 & 0 \\ 1 & 1 \end{pmatrix}, \qquad B = \begin{pmatrix} 3 & 0 \\ 2 & 2 \end{pmatrix}$$

(a) Show that there are two economic expansion rates, $\alpha = 3$ and $\alpha = 2$.

(b) Show that there are two subeconomies and find solutions for each.

(c) Show that when the whole economy is run, $\alpha = 2$ and good 1 is overproduced and hence is free.

(d) Show that total aggregation of both processes and goods artificially raises the expansion rate to $\alpha = 7/3$.

7. Consider the ratios b_k/a_k for $k = 1, \ldots, r$. Suppose that b_1/a_1 is the largest and that b_r/a_r is the smallest of these.

(a) Show by direct calculation that

$$\frac{b_1}{a_1} \geq \frac{b_1 + b_r}{a_1 + a_r} \geq \frac{b_r}{a_r}$$

(b) Show by direct calculation that

$$\frac{b_1}{a_1} \geq \frac{b_1 + b_2 + \ldots + b_r}{a_1 + a_2 + \ldots + a_r} \geq \frac{b_r}{a_r}$$

8. Consider the economy with the following matrices:

$$A = \begin{pmatrix} 1 & 0 \\ 1 & 1 \end{pmatrix}, \qquad B = \begin{pmatrix} 2 & 0 \\ 4 & 1 \end{pmatrix}$$

   (a) Show that there are two economic expansion rates, $\alpha = 2$ and $\alpha = 1$.
   (b) Find solutions for the resulting subeconomies.
   (c) Perform total processes and goods aggregation and show that the resulting expansion rate is greater than either of the rates in (a).
   (d) Use this example to show that the assumption that M_α is totally disconnected cannot be dropped from the statement of Theorem 5-4.
   (e) What happens if we make $a_{21} = 4$ and $b_{21} = 1$?

9. In Example 5-3, suppose that we have the consumption vector $h = (1,1,4)$. Show that by reducing its expansion rate to 9/7 the economy can consume one unit of wheat, one chicken, and four eggs during each time period.

10. Solve subeconomy (c) of Section 4.

11. Solve subeconomy (d) of Section 4.

12. By finding the first derivative of

$$\alpha = \frac{25t + 27}{20t + 3}$$

   show that α is a decreasing function of t when $t \geq 0$.

13. Show that, for subeconomy (f), when $t_2^p = 1$ and $t_3^p = t_3^n = t$, then

$$\alpha = \frac{25t + 29}{18t + 10}$$

   Show that α is a decreasing function of t and comment on the result.

14. In Example 5-6, show that the open economy is satisfied by the following two sets of conditions:

   (a) $$u = v = 1, \quad \alpha = 3.$$

   This is a closed economy.

   (b) $$u = v = 1/2, \quad \alpha = 3.5$$

   This is an open economy.

15. In Example 5-6, show that the following conditions must hold for the economy to import both chickens and eggs:

$$\frac{5 - \alpha}{\alpha - 1} \leq \frac{u}{v} \leq \frac{\alpha}{3}$$

Check that these conditions hold for both parts of Exercise 14.

6

Private and Public Consumption and Savings in the Closed Model

1. Axioms and Assumptions

In the models of the previous chapters we discussed economies whose sole purpose was to grow successively larger from one time period to another. Consumption, if any, was treated merely as a necessary part of the input matrix, and no discretionary consumption was allowed.

In this chapter we add the possibility of drawing off part of the production to be used for public or private consumption, defense, foreign aid, etc., to the KMT economic model of Chapter 2. (In Chapter 7 we will consider a similar extension for the open model of Chapter 4.)

As in the original model of Chapter 2, we let A and B be non-negative $m \times n$ matrices whose entries are the input and output coefficients of the various industries, respectively. We introduce an additional non-negative $m \times n$ matrix H whose entries will be interpreted as the maximum amounts of optional consumption or surplus, in real terms, that are permitted in the model. Thus h_{ij} is the maximum amount of good j that can be consumed by the workers and stockholders of industry i if that industry is run at unit intensity. We do not describe the exact processes by which these goods are declared surplus and available for consumption or the way they are distributed among these persons. Our model, in fact, does not explicitly assign identities to persons. Note that this maintains the same limitations in consideration of technology that our previous models had.

We also assume that there are two non-negative numbers c and s, called the consumption and capital accumulation (savings) coefficients, respectively. We assume for mathematical purposes that

$$0 \le c \le 1 \quad \text{and} \quad 0 \le s \le 1 \tag{1}$$

We frequently make the stronger but economically reasonable assumption that a fraction c of the surplus is consumed (i.e., withdrawn from the input-output process) and that the remainder $s = 1 - c$ is added to capital stocks. Most of our examples will satisfy the latter assumption.

As in Chapter 2, we let α and β be the expansion and interest factors, respectively. We let x be the $1 \times m$ intensity vector, and we let y be the $n \times 1$ price vector. These vectors are assumed to be normalized so that they are

This chapter, except for Section 5, is largely based on our paper [90].

probability vectors. Then the equilibrium conditions that the model must satisfy are given by the following axioms:

Axiom (CC1): $x[B - \alpha(A + cH)] \geq 0$

Axiom (CC2): $[B - \beta(A + sH)]y \leq 0$

Axiom (CC3): $x[B - \alpha(A + cH)]y = 0$

Axiom (CC4): $x[B - \beta(A + sH)]y = 0$

Axiom (CC5): $xBy > 0$

The first axiom states that the output of a given time period must be enough to provide the inputs of the next time period (including the reproduction of the workers) plus the surplus consumption of the workers. The second axiom states that the value of the outputs must be enough to cover the capitalized value of the inputs plus the excess profits. Axiom (CC3) says that overproduced goods should obtain zero price (the free disposal condition). And Axiom (CC4) says that inefficient industries should be used with zero intensity. Finally, Axiom (CC5) says that the production-pricing structure must be such that something of value is produced.

As in Chapter 2, additional assumptions have to be made in order that solutions to (CC1) through (CC5) must necessarily exist. These are:

(A1) $\qquad\qquad\qquad\qquad \nu(B) > 0$

(A2) $\qquad\qquad\qquad\qquad \nu(-A) < 0$

(A3) $\qquad\qquad\qquad\qquad A + B + H > 0$

The interpretations of (A1) and (A2) are as before, namely, (A1) says that B has no zero columns, which means that every good can be produced by some process, while (A2) says that A has no zero rows, meaning that every process requires a positive amount of some input. Condition (A3), which is similar to the original von Neumann condition $A + B > 0$, prevents the economy from breaking up into disconnected subeconomies. Here it is an assumption of convenience and it can be easily removed. However, we make this assumption in this chapter since our principal interest is to discuss the economic implications of an economy that is either connected by technological requirements ($A + B > 0$) or at least by ubiquitous tastes of the workers in all industries (condition A3). In Section 6 we show that the "tastes" of the public sector may also have a unifying effect on different areas of the economy.

To reiterate the above points, let us note that at least three kinds of "subeconomies" may be distinguished: technological subeconomies, private consumption subeconomies, and public consumption subeconomies. Thus looking at only one of these factors may permit breaking up the economy in various ways, but looking at them simultaneously may, in effect, tie them all together into a single economy. As far as we know, these ideas were stated in 1967 in [90] for the first time for economics in a technically precise manner. We would like to note the remarkably strong similarity of this procedure to the method of composition and decomposition of n-person games (see [106]; as summarized on pp. 340-341 there).

2. Elementary Examples

Although these axioms seem quite plausible given the results of the preceding chapters, we see that the addition of the decision variable $c = 1 - s$ makes substantial changes in the solutions which in turn require new kinds of economic interpretations. The first four examples are based on the chicken-and-eggs example from Chapter 2. The matrices we will use are:

$$
\begin{array}{cc}
 & \begin{array}{cc} \text{Chicken} & \text{Egg} \end{array} \\
\begin{array}{c} \text{Laying} \\ \\ \text{Hatching} \end{array} \quad B = & \begin{pmatrix} 1 & 12 \\ 5 & 0 \end{pmatrix}
\end{array}, \quad
\begin{array}{cc}
 & \begin{array}{cc} \text{Chicken} & \text{Egg} \end{array} \\
A = & \begin{pmatrix} 1 & 0 \\ 1 & 4 \end{pmatrix}
\end{array},
$$

$$
\begin{array}{cc}
 & \begin{array}{cc} \text{Chicken} & \text{Egg} \end{array} \\
H = & \begin{pmatrix} 2 & 4 \\ 2 & 4 \end{pmatrix}
\end{array}
$$

In other words, we assume that the workers and stockholders of both the laying and hatching industries are given real goods in the proportion of 2 chickens to 4 eggs to use in any combination they wish for consumption or reinvestment. We now solve the model for various choices of c and s.

Example 6-1. Suppose that $c = s = 1/2$. Then

$$
A + cH = A + sH = \begin{pmatrix} 2 & 2 \\ 2 & 6 \end{pmatrix}
$$

so that Axioms (CC1) through (CC5) becomes exactly those of a KMT model with input matrix $A' = A + cH$. Here the solution is easily found to be $\alpha = \beta = 3/2$ and

$$x = (½, ½), \qquad y = \begin{pmatrix} 9/11 \\ 2/11 \end{pmatrix}$$

Thus we see that adding consumption to the model has decreased the expansion rate from $\alpha = 3$ (see Example 2-1) to $\alpha = 3/2$. The optimal intensity vector is the same as before, but the chicken-egg price ratio has decreased from $6:1$ to $9:2$. Figure 6-1 shows production and consumption over time, given that we start with 40 chickens and 80 eggs that are to be used in the production processes. Observe that in Period 1, 20 of the 40 chickens are used in the laying industry and the remaining 20 chickens, together with the 80 eggs, are used in the hatching industry. At the end of Period 1 there are 120 chickens and 240 eggs. Of these, 60 chickens and 120 eggs are consumed and the rest are used to run the laying and hatching industries at intensities of 30 each for Period 2. The transition from Period 2 to Period 3 is similar. The arrow diagram in Figure 6-2 makes this production-consumption process clear.

Example 6-2. Assume that $c = 0$ and $s = 1$. To satisfy Axioms (CC1) and (CC3), we solve the game

$$B - \alpha A = \begin{pmatrix} 1 - \alpha & 12 \\ 5 - \alpha & -4\alpha \end{pmatrix}$$

and find $\alpha = 3$ and $x = (½, ½)$. To satisfy Axioms (CC2) and (CC4), we solve the game

$$B - \beta(A + H) = \begin{pmatrix} 1 - 3\beta & 12 - 4\beta \\ 5 - 3\beta & -8\beta \end{pmatrix}$$

and find that $\beta = 1$ and

$$y = \begin{pmatrix} 4/5 \\ 1/5 \end{pmatrix} .$$

It is easy to check that Axiom (CC5) holds, so the above solutions satisfy all the axioms. Note that $3 = \alpha > \beta = 1$ so that although the economy is tripling its real goods output, the price structure is such that the value of the inputs needed to get one unit of output is exactly equal to the value of the unit of output (values are calculated using the model's prices). Figure 6-3 shows production and consumption over time, given that we start with 40 chickens and 80 eggs that are to be used in the production process.

Note that the production process is exactly that of the original chicken-

	Period 1		Period 2		Period 3		
	Begin	End	Begin	End	Begin	End	
Laying	20		30		45		
Hatching	20		30		45		
Chickens produced		120		180		270	...
Eggs produced		240		360		540	
Chickens consumed		60		90		135	
Eggs consumed		120		180		270	

Figure 6-1

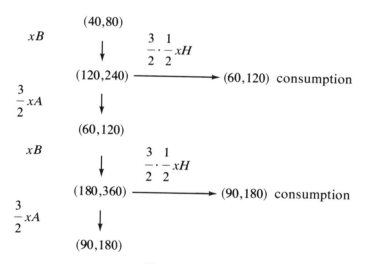

Figure 6-2

and-egg example of Chapter 2. However, the decision to reinvest rather than to consume now resides in the consumers hands. The very fact that they have made this consumption-investment decision in this way has caused the extreme distortion in the interest factor and price structure, as compared to the former interest and price structure.

This is a wholly unexpected and surprising phenomenon derived from economically plausible axioms by a mathematically rigorous procedure, (to which reference was already made in Chapter 1) and that could not be anticipated by merely verbal analysis or intuition.

	Period 1		Period 2		Period 3	
	Begin	End	Begin	End	Begin	End
Laying	20		60		180		
Hatching	20		60		180		
Chickens produced		120		360		1040	...
Eggs produced		240		720		2160	
Chickens consumed		0		0		0	
Eggs consumed		0		0		0	

Figure 6-3

Example 6-3: Assume that $c = 1$, $s = 0$. Here we consume all of H and reinvest nothing. To satisfy Axioms (CC1) and (CC3) we solve the game

$$B - \alpha (A + H) = \begin{pmatrix} 1 - 3\alpha & 12 - 4\alpha \\ 5 - 3\alpha & - 8\alpha \end{pmatrix}$$

and find $\alpha = 1$, $x = (\frac{1}{2}, \frac{1}{2})$. To satisfy Axioms (CC2) and (CC4) we solve the game

$$B - \beta A = \begin{pmatrix} 1 - \beta & 12 \\ 5 - \beta & -4\beta \end{pmatrix}$$

and obtain $\beta = 3$ and

$$y = \begin{pmatrix} 6/7 \\ 1/7 \end{pmatrix}.$$

Here $1 = \alpha < \beta = 3$ and both the price and intensity vectors are exactly the same as in the chicken and eggs example of Example 2-1.

The production and consumption patterns over time are shown in Figure 6-4, starting with 40 chickens and 80 eggs that are to be used in the production process.

Note that although $\alpha = 1$ so that the economy is completely stationary, the value of one unit of output is three times the total value of the inputs needed to produce it when the values are calculated using the prices of the model. Again, there is extreme distortion in the relative price structure due to the presence of a decision maker.

	Period 1		Period 2		Period 3	
	Begin	End	Begin	End	Begin	End
Laying	20		20		20	
Hatching	20		20		20	
Chickens produced		120		120		120
Eggs produced		240		240		240
Chickens consumed		80		80		80
Eggs consumed		160		160		160

Figure 6-4

Example 6-4: As a somewhat more typical example, let $c = \frac{3}{4}$ and $s = \frac{1}{4}$. Then solving

$$B - \alpha(A + (\tfrac{3}{4})H) = \begin{pmatrix} 1 - (5/2)\alpha & 12 - 3\alpha \\ 5 - (5/2)\alpha & -7\alpha \end{pmatrix}$$

gives

$$\alpha = 6/5 = 1.2 \quad \text{and} \quad x = (1/2, 1/2)$$

Similarly, solving

$$B - \beta(A + (\tfrac{1}{4})H) = \begin{pmatrix} 1 - (3/2)\beta & 12 - \beta \\ 5 - (3/2)\beta & -5\beta \end{pmatrix}$$

gives

$$\beta = 2 \quad \text{and} \quad y = \begin{pmatrix} 5/6 \\ 1/6 \end{pmatrix}$$

In Figure 6-5 we have listed the production and consumption pattern over time, starting with 50 chickens and 100 eggs that are to be used in the production process.

We will return to these examples in Sections 4 and 5 where we provide a theoretical setting and prove general theorems of which these are specific instances. We simply remark for now that the determination of c and s may be influenced by such things as the age distribution of the population, foreign investment or disinvestment, public consumption, etc.

	Period 1		Period 2		Period 3		
	Begin	End	Begin	End	Begin	End	
Laying	25		30		36		
Hatching	25		30		36		
Chickens produced		150		180		216	. . .
Eggs produced		300		360		432	
Chickens consumed		90		108		129	
Eggs consumed		180		216		259.2	

Figure 6-5

Example 6-5: To illustrate a slightly larger model, we present a simple three-industry, three-product economy first without and then with consumption and savings. In the model there are three products, food, entertainment, and diamonds, and three industries, one that produces each of the products. The input and output matrices are:

	A matrix			B matrix		
	F	E	D	F	E	D
Food industry	10	0	0	40	0	0
Entertainment industry	2	10	0	0	20	0
Diamond industry	1	0	10	0	0	12

In this model, $\alpha = \beta$ and there are clearly three different feasible expansion (and interest) rates. These together with their solutions are:

1. $\alpha = 4$; $x = (1,0,0)$ and y is an arbitrary column probability vector
2. $\alpha = 2$; $x = (a, 1 - a, 0)$, where $1/6 \leq a \leq 1$ and $y = (0,b,1 - b)$, where b satisfies $0 \leq b \leq 1$
3. $\alpha = 1.2$; $x = (a_1,a_2,1 - a_1 - a_2)$, where $29.2a_1 + 3.6a_2 \geq 1.2$ and $a_1 \geq 0$, $a_2 \geq 0$; and

$$y = \begin{pmatrix} 0 \\ 0 \\ 1 \end{pmatrix}$$

These solutions are somewhat unsatisfactory since food has positive price when only the food industry is run; but if any other industry is also run, the price of food is zero. (These zero price situations can be handled by using the methods given in Chapters 2 and 5 or else by going over to the open model of Chapter 4.)

Suppose now that the H matrix of the economy is given by

$$H = \begin{pmatrix} 0.6 & 0.4 & 0.1 \\ 0.8 & 0.2 & 0.2 \\ 0.9 & 0.3 & 0.3 \end{pmatrix}$$

and $c = 0.8$ and $s = 0.2$. We now see that the technological subeconomies in the previous example have vanished since $A + B + H > 0$ and there is only a single economy in which (A3) holds. Thus, by permitting the workers and stockholders in the various industries to take their remuneration partly in each of the three products of the economy, to consume part of it, and to invest part of it, we have tied the economy together and achieved a unique expansion and interest rate. We indicate the solution to this example in Section 4, and it will be seen that $\alpha < \beta$.

3. Existence Theorem

The purpose of this section is to show that there are economic solutions to the model defined by Axioms (CC1) through (CC5) when (1) and Assumptions (A1), (A2), and (A3) hold.

We begin by noting that when $c = s$, Axioms (CC1) through (CC5) become just those of the KMT model of Chapter 2 with the replacement of the input matrix A by $A + cH = A + sH$. Hence the existence theorem of that chapter gives the following result:

Lemma 6-1: If $c = s$ and (A1) and (A2) hold [(A3) is not needed here], then there is an economic solution to (CC1) through (CC5) for which $\alpha = \beta$.

We prove in Theorems 6-1 and 6-2 that we can obtain economic solutions to the model for any s, c, and H satisfying the stated assumptions. But first we draw some logical consequences of the assumption of existence of such solutions.

Lemma 6-2: Assume that there is a solution to the model defined by Axioms (CC1) through (CC5).

It follows that

(a) If $c \geq s$, then $0 < \alpha \leq \beta$.

(b) If $c \leq s$ then $\alpha \geq \beta > 0$.

Proof: These consequences follow immediately from the following formulas:

$$\alpha = \frac{xBy}{x(A + cH)y} \tag{2}$$

$$\beta = \frac{xBy}{x(A + sH)y} \tag{3}$$

which are immediately deducible from (CC3) and (CC4). The positivity of α and β follows, as in Chapter 2, from Axiom (CC5) and Assumptions (A1) and (A2), as does the nonzero property of the denominators in (2) and (3). This completes the proof.

Next we define the following matrix games:

$$M(\alpha) = B - \alpha(A + cH) \tag{4}$$

$$M(\beta) = B - \beta(A + sH) \tag{5}$$

which will be used later in the theorems and solution algorithm for the model. Note that $M(\alpha)$ and $M(\beta)$ each considered by itself is an ordinary KMT model which, by the above assumptions will have a unique expansion factor that is equal to its interest factor. Denote by α' the unique expansion (interest) factor of $M(\alpha)$ and denote by β' the unique interest (expansion) factor of $M(\beta)$.

Lemma 6-3: If there is an economic solution to (CC1) through (CC5), then $\alpha \leq \alpha'$ and $\beta \geq \beta'$.

Proof: By the analysis of Chapter 2, the number α' is chosen so that the value of the game $M(\alpha')$ is zero. If (CC1) holds, then the value of the game $M(\alpha)$ is positive or zero. Since A and H are non-negative matrices and c is a non-negative number, and since α' is unique, the inequality $\alpha > \alpha'$ would imply that the value of $M(\alpha)$ is negative contrary to the assumption that Axiom (CC1) is satisfied. Hence, $\alpha \leq \alpha'$. The proof that $\beta \geq \beta'$ is similar.

The results of the first three lemmas permit us to draw Figure 6-6, which illustrates the effects of c and s on the expansion and interest factors. The 45° line represents the situation in which $c = s$ and therefore $\alpha = \beta$. The point $c = s = 0$ represents the original von Neumann model and the model with outside demand that we discussed in Chapter 5. The other diagonal line of the square is the case for which $c + s = 1$, which is probably that of most economic interest. The additional reasonable assumption that $c > s$ indicates that the region in the lower right-hand triangle of the square is desired. Finally, if we restrict ourselves to the subset of this triangle that is

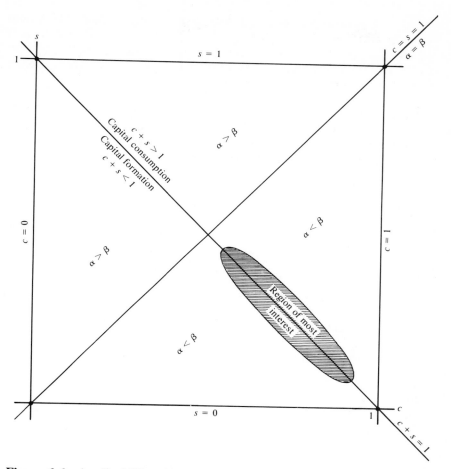

Figure 6-6. Applicability of Expansion Models for Various Values of c and s.

close to the line $c + s = 1$, the area shaded in Figure 6-6, then we have the region of most probable economic interest.

Of course, the economist is much more interested in the corresponding variation of expansion and interest factors α and β. The corresponding figure is a mapping of the square in Figure 6-6, and in the course of the mapping some of the straight lines may become curves (see Example 6-6 and Figure 6-7 in the next section). We do not know at present exactly how the general case is characterized, and this awaits further study and computation.

We now present two theorems that give various methods for finding solutions to (CC1) through (CC5). The first theorem gives a sufficient condition for the solution to $M(\alpha)$ and $M(\beta)$ to be solutions to (CC1) through (CC5). The second theorem gives an algorithm for finding solutions even when the first theorem does not apply.

Theorem 6-1: Let x and α^* be solutions to $M(\alpha)$ and y and β^* be solutions to $M(\beta)$. Then if the positive components of x correspond to active[a] row strategies in $M(\beta)$ and the positive components of y correspond to active column strategies in $M(\alpha)$, these quantities x, y, α^*, and β^* are solutions to (CC1) through (CC5).

Proof: Since x and α^* are solutions to $M(\alpha)$, we have

$$xM(\alpha^*) = x[B - \alpha^*(A + cH)] \geq 0 \tag{6}$$

which is (CC1). Similarly y and β^* solve $M(\beta')$ so we have

$$M(\beta^*)y = [B - \beta^*(A + sH)]y \leq 0 \tag{7}$$

which is (CC2). If column j is an active column strategy in $M(\alpha^*)$, then the jth inequality of (6) is satisfied as an equality, as is shown in Appendix 1. By assumption, $y_j > 0$ means that column j is active in $M(\alpha^*)$; it follows that

$$xM(\alpha^*)y = x[B - \alpha^*(A + cH)]y = 0 \tag{8}$$

which is (CC3). Similarly, if row i is an active row strategy in $M(\beta^*)$, then, as shown in Appendix 1, the ith inequality of (7) is satisfied as an equality. By assumption, $x_i > 0$ means that row i is active in $M(\beta^*)$; it follows that

$$xM(\beta^*)y = x[B - \beta^*(A + sH)]y = 0 \tag{9}$$

which is (CC4). Finally, (A2) and the fact that x and y are probability vectors imply that (CC5) holds, completing the proof of the theorem.

Corollary: If all pure strategies in both $M(\alpha)$ and $M(\beta')$ are active, then x, y, α^*, and β^* (defined in the statement of Theorem 6-2) provide solutions to (CC1) through (CC5).

Note that Examples 6-1 through 6-4 of Section 2 all satisfy the corollary. In fact, the solution technique used in that section is exactly that described in Theorem 6-1. Further computations with this class of examples are made in Example 6-6 of Section 4.

Not every economic model will satisfy the hypotheses of Theorem 6-1. Hence it is necessary to provide a solution technique for solving the general

---

[a] An active pure (row or column) strategy is a pure strategy that is used with non-negative weight in some optimal mixed strategy. Further explanation and examples are given in Appendix 1.

case. An algorithm for finding solutions for the general case is supplied as a constructive proof of the next theorem.

Theorem 6-2: Every model, (CC1) through (CC5), satisfying Assumptions (A1) through (A3) has an equilibrium solution.

Proof: We remark first of all that if $m = n = 1$, then Theorem 6-1 can be applied to show that there is a solution.

Suppose that at least one of m and n is greater than one. We specify below an algorithm that will always find at least one, and possibly many, solutions.

Algorithm [For finding solutions to (CC1) through (CC5)]

1. Solve $M(\alpha)$ and $M(\beta)$ as ordinary KMT models; let the solutions be x, α^* and y, β^*.
2. If x, α^*, y, β^* satisfy the hypotheses of Theorem 6-1, then they provide solutions to the model. Stop.
3. If x, α^*, y, β^* do not satisfy the hypotheses of Theorem 6-1, then do one of the following:
   (a) Impose a constraint $x_i = 0$ corresponding to a zero component of the solution for x in $M(\alpha)$ or $M(\beta)$. The easiest way to do this is to cross out row i of $M(\alpha)$ and $M(\beta)$.
   (b) Impose a constraint $y_j = 0$ corresponding to a zero component to the solution for y in $M(\alpha)$ or $M(\beta)$. The easiest way to do this is to cross out column j of $M(\alpha)$ and $M(\beta)$.
4. Go to step 1.

The algorithm is certain to stop after a finite number of steps, as can be seen by the following argument. The algorithm will never remove a final remaining row or a final remaining column, since they never correspond to zero components. Each time the algorithm goes through step 3 either a row or a column of both $M(\alpha)$ and $M(\beta)$ are eliminated, so that $m + n$ is reduced by 1 each time. Thus after a finite number of steps we arrive either at the case $m = n = 1$, which has a solution as discussed above, or at some earlier time we terminate at step 2 of the algorithm with the solution. See Example 6-7 in the next section for an application of the algorithm.

By enumerating all the possible ways of imposing the constraints in step 3 one can determine all possible solutions to (CC1) through (CC5). As noted, there is certain to be at least one solution, but there may also be many solutions to the model. Some of these solutions will be economically meaningful and some not. Further discussion of the selection of one of the several possible economic solutions is given after Example 6-7 in the next section and in Section 6.

4. More Complicated Examples

In order to show more clearly the complexity of the present model, we give additional examples that bring out various points of interest.

Example 6-6: We return to the chicken and eggs economy treated in Examples 1 through 4, but here we keep the consumption and savings coefficients as parameters. Then we have as the two KMT models:

$$M(\alpha) = \begin{pmatrix} 1 - \alpha(1 + 2c) & 12 - 4\alpha c \\ 5 - \alpha(1 + 2c) & -4\alpha(1 + c) \end{pmatrix} \tag{10}$$

$$M(\beta) = \begin{pmatrix} 1 - \beta(1 + 2s) & 12 - 4\beta s \\ 5 - \beta(1 + 2s) & -4\beta(1 + s) \end{pmatrix} \tag{11}$$

If we choose

$$\alpha^* = \frac{3}{1 + 2c} \tag{12}$$

(the reason for this choice will be explained in Section 5), then $M(\alpha^*)$ becomes

$$M(\alpha^*) = \begin{pmatrix} -2 & d \\ 2 & -d \end{pmatrix}, \quad \text{where } d = \frac{12(1 + c)}{1 + 2c} \tag{13}$$

so that $x = (1/2, 1/2)$ is an optimal strategy in the resulting game. Similarly, if we choose

$$\beta^* = \frac{3}{1 + 2s} \tag{14}$$

(the reason for this choice will also be explained in Section 5), then $M(\beta^*)$ becomes

$$M(\beta^*) = \begin{pmatrix} -2 & e \\ 2 & -e \end{pmatrix}, \quad \text{where } e = \frac{12(1 + s)}{1 + 2s} \tag{15}$$

and $y = (e/e + 2), 2/(e + 2))$ is an optimal strategy in the resulting game. Because both strategies are completely mixed, the other equations of the model are also satisfied for all c and s. In Figure 6-7 we have sketched the curve of β versus α for the condition $c + s = 1$. To derive the equation, note that

$$1 + 2c = \frac{3}{\alpha^*}$$

$$1 + 2s = \frac{3}{\beta^*}$$

Adding these equations together and using $c + s = 1$ gives us

$$2 + 2 = 3\left(\frac{1}{\alpha^*} + \frac{1}{\beta^*}\right)$$

and solving for β^*, we have

$$\beta^* = \frac{3\alpha^*}{4\alpha^* - 3} \tag{16}$$

which is the hyperbola sketched in Figure 6-7. Note that in the case of Example 6-2 of Section 6-2 when $c = 0$ and $s = 1$ (e.g., low consumption and high savings) we obtain $\alpha = 3$ and $\beta = 1$ (i.e., high expansion rate and low interest rate). Also, the case treated in Example 6-3 of Section 6-2, $s = 0$ and $c = 1$, results in $\alpha = 1$ and $\beta = 3$ (i.e., low expansion rate and high interest rate). These results are intuitively reasonable.

Observe that the line $c + s = 1$ of Figure 6-6 has been transformed into the hyperbola of Figure 6-7. The lines $c = 0, 1$ and $s = 0, 1$ which delimit the square in Figure 6-6 go into the correspondingly marked straight lines in Figure 6-7, p. 116.

Example 6-7: The next example demonstrates the necessity for the algorithm presented in the proof of Theorem 6-2. It shows that the solution to the model involves the choice of an optimal strategy for the row player in the game $M(\alpha)$, and an optimal strategy for the column player in the game $M(\beta)$. In the example, this pair of choices can be made in two different ways, each leading to a different economic solution of the model. Later, we shall remark further on the question of choice of solution.

The technological matrices for the example are:

$$B = \begin{pmatrix} 20 & 0 \\ 1 & 20 \end{pmatrix}, \quad A = \begin{pmatrix} 10 & 0 \\ 0.1 & 1 \end{pmatrix}, \quad H = \begin{pmatrix} 1 & 0 \\ 2 & 50 \end{pmatrix}$$

We choose $c = 0.1$ and $s = 0.9$ so that

$$M(\alpha) = \begin{pmatrix} 20 - 10.1\alpha & 0 \\ 1 - 0.3\alpha & 20 - 6\alpha \end{pmatrix} \tag{17}$$

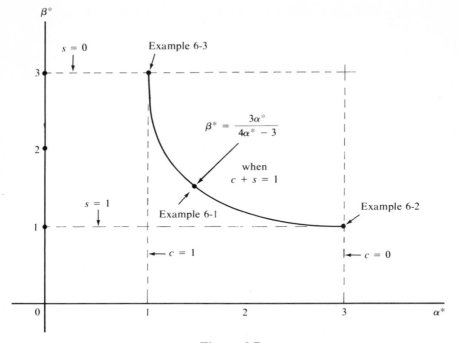

Figure 6-7

$$M(\beta) = \begin{pmatrix} 20 - 10.9\beta & 0 \\ 1 - 1.9\beta & 20 - 46\beta \end{pmatrix} \tag{18}$$

The solution to the model $M(\alpha)$ is given by

$$\alpha = 10/3 = 3.333, \quad x = (0,1), \quad \text{and } y = \begin{pmatrix} 0 \\ 1 \end{pmatrix} \tag{19}$$

while the solution to the $M(\beta)$ economy is

$$\beta = 20/10.9 = 1.835, \quad x = (1,0), \quad \text{and } y = \begin{pmatrix} 1 \\ 0 \end{pmatrix} \tag{20}$$

which are clearly incompatible. Utilizing the algorithm of the previous selection we can impose either the constraint $x_1 = 0$ or $y_2 = 0$. The first constraint makes the above solution to $M(\alpha)$ to be optimal with $\beta = 20/46 =$ .435. The second constraint makes the solution to $M(\beta)$ be optimal with $\alpha = 200/101 = 1.98$. Hence we have a case in which there are two and only two solutions which are quite different in character, and there is no reason to prefer one over the other.

The question of choice of solution arises. A choice is impossible within the rules of the game, i.e., there is no way of preferring one outcome over another. It would require an outside agency, say the government or some ideologically controlled board to choose one rather than the other for reasons which have nothing whatsoever to do with the game as such. The choice is, at any rate, *not* made by members of the economy. Although this is a two-person setup, the situation is reminiscent of the solution concept of a cooperative (i.e., essential) *n*-person game, where the solution consists by necessity of a set of more than one imputation that do not dominate each other and among which there is no choice possible. Game theory shows that it is impossible to indicate which of the imputations belonging to the solution set will actually materialize in an essential *n*-person game. It is noteworthy that a similar occurrence is to be observed here. This is fundamentally different from the processes described by classical mechanics and *a fortiori* by classical economics.

Applied to the present case, the above result means that the frequently made assumption *that the economy must automatically go to a unique "efficiency point"*[b] is not, in general, true for the simple reason that no such point necessarily exists. In the above counterexample there is no way of choosing between the two possible states unless the indicated outside factors are brought into play or entirely new ideas are formulated. That this example could be found establishes a tie to the conceptual world of game theory when the latter is used as a model of economic reality rather than merely as a tool of mathematical analysis. In game theory no imputation in a solution set is "better" than any other, which implies that only an arbitrary choice among them is possible.

Example 6-8: We indicate the solution to the diamonds example discussed in Example 6-5 using techniques that will be discussed in Chapter 8.

The solution to the example was found using a computer. They are:

$$\alpha = 1.1705$$

$$\beta = 1.1927$$

$$\text{Activity vector} = (0.0689, 0.0343, 0.8968)$$

$$\text{Price vector} = (0.0009, 0.0061, 0.9930)$$

Thus we see that diamonds are priced very much more highly than either food or entertainment; entertainment is priced nearly seven times higher than food; and the food industry is operated at nearly twice the level of the

---

[b] Compare Chapter 1, page 6.

entertainment industry, but at less than a twelfth of the level of the diamond industry. Intensity of operation of an industry should, of course, be measured in terms of the level of sophistication of technique as well as physical effort.

The numerical data were chosen rather arbitrarily, but the above example suffices to show the following: (a) the demand matrix has tied the economy together so that unique expansion and interest rates occur, and (b) the model is capable of fast computation on an electronic computer. By the use of the fastest computers now available, it would be possible to find numerical solutions to methods having values of m and n ranging in the thousands.

5. Consumption of Excess Production and Excess Value

So far we have not made restrictions on the choice of the optional consumption matrix H. Yet it is clear that some choices of H are not economically meaningful and would lead to economically unacceptable models. In this section we present some new results (which did not appear in [90], which give ways of choosing H such that it will be certain to lead to economically reasonable models.

We begin by defining the *excess production vector*

$$h = x (B - A) \tag{21}$$

where x is a given intensity vector. Since xB represents the outputs, given inputs xA, it follows that $h = xB - xA$ is the production of goods that are in excess over the amount needed to maintain a stationary economy (including the "reproduction" of the workers). Thus, for example, if we choose to consume all of H—which is everything in excess of xA,—we can maintain a stationary economy with xA as inputs for each time period.

With the choice of h as in (21), we define the $m \times n$ matrix h as

$$H = f \cdot h \tag{22}$$

where f is an m-component column vector of all ones. The reader should verify that this was the way H was chosen in Section 2.

Suppose that x and α solve the KMT model given by

$$M(\alpha) = B - \alpha A \tag{23}$$

This means that x and α satisfy

$$x(B - \alpha A) \geq 0 \tag{24}$$

We now want to solve

$$x^*[B - \alpha^*(A + cH)] \geq 0 \qquad (25)$$

where H is given by Equation (22). We show that we can choose $x^* = x$. Making this substitution and multiplying out (25) yields

$$xB - \alpha^*(xA + cxH) \geq 0$$

$$(26)$$

Substituting in (22) and using $xf = 1$ gives

$$xB - \alpha^*(xA + ch) \geq 0 \qquad (27)$$

Substituting (21) and collecting like terms gives

$$(1 - \alpha^*c)xB - \alpha^*(1 - c)\, xA \geq 0 \qquad (28)$$

Then, assuming $1 - \alpha^*c > 0$ (see Exercise 11) we divide (28) by $(1 - \alpha^*c)$ to obtain

$$xB - \left(\frac{\alpha^*(1 - c)}{1 - \alpha^*c}\right) xA \geq 0 \qquad (29)$$

Comparing (24) and (29) we see that if we choose α to satisfy

$$\alpha = \frac{\alpha^*(1 - c)}{1 - \alpha^*c} \qquad (30)$$

then x and α^* solve (25). By solving (30) for α^* we get

$$\alpha^* = \frac{\alpha}{1 + c(\alpha - 1)} \qquad (31)$$

The reader can verify that the choice of α^* in Example 6-6 of the previous section was made by using Formula (31).

We must now carry out the same analysis for the KMT model.

$$M(\beta^*) = B - \beta^*[A - sH] \qquad (32)$$

It can be shown that the solution is given by the same activity vector x and β^* chosen by the formula

$$\beta^* = \frac{\beta}{1 + s(\beta - 1)} \qquad (33)$$

where $\beta = \alpha$ in the KMT model of (23) (see Exercise 12). The price vector y must be found by solving $M(\beta^*)\, y \leq 0$.

Using $c + s = 1$ and $\alpha = \beta$, the following relationship between α^* and β^* can be derived (see Exercise 13).

$$\beta^* = \frac{\alpha\,\alpha^*}{(\alpha + 1)\alpha^* - \alpha} \qquad (34)$$

Again the locus of this equation is a hyperbola in α^*, β^* space, as was illustrated in Figure 6-7 of the previous section.

The above calculations now permit us to state the following theorem.

Theorem 6-3: If the economy makes its excess consumption proportional to the excess production vector, that is, if the excess consumption matrix H is chosen as in (21) and (22), then the solution of the model consists of the same activity vector x, the expansion factor α^* in (31), the interest factor β^* in (33) and the price vector y which solves $M(\beta^*)y \leq 0$.

Proof: As shown above, x is optimal in both $M(\alpha^*)$ and $M(\beta^*)$. Because x is optimal in $M(\alpha^*)$, Axiom (CC1) holds. The price vector y was chosen to be optimal in $M(\beta^*)$, so Axiom (CC2) holds. Because x is also optimal in $M(\beta^*)$, Axiom (CC4) holds. Because x is optimal in $M(\beta^*)$, we know that $y_j > 0$ only if the jth inequality of $xM(\beta^*) \geq 0$ is satisfied as an equality, but because x is also optimal in $M(\alpha^*)$ the jth inequality of $xM(\alpha^*) \geq 0$ is also satisfied as an equality, since they both can be related back to (23). Thus Axiom (CC3) also holds. Finally, Assumption (A3) shows that Axiom (CC5) also holds, completing the proof of the theorem.

A completely symmetric theorem can be derived by starting with the definition

$$h = (B - A)\, y \tag{35}$$

That is, h is now chosen to be the *excess value vector*. Letting e be an n-component row vector of all ones, we define

$$H = he \tag{36}$$

Then with y and α being solutions to the KMT model of (23), it can be shown that y solves both the KMT models $M(\alpha^*) = B - \alpha^*(A + cH)$ and $M(\beta^*) = B - \beta^*(A + sH)$, where α^* and β^* are as given in (31) and (34). (See Exercise 14).

Thus we can state the following theorem which is symmetric to Theorem 6-3.

Theorem 6-4: If the economy makes its excess consumption proportional to the excess value vector, that is, if the excess consumption matrix H is chosen as in (35) and (36), then the solution of the model consists of the same price vector y, the expansion factor α^* in (31), the interest factor β^* in (33) and the activity vector x which solves $xM(\alpha^*) \geq 0$.

The details of the proof of this theorem are asked for in Exercise 15.

Some interpretive comments on Theorems 6-3 and 6-4 are in order. Note that when H is chosen as in (21) and (22), the workers in each industry have the vector of real goods for their consumption, and this vector of real goods is proportional to the excess production of each good. In this case, the production plan x remains unchanged but the price vector y is affected by the specific choices of c and s. This was already illustrated in Example 6-6 of the previous section.

On the other hand, when H is chosen as in (35) and (36), the workers in each industry have excess consumption proportional to the value of excess production of that industry. Here the price vector y remains unchanged but the activity vector x is affected by the specific selections of c and s.

One might consider what kinds of social institutions would lead to one or the other of these possibilities or even to some entirely different choice of H. This is an interesting matter for further study.

6. The Public Sector Model

The reader will have observed that our model—closed or open—does not have money in it. The question of how to introduce money into such models is, as far as we know, completely unsolved.[e] Our mechanism for paying workers and stockholders was to reimburse them with real goods, in proportions according to their tastes. Then we let them consume or reinvest their holdings as they desired. The same may be done for the public sector; that is, we may permit the 'government' to acquire (say, by its tax power) part of the output of the economy in real goods according to its public 'preferences' and consume or reinvest it as it sees fit.

To be specific, let c' and s' be the consumption and savings coefficients of the public sector, and let G be the matrix which indicates the real goods payments of the economy to the government. We shall assume that c' and s' are non-negative, but not necessarily bounded above by 1. It is well known that governments can spend more than their total revenue. The equations that govern the new model are:

Axiom (CG1): $x[B - \alpha(A + cH + c'G)] \geq 0$

Axiom (CG2): $[B - \beta(A + sH + s'G)]y \leq 0$

Axiom (CG3): $x[B - \alpha(A + cH + c'G)]y = 0$

Axiom (CG4): $x[B - \beta(A + sH + s'G)]y = 0$

---

[e] Newton developed his mechanics without considering light. It took several centuries for physics to account properly for light phenomena. Let us hope that money can be fitted into the present models in a shorter time!

Axiom (CG5): $xBy > 0$

We also make Assumptions (A1) and (A2). However, we will replace (A3) by

(A4) $A + B + H + G > 0$

These eight conditions characterize the new model.

Although the new model differs in only relatively minor respects from the previous one, it opens several important possibilities. We first note that condition (A4) can hold even if (A3) does not. In other words, the governmental "tastes" can unify an economy that would otherwise be disconnected. In real economies it is observed that only the government is willing to pay (in real terms) for such things as roads, community welfare, defense weapons, etc. Second, the new model now permits the government, through its choice of c' to influence the expansion rate α, and through its choice of s', similarly, to influence the interest rate β of the economy. Even further, the government can change G by changing its tax policies and influence both these factors simultaneously. Exactly how these changes come about is completely determined by the equations of the model. It is clear, without formal proof, that increasing c' will decrease α, and increasing s' will decrease β, while multiplying the matrix G by a number larger than 1 will decrease both of these factors simultaneously. All these conclusions seem to be in complete agreement with conclusions from other parts of economics.

We conclude by reworking the example of Section 3 assuming that the government has a taste matrix:

$$G = \begin{pmatrix} 0.3 & 0 & 0 \\ 0 & 0.1 & 0 \\ 0 & 0 & 0.2 \end{pmatrix}$$

We also assume that $c' = 1.2$ and $s' = 0$; that is, a case of deficit spending in real goods and services. The solution to the model for the interest rate and price vector is exactly the same as that in Example 4-8 of Section 4, since $s' = 0$. The solution for expansion factor and activity vector, however, has been slightly changed:

$\alpha = 1.1660$ and   activity vector $= (0.0687, 0.0340, 0.8973)$

Note that the activity vector is, to three decimal places of accuracy, the same as before, while the expansion factor has been decreased by 0.005.

The important problem of adding consumption to the von Neumann model has been widely studied by many authors. We have not attempted to give an exhaustive account here. A reader who is interested in pursuing the matter further may wish to consult the following papers and books: Malinvaud [72], Morishima [99, 100, 101, 102], Frisch [22], Los [64], and Bromek [7, 8]. In [4] Bauer gives excellent summaries of and comparisons among these models.

Exercises

1. (a) Verify the entries in Figure 6-1.
   (b) Verify the entries in Figure 6-3.
   (c) Verify the entries in Figure 6-4.
   (d) Verify the entries in Figure 6-5.
2. Consider the chicken-and-eggs economy, but with consumption matrix

$$H = \begin{pmatrix} 2 & 16 \\ 2 & 16 \end{pmatrix}$$

If $c = s = 1/2$, show that the solution is

$$\alpha = 1, \quad x = (3/4, 1/4), \quad y = (4/5, 1/5)'$$

3. In Exercise 2, assume that $c = 0$, $s = 1$. Show that the solution is

$$\alpha = 3, \quad x = (1/2, 1/2), \quad y = (.7818, .2182)'$$

   Interpret this solution.
4. In Exercise 2, assume that $c = 1$, $s = 0$. Show that the solution is

$$\alpha = .5826, \quad x = (.8131, .1869), \quad y = (6/7, 1/7)'$$

   Interpret this solution.
5. Verify the solutions indicated for Example 6-5.
6. Show that the choice of α^* in (12) leads to the game in (13) and that $x = (1/2, 1/2)$ is optimal for the latter.
7. Show that the choice of β^* in (14) leads to the game in (15) and that

$$y = (e/(e + 2), \quad 2/(e + 2))$$

   is optimal for the latter.
8. Show that the expression for β^* in (16) is correct.
9. Show that the quantities in (19) solve the game in (17).
10. Show that the quantities in (20) solve the game in (18).
11. (a) Derive (29) from (28), assuming that $c < 1/\alpha^*$.
    (b) Derive (30).
    (c) Derive (31).

12. Derive (33).

13. Put $\alpha = \beta$ into (31) and solve for c; put $\alpha = \beta$ into (33) and solve for s; now use $c + s = 1$ and derive (34).

14. Assume that h and H are defined as in (35) and (36); let y and α be solutions to the KMT model of (23).

   (a) Show that y solves $M(\alpha^*) = B - \alpha^*(A + cH)$, where α^* is given in (31).

   (b) Show that y solves $M(\beta^*) = B - \beta^*(A + cH)$, where β^* is given in (34).

15. Prove Theorem 6-4 by developing an argument parallel to the proof of Theorem 6-3.

16. Show that if $\alpha = \beta$ and $c + s = 1$, the following relationship holds between α^* and β^* in both the excess production and excess value cases:

$$\frac{1}{\alpha^*} + \frac{1}{\beta^*} = \frac{\alpha + 1}{\alpha}$$

7

Private and Public Consumption and Savings in the Open Model

1. Consumption and Savings in the Open Model

We now add consumption and savings to the open (MT) model following the same procedures used in that respect for the closed model. It turns out that the technical problems encountered in adding consumption and savings to the open model are much simpler than those for the closed model. We will also be able to extend to the open model the excess consumption results obtained in the previous chapter for the closed model.

As in the previous chapter, we will let A, B, and H be non-negative $m \times n$ matrices and interpret them, as before, as the input, output, and consumption matrices. We also have the non-negative numbers c and s representing consumption and capital accumulation coefficients. We define the matrices as follows:

$$M(\alpha) = B - \alpha(A + cH) \qquad (1)$$

$$M(\beta) = B - \beta(A + sH) \qquad (2)$$

and with these state the usual seven axioms of the open model.

Axiom (OC1): $xM(\alpha) = w^e - w^i$

Axiom (OC2): $M(\beta)y = z^p - z^n$

Axiom (OC3): $w^e p^e = w^i p^i$

Axiom (OC4): $t^p z^p = t^n z^n$

Axiom (OC5): $xBy > 0$

Axiom (OC6): $t^n \leq x \leq t^p$

Axiom (OC7): $p^e \leq y \leq p^i$

The interpretations of these axioms are the same as in Chapter 4.

As in Chapter 6 we no longer assume that $\alpha = \beta$, since the presence of consumption and savings causes these two to diverge. However, the problem of finding solutions to the open model with consumption is easier than in the closed model, as we now describe.

To find an intensity vector x satisfying Axioms (OC1), (OC3), and (OC6), we solve the minimizing linear programming problem given in (3).

$$
\left.
\begin{aligned}
\text{Minimize} \quad & -w^e p^e + w^i p^i \\
\text{Subject to} \quad & \\
x\,M(\alpha) - w^e + w^i &= 0 \\
-x \qquad\qquad &\geq -t^p \\
x \qquad\qquad &\geq t^n \\
w^e, w^i &\geq 0
\end{aligned}
\right\} \tag{3}
$$

where $M(\alpha)$ is defined in (1). We select α so that the value of the objective function of (3) is zero in order to satisfy Axiom (OC3). Similarly, to find a price vector y satisfying Axioms (OC2), (OC4), and (OC7), we solve the maximizing linear programming problem given in (4).

$$
\left.
\begin{aligned}
\text{Maximize} \quad & -t^p z^p + t^n z^n \\
\text{Subject to} \quad & \\
M(\beta)y - z^p + z^n &= 0 \\
-y \qquad\qquad &\leq -p^e \\
y \qquad\qquad &\leq p^i \\
z^p, z^n &\geq 0
\end{aligned}
\right\} \tag{4}
$$

where $M(\beta)$ is defined in (2). We select β so that the value of the objective function of (4) is zero in order to satisfy Axiom (OC4).

Axiom (OC5) is easily satisfied by assuming, if necessary, that each zero component of p^e is slightly positive. This assumption can be used in place of (A3) of Chapter 6.

Note that no special algorithm is needed here to find solutions to the open model with consumption. Essentially all that we have to do is to solve two open models represented by the linear programming models (3) and (4). On the other hand, the results of Chapter 4 that relate the x and y solutions through the complementary slackness properties of linear programming are lost in whole or in part for the present model, depending on the structure of the H matrix. It is difficult to make any general statements about how the solutions change unless some assumptions are made about the H matrix. In the next section we will see that the excess consumption conditions used in Chapter 6 carry over easily to the present case.

2. Consumption of Excess Production and Excess Value in the Open Model

As in Chapter 6, we first define the *excess production vector*

$$h = x(B - A) \qquad (5)$$

where x is a solution intensity vector normalized to be a probability vector. As before, $h = xB - xA$ represents the production of goods that are in excess over the amount needed to maintain a stationary economy. Similarly, we define the $m \times n$ matrix

$$H = fh \qquad (6)$$

where f is an m-component column vector of all ones.

Suppose that x, w^e, w^i, and α solve the open model whose matrix is

$$M(\alpha) = B - \alpha A \qquad (7)$$

Then it follows that

$$x(B - \alpha A) = w^e - w^i \qquad (8)$$

We now want to solve

$$x^*[B - \alpha^*(A + cH)] = w^{e*} - w^{i*} \qquad (9)$$

where H is given by (6). We show that we can choose $x^* = x$. Making this substitution and multiplying out (9) gives

$$xB - \alpha^*(xA + cxH) = w^{e*} - w^{i*} \qquad (10)$$

Substitution in (6) and using $xf = 1$ gives

$$xB - \alpha^*(xA + ch) = w^{e*} - w^{i*} \qquad (11)$$

Substituting in (5) and collecting like terms gives

$$(1 - \alpha^*c)\, xB - \alpha^*(1 - c)xA = w^{e*} - w^{i*} \qquad (12)$$

Then, assuming $1 - \alpha^*c > 0$ (see Exercise 3), we divide (12) by $(1 - \alpha^*c)$ to obtain

$$xB - \frac{\alpha^*(1 - c)}{1 - \alpha^*c} xA = \frac{1}{1 - \alpha^*c} w^{e*} - \frac{1}{1 - \alpha^*c} w^{i*} \qquad (13)$$

Comparing (13) and (8) we see that if we choose α^*, w^{e*}, and w^{i*} to satisfy

$$\alpha = \frac{\alpha^*(1 - c)}{1 - \alpha^*c} \qquad (14)$$

$$\frac{1}{1 - \alpha^*c} w^{e*} = w^e \qquad (15)$$

$$\frac{1}{1 - \alpha^*c} w^{i*} = w^i \tag{16}$$

then x, w^{i*}, w^{e*}, and α^* solve (9). Solving for these quantities from (14) through (16) gives the following desired solutions:

$$\alpha^* = \frac{\alpha}{1 + c(\alpha - 1)} \tag{17}$$

$$w^{e*} = (1 - \alpha^*c)w^e \tag{18}$$

$$w^{i*} = (1 - \alpha^*c)w^i \tag{19}$$

In other words, the solution to the open model (8) yields, with appropriate modifications, the (unique) solution to the open model with consumption (9).

Specific numerical examples of this relationship are given in the next section.

We must now analyze the price solution for the open model:

$$M(\beta^*)y = [B - \beta^*(A + sH)]\, y = z^{p*} - z^{n*} \tag{20}$$

It can be shown that the solution is given by the same activity vector x and interest factor β^* given by the following formula:

$$\beta^* = \frac{\beta}{1 + s(\beta - 1)} \tag{21}$$

Once β^* is known, the vectors y, z^{p*}, and z^{n*} can be determined by solving the linear programming problem, (4).

Given $c + s = 1$ and $\alpha = \beta$, the relationship connecting α^* and β^* of Equation (34) of Chapter 6 can be shown to hold. (see Exercise 6).

We can now state a theorem that is completely analogous to Theorem 6-4.

Theorem 7-1: If the economy makes its excess consumption proportional to the excess production vector, that is, if the excess consumption matrix H is chosen as in (5) and (6), then the solution of the model (8) is found as follows: The same x that solves (7), α^*, w^{e*}, w^{i*} are the same as those given in (17) through (19); β^* is given by (21); and y^*, x^{p*}, x^{n*} are found as solutions to the linear programming problem (4) with this value of β^*.

The proof of this theorem is asked for in Exercise 7.

A completely symmetric theorem can be derived by starting with the following definition:

$$h = (B - A)y \tag{22}$$

That is, h is now chosen to be the *excess value vector*. Letting e be an

n-component row vector of all ones, we define

$$H = he \tag{23}$$

With y and α being solutions to the open model given by

$$M(\beta)y = (B - \beta A)y = z^p - z^n \tag{24}$$

y solves both the open models with matrices $M(\alpha^*) = B - \alpha^*(A + cH)$ and $M(\beta^*) = B - \beta(A + sH)$, where α^* and β^* are given by Formulas (17) and (21). The rest of the solution is given by

$$z^{p*} = (1 - \beta^*s)z^p \tag{25}$$

$$z^{n*} = (1 - \beta^*s)z^n \tag{26}$$

Given α^* from (17), the values of x^*, w^{e*} and w^{i*} are found by solving linear program (3). Thus we can state the following theorem, which is analogous to Theorem 6-5.

Theorem 7-2: If the economy makes its excess consumption proportional to the excess value vector, that is, if the excess consumption matrix H is chosen as in (24) and (25), then the solution of model (20) consists of the same price vector y that solves the open model of (7) and (24); β^*, x^{p*}, z^{n*} are as given by (21), (25), (26); α^* is given by (17); and x, w^{e*}, w^{i*} are found by solving (3) with this value of α^*.

The proof of this theorem is asked for in Exercise 8.

Specific numerical illustrations of Theorem 7-2 are presented in the next section.

3. Examples

We will return to the elementary examples of Chapter 4 and rework them after we add consumption and savings.

Example 7-1: The chicken and the egg example of Example 4-1 had

$$M_\alpha = \begin{pmatrix} 1 - \alpha & 12 \\ 5 - \alpha & -4\alpha \end{pmatrix}$$

with constraints

$$2 \le x_1 \le 3$$

$$0 \le x_2 \le 1$$

$$5 \le y_1 \le 6$$

$$2 \le y_2 \le 3$$

The optimum solution was found to be $\alpha = 5$ and

$$x = (3,0), \quad w^e = (0,36), \quad w^i = (12,0)$$

$$y = \begin{pmatrix} 6 \\ 2 \end{pmatrix}, \quad z^p = \begin{pmatrix} 0 \\ 0 \end{pmatrix}, \quad z^n = \begin{pmatrix} 0 \\ 40 \end{pmatrix}$$

Let us rework the problem using the excess production-consumption scheme we used in Section 2. If we normalize x to be a probability vector, it becomes $x = (1,0)$ so that the excess production vector becomes

$$h = x(B - A) = (1,0) \begin{pmatrix} 0 & 12 \\ 4 & -4 \end{pmatrix} = (0, 12)$$

Thus the matrix H is

$$H = fh = \begin{pmatrix} 0 & 12 \\ 0 & 12 \end{pmatrix}$$

If we assume that $c = 1/2 = s$, then

$$M(\alpha^*) = B - \alpha^*(A + cH) = \begin{pmatrix} 1 - \alpha^* & 12 - 6\alpha^* \\ 5 - \alpha^* & -10\alpha^* \end{pmatrix}$$

The formulas of the preceding section give

$$\alpha^* = \frac{\alpha}{1 + c\,(\alpha - 1)} = \frac{5}{1 + (1/2)\,(4)} = \frac{5}{3}$$

so that $1 - \alpha^*c = 1 - (5/3)\,(1/2) = 1/6$. Hence the rest of the solution becomes, after returning to the unnormalized x vector,

$$x^* = x = (3, 0)$$

$$w^{e*} = \frac{1}{6}w^e = (0, 6)$$

$$w^{i*} = \frac{1}{6}w^i = (2, 0)$$

$$\beta^* = \frac{5}{3}$$

We now calculate y^*, z^{p*} and z^{n*} as solutions to the linear programming problem (4) with this value of β^*. The solutions are easily found to be

$$y^* = \begin{pmatrix} 6 \\ 2 \end{pmatrix}, \quad z^{p*} = \begin{pmatrix} 0 \\ 0 \end{pmatrix} \quad \text{and} \quad z^{n*} = \begin{pmatrix} 0 \\ 20/3 \end{pmatrix}$$

Example 7-2: Let us rework Example 4-2 again using the first excess production scheme of the previous section. The only change in data is $t_1^n = 1$. The old solution was $\alpha = 15/4$ and

$$x = (3, 1), \quad w^e = (0, 21), \quad w^i = (7, 0)$$

$$y = \begin{pmatrix} 6 \\ 2 \end{pmatrix}, \quad z^p = \begin{pmatrix} 15/2 \\ 0 \end{pmatrix}, \quad z^n = \begin{pmatrix} 0 \\ 45/2 \end{pmatrix}$$

Normalizing x we have $x = (3/4, 1/4)$ so that the excess production vector becomes

$$h = x(B - A) = (3/4, 1/4) \begin{pmatrix} 0 & 12 \\ 4 & -4 \end{pmatrix} = (1, 8)$$

Thus the H matrix becomes

$$H = \begin{pmatrix} 1 & 8 \\ 1 & 8 \end{pmatrix}$$

Again assuming that $c = 1/2 = s$, then

$$M(\alpha^*) = \begin{pmatrix} 1 - (3/2)\alpha^* & 12 - 4\alpha \\ 5 - (3/2)\alpha^* & -8\alpha^* \end{pmatrix}$$

The formulas of the preceding section give

$$\alpha^* = \frac{\alpha}{1 + c(\alpha - 1)} = \frac{15/4}{1 + (1/2)(11/4)} = \frac{15/4}{19/8} = 30/19$$

so that $1 - \alpha^* c = 1 - (30/19)(1/2) = 4/19$. Hence we can calculate, after returning x to its unnormalized form,

$$x^* = x = (3,1)$$

$$w^{e*} = \left(\frac{4}{15} \right) w^e = \left(\frac{4}{15} \right) (0,21) = (0, 28/5)$$

$$w^{i*} = \left(\frac{4}{15} \right) w^i = \left(\frac{4}{15} \right) (7,0) = (28/15, 0)$$

$$\beta^* = 30/19$$

We calculate y^*, z^{p*} and z^{n*} as solutions to the linear programming problem (4) with this value of β^*. The solutions are

$$y^* = \binom{6}{2}, \quad z^{p*} = \binom{60/19}{0}, \quad z^{n*} = \binom{0}{180/19}$$

Example 7-3: Let us rework Example 7-1 using the second excess consumption scheme of Section 2. First we normalize y so that it becomes the probability vector

$$y = \binom{3/4}{1/4}$$

Then the excess value vector becomes

$$h = (B - A)y = \begin{pmatrix} 0 & 12 \\ 4 & -4 \end{pmatrix} \binom{3/4}{1/4} = \binom{3}{2}$$

Thus the matrix H is

$$H = he = \begin{pmatrix} 3 & 3 \\ 2 & 2 \end{pmatrix}$$

If we assume that $c = 1/2 = s$, then

$$M(\beta^*) = B - \beta^*(A + sH) = \begin{pmatrix} 1 - (5/2)\beta^* & 12 - (3/2)\beta^* \\ 5 - 2\beta^* & -5\beta^* \end{pmatrix}$$

The formula derived in Section 2 gives

$$\beta^* = \frac{\beta}{1 + s(\beta - 1)} = \frac{5}{1 + (1/2)(4)} = 5/3$$

so that $1 - \beta^*s = 1 - (5/3)(1/2) = 1/6$. After returning to the unnormalized y vector, the rest of the solution becomes $\alpha^* = 5/3$,

$$y^* = y = \binom{6}{2}, \quad z^{p*} = \binom{0}{0}, \quad z^{n*} = \binom{0}{20/3}$$

Next we calculate x^*, w^{e*}, and w^{i*} by solving the linear programming problem (3) with this value of α^*. They are found to be $x^* = (3,0)$, $w^{e*} = (0, 57/2)$, $w^{i*} = (19/2, 0)$. The reader can check that the balance of payments conditions holds.

Example 7-4: Let us rework Example 7-2 using the excess value consumption scheme of Section 2. The original solution to the model was given there. Normalizing, we have

$$y = \begin{pmatrix} 3/4 \\ 1/4 \end{pmatrix}$$

so that the excess value vector and matrix H are

$$h = (B - A)y = \begin{pmatrix} 3 \\ 2 \end{pmatrix}, \qquad H = \begin{pmatrix} 3 & 3 \\ 2 & 2 \end{pmatrix}$$

as before. Thus, using the formulas of Section 2, we have

$$y^* = \begin{pmatrix} 6 \\ 2 \end{pmatrix}, \qquad z^{p*} = \begin{pmatrix} 30/19 \\ 0 \end{pmatrix}, \qquad z^{n*} = \begin{pmatrix} 0 \\ 90/19 \end{pmatrix}$$

and $\alpha^* = \beta^* = 30/19$. Finally, solving for the rest of the quantities, we get

$$x^* = (3,1), \quad w^{e*} = (0,21), \quad w^{i*} = (7,0)$$

Note that here production, exports, and imports remain unchanged, but the expansion and interest rates and positive and negative profits are all reduced.

Our discussion of consumption in the open model has been necessarily brief. However, we have illustrated that the computations—while somewhat involved—are straightforward. By making use of large-scale linear programming codes and modern computers, it is possible in the same way to model consumption in economics having thousands of activities and goods. As remarked earlier, the principal difficulty in carrying out such modelling resides in the effort needed for data collection—not primarily in the effort needed for solving the resulting computational problems.

Exercises

1. Show that the initial tableau of the linear program in (3) is

x	$B - \alpha(A + cH)$	$-I$	I	$= 0$
w^e	$-I$			$\leq -p^e$
w^i	I			$\leq p^i$
	$= 0$	$\geq -t^p$	$\geq t^n$	

2. Show that the initial tableau of the linear program in (4) is

	y	z^p	z^n	
	$B - \beta(A + sH)$	$-I$	I	$= 0$
	$-I$			$\leq -p^e$
	I			$\leq p^i$
	$= 0$	$\geq -t^p$	$\geq t^n$	

3. Assume that $c < 1/\alpha^*$ and derive (13) from (12).
4. Show that (14) through (16) solve (9).
5. Show that (21) gives the correct value for β^*.
6. If $c + s = 1$ and α^*, β^* are chosen as in (17) and (21), show that relationship (34) of Chapter 6 holds.
7. Prove Theorem 7-1.
8. Prove Theorem 7-2.
9. Verify the calculations in Example 7-1.
10. Verify the calculations in Example 7-2.
11. Verify the calculations in Example 7-3.
12. Verify the calculations in Example 7-4.
13. If $\alpha = \beta$ and $c + s = 1$, show that the following relationship holds in both the excess production and excess value cases:

$$\frac{1}{\alpha^*} + \frac{1}{\beta^*} = \frac{\alpha + 1}{\alpha}$$

8 Stepwise Construction of Simple Economic Models

1. Introduction

In the past few decades the use of linear programming models for analyzing large industrial operations has become commonplace. For instance, most oil companies use linear programming models having thousands of variables to control their oil refineries, even though these refineries are not linear devices. Such nonlinearities, when important, can be included by means of piece-wise linear approximation techniques and other devices well known in the mathematical programming literature.

However, the corresponding uses of linear programming for economic applications have hardly begun. The book [20] by R. Dorfman, P. Samuelson, and R. Solow and the recent book [32] by L.M. Goreux and A. Manne are notable exceptions.

In the present chapter we carry out a step-by-step construction of a simple model of an economy that includes most of the industries and goods that occur in our modern economy. We do this to illustrate both the economic structure and the use of linear programming techniques for modelling it. In an actual application, we would have to deal with models having thousands of variables, as is done successfully in business uses of linear programming, for example, by the above mentioned oil industries.

Of course, the numbers we use for our models are chosen merely for numerical convenience. The task of collecting and evaluating the data necessary and computing solutions for a full scale expanding economic model of, for instance, the United States economy, is formidable and would require the efforts of many persons and institutions over long periods of time. The same difficulties have arisen in the industrial models referred to previously. Doubtlessly the same kinds of techniques found useful for overcoming the latter difficulties will also be useful for the former.

It is well known that (Leontief) input-output models of (no joint-production) economies with matrices of about 200×200 have been constructed for various real economies. Such models are very useful. The model we propose has, besides its input-output properties, the following additional features: prices, economic expansion, joint production, control variables, and certain optimization properties. (We will present further relations between these two models in Chapter 13.)

Other well-known kinds of large-scale economic models are the

135

econometric models presently used to predict outputs of various sectors of the economy. Some of these models are rather sophisticated, but they do not possess the special features of our model just mentioned either.

In the succeeding sections of this chapter, we will discuss a rural economic model, technological change, then an urban model, and then larger models that incorporate service industries and goods, governmental operations, and waste disposal activities. Some of these models will be closed and some open.

2. A Rural Economy

We begin with the construction of a simple stationary rural economy whose input and output matrices are shown in Figure 8-1. If we consider this as a

$$
\begin{array}{cc}
& \begin{array}{cc} Food & Labor \end{array} \\
\begin{array}{c} Farming \\ \\ Rural\ labor \end{array} & A = \begin{pmatrix} 1 & 1 \\ 1 & 0 \end{pmatrix}
\end{array}
\qquad
\begin{array}{cc}
\begin{array}{cc} Food & Labor \end{array} \\
B = \begin{pmatrix} 2 & 0 \\ 0 & 1 \end{pmatrix}
\end{array}
$$

Figure 8-1

simple KMT model, it is easy to see (Exercise 1) that its solution is given by

$$\alpha = 1, \quad x = (1/2, 1/2), \quad y = (1/2, 1/2), \tag{1}$$

Thus if we begin with 1000 units of food and 1000 workers, we use the 1000 units of food (for seed and animal feed), and produce 2000 units of food at the end of the first time period. Of this, we give 1000 units of food to the laborers to consume, and the economy utilizes the remaining 1000 units of food for the next period's farming activities, etc.

We thus see that our first model is that of a stationary farming economy that can go on forever while remaining the same size. It does not influence, nor is it influenced by, the outside world.

3. Technological Change

Suppose now that there is technological change and a new kind of farming, which we call agribusiness, has been developed but not yet introduced. Let us show how this kind of technological change can be inserted into the model of Section 2. We will only sketch the ideas here to keep the size of the model down. (In the next section and again in Chapter 10 we discuss the same topic further.)

Suppose that the rural model of the previous section was based on horse drawn agricultural equipment, natural seeds, and fertilizers, while the new agribusiness requires tractors, hybrid seeds, and artificial fertilizers. Thus the new agriculture industry requires many more inputs from the industrial sector of the economy than did the previous kind of agriculture. We will not specifically indicate these dependencies in the model now in order to keep the model size small. However, these dependencies will become visible in the input coefficients of the model in the next section.

Let us suppose that the input and output matrices of the agribusiness model are as given in Figure 8-2. It is easy to show (see Exercise 2) that the solution to this model is as given in (2).

$$
\begin{array}{cc}
& \begin{array}{cc} Food & Labor \end{array} \\
\begin{array}{c} \text{Farming} \\ \\ \text{Rural labor} \end{array} & A = \begin{pmatrix} 1 & 1 \\ \\ 2 & 0 \end{pmatrix}
\end{array}
\qquad
\begin{array}{cc}
& \begin{array}{cc} Food & Labor \end{array} \\
B = \begin{pmatrix} 6 & 0 \\ \\ 0 & 2 \end{pmatrix}
\end{array}
$$

Figure 8-2

In words, the expansion rate

$$\alpha = 2, \quad x = (1/2,\ 1/2), \quad y = (1/3,\ 2/3)', \tag{2}$$

of the agribusiness economy is 2, both farming and labor industries are run with equal intensities, and labor is (relatively) twice as valuable as food. (In the rural model of the previous section, labor and food were equally valuable.)

Of course, even if the methods of agribusiness were known completely it would not be possible to implement them instantaneously. We next show how to develop a larger model that contains both kinds of agricultural activities and include constraints on the agribusiness activities in the new model. These constraints are initially tight, but they can gradually be relaxed to indicate that the agribusiness activities are becoming used in the economy.

Figure 8-3 shows (part of) the initial linear programming tableau M_α of the new model. Note that the model is now 4×4. The first two columns are constructed from the models in Figures 8-1 and 8-2. The last two columns give (after multiplying through by -1) the constraints

$$x_1 \le \delta, \quad x_2 \le \delta \tag{3}$$

Initially we set $\delta = 0$ to indicate that only the rural economy can operate. The solution for this model gives $\alpha = 1$. Then as we gradually increase δ, the agribusiness sector of the economy takes over more and more of the food production. When δ reaches a sufficiently large value (actually $\delta = 1/2$ is enough; see Exercise 3) the entire food production of the economy is

	Food	Labor	Agribusiness Constraints	
Agribusiness $\Big\{$	$6-\alpha$	$-\alpha$	-1	0
	-2α	2	0	-1
Rural economy $\Big\{$	$2-\alpha$	$-\alpha$	0	0
	$-\alpha$	1	0	0
	≥ 0	≥ 0	$\geq -\delta$	$\geq -\delta$

Figure 8-3

performed by the agribusiness sector. Here the expansion rate of the economy is $\alpha = 2$.

At the point at which the rural industries become inefficient, they are no longer used in the economy. However, they remain as potential activities in case the economy is for some reason forced to contract or is compressed. (We will discuss the latter possibilities further in Chapter 10.)

The above discussion of technological innovation in expanding economy models is only a sketch and far from complete. We hope to take up this point again at some later occasion.

4. The Urban Model

As the next step in the model construction we add an urban economy containing an agribusiness to the rural economy previously discussed. Because the original rural economy is inefficient relative to the agribusiness, we will not even show it. Also, we change the agribusiness input and output coefficients from those of the previous section to make the agribusiness (a) capable of faster expansion and (b) include its urban inputs that were omitted from the previous example. The new agribusiness coefficients appear in rows 1 and 2 of Figure 8-4.

In Figure 8-4 we show the M_α matrix for the new model. Note that the output coefficients have positive sign and the input coefficients have negative sign and are multiplied by the expansion coefficient α. The names of the activities are shown to the left and the names of the goods at the top of the matrix.

The reader may question how the numbers of Figure 8-4 were chosen. We simply entered the kinds of industries and goods that seemed plausible for such an economy, and then we chose input and output coefficients that also seemed plausible. We would not argue strongly for the choice of these

	1 Food	2 Labor (Rural)	3 Transp. (Rail)	4 Transp. (Auto)	5 Raw mat'ls.	6 Household goods	7 L. Ind. goods	8 H. Ind. goods	9 Labor (Urban)
1. Food	$12-2\alpha$	-2α					$-\alpha$	$-\alpha$	
2. Labor (Rural)	-4α	14		$-\alpha$		$-\alpha$	$-\alpha$		
3. Transportation (Rail)			$23-\alpha$		-3α		-2α	-7α	
4. Transportation (Auto)				$43-\alpha$	-7α		-11α	-4α	-13α
5. Raw Materials			-12α	-4α	45		-2α	-11α	-16α
6. Industry (Light)			-2α	-8α	-6α	8	$33-9\alpha$	-7α	-14α
7. Industry (Heavy)			-12α	-3α	-11α	6	-2α	$38-5\alpha$	-10α
8. Labor (Urban)	-3α	-2α		-2α		-2α	$-\alpha$		12

Figure 8-4

particular numbers. A reader who questions or objects to the numbers chosen is encouraged to change them and resolve the problem in the manner to be described. In any case, the results of this and later models to be described should be considered as illustrative and not necessarily realistic.

The solution to the model of Figure 8-4 was obtained by using the binary search technique described in Chapter 3. (It is clear from the structure of the M_α matrix in Figure 8-4 that the expansion factor is unique.) A small time-shared computer was used for the calculation, and the third method described in Chapter 3 for solving fair matrix games was used for the actual problem formulation. By solving 21 linear programming problems of size 8×9, it was possible to obtain solutions accurate to five significant figures, which was about the maximum accuracy possible with the computer used. It is to be emphasized that the calculations for this small model are quite easy, and that they would not be any harder in principle (although certainly in detail) for much larger problems.

The solutions to the problem of Figure 8-4 are shown in Figures 8-5 and 8-6. The optimum expansion coefficient is $\alpha = 1.15076$.

The corresponding optimum intensity vector is shown in Figure 8-5. Note that the sum of the intensities is 100,000, so that we can interpret each intensity as the part of a \$100,000 budget that is spent on the operation of each industry. In particular, the intensity associated with the rural and urban labor activities can be interpreted as wage bills. In the last column of Figure 8-5 we have computed the ratio of each intensity to that of urban labor in order to be able to compare this solution with those of models we develop later in the chapter.

The optimum price vector is shown in Figure 8-6. Again, the sum of the prices is 100,000, so the individual prices can be determined as the relative prices in the economy of each kind of good. The price of household goods is 0, indicating that they are over produced. We can expect at least one good to have zero price since we have 8 industries and 9 goods, and from well-known linear programming results we know that there can be at most 8 basic variables, so that the other one is nonbasic and hence zero. One way around this difficulty is to add a lower bound constraint on the price of household goods which will make its price positive. This can be interpreted, as in Chapter 4, as the export price for these goods. If this is done (see Exercise 4), there will be 9 rows and 9 columns, and hence (both technically and economically) positive prices for all goods are possible.

In the last column of Figure 8-6 we have recorded the ratios of each price to the price of urban labor. These ratios may be interpreted as the number of units of work needed by such labor to purchase a unit of the corresponding good.

Industries	Solution	Ratios
1. Food	17,239	.4707
2. Labor (Rural)	8,854	.2418
3. Transportation (Rail)	9,400	.2567
4. Transportation (Auto)	5,746	.1569
5. Raw materials	5,356	.1463
6. Industry (Light)	8,719	.2381
7. Industry (Heavy)	8,064	.2202
8. Labor (Urban)	36,622	1.0000

Figure 8-5

Prices	Solution	Ratios
1. Food	5,952	.7584
2. Labor (Rural)	5,121	.6525
3. Transportation (Rail)	11,673	1.4874
4. Transportation (Auto)	15,249	1.9430
5. Raw materials	14,234	1.8137
6. Household goods	0	0
7. Light ind. goods	23,244	2.9618
8. Heavy ind. goods	16,679	2.1253
9. Labor (Urban)	7,848	1.0000

Figure 8-6

5. Addition of Service and Luxury Industries

In the previous section we compared an urban model to the previous rural model and found that the agribusiness sector of the new urban model dominated the previous rural model. We also found that the expansion factor went from $\alpha = 1$ to $\alpha = 1.15076$, that is, the economy changed from a stationary zero-growth rate economy to a more complicated economy capable of growing at a rate of more than 15% per year. Every industry and good of the rural-urban economy is necessary for its operation in the sense that the elimination of one of these industries or goods would make the economy collapse, because each industry produces at least one good that is essential for the functioning of at least one other industry, and each good is required in an essential manner by at least one industry. Treated as a whole, the urban economy is productive.

Suppose that the laborers in the urban model require services and luxuries, in addition to the essentials of food, clothing, housing, and transportation provided by the urban economy. The services might include governmental services, recreational facilities, medical care, personal grooming services, retirement benefits, etc., while the luxury goods could include cosmetics, jewelry, recreational vehicles, certain books, entertainment, etc. These activities contribute to the "quality of life" but are not productive in the sense that the total value of their outputs is less than the total value of their inputs. Hence the economy will not operate these activities unless forced to do so.

There are at least two ways of making the economy operate the service and luxury activities. One way would be to put a positive lower bound on each of their intensities, as we did in the open model of Chapter 4. The other way is to have the rural and urban laborers demand some services and luxuries. We choose the latter device to keep the model within the KMT framework.

The input-output matrix M_α for the enlarged model is shown in Figure 8-7. Note that two new industries—services and luxuries—have been added as have two new "goods" services and luxury goods. Appropriate input and output coefficients appear in the matrix. Note that rural labor demands 2 units of luxury goods when operated at intensity 1 while urban labor demands 5 units of services and 4 units of luxury goods under similar conditions. Because of these demands, the service and luxury industries will be forced to operate with positive intensity if the economy is to work.

The solutions to the model of Figure 8-7 are shown in Figures 8-8 and 8-9. The new expansion factor is now $\alpha = 1.06956$; the expansion rate has dropped from 15.08% to 6.96% due to the production and consumption of services and luxuries. In Figure 8-8, the optimum intensities are given, as well as the ratios of these intensities to the urban labor intensity. And Figure 8-9 gives the optimum prices, and the ratios of these prices to the urban labor price. Note that it is again true that household goods have zero price.

In Section 8 of this chapter, we compare in more detail this solution with the previous and later solutions. For the present, the reader may make such comparisons for himself.

	1. Food	2. Labor (Rural)	3. Transp. (Rail)	4. Transp. (Auto)	5. Raw Mat'ls	6. Household goods	7. L. Ind. goods	8. H. Ind. goods	9. Labor (Urban)	10. Services	11. Luxury goods
1. Food	$12-2\alpha$	-2α					$-\alpha$	$-\alpha$			
2. Labor (Rural)	-4α	14		$-\alpha$		$-\alpha$	$-\alpha$				-2α
3. Transportation (Rail)			$23-\alpha$		-3α		-2α	-7α			
4. Transportation (Auto)				$43-\alpha$	-7α		-11α	-4α	-13α		
5. Raw Materials			-12α	-4α	45		-2α	-11α	-16α		
6. Industry (Light)			-2α	-8α	-6α	8	$33-9\alpha$	-7α	-14α		
7. Industry (Heavy)			-12α	-3α	-11α	6	-2α	$38-5\alpha$	-10α		
8. Labor (Urban)	-3α	-2α		-2α		-2α	$-\alpha$		12	-5α	-4α
9. Services Industry				-3α			-5α		-25α	180	
10. Luxuries industry				-4α	-9α		-8α		-19α		76

Figure 8-7

Industries	Solution	Ratios
1. Food	16,087	.4195
2. Labor (Rural)	8,317	.2169
3. Transportation (Rail)	7,746	.2020
4. Transportation (Auto)	5,570	.1453
5. Raw materials	4,996	.1303
6. Industry (Light)	8,600	.2243
7. Industry (Heavy)	6,805	.1775
8. Labor (Urban)	38,347	1.0000
9. Services industry	1,139	.0297
10. Luxuries industry	2,393	.0624

Figure 8-8

Prices	Solution	Ratios
1. Food	4,872	.4834
2. Labor (Rural)	5,182	.5142
3. Transportation (Rail)	9,673	.9598
4. Transportation (Auto)	13,416	1.3312
5. Raw materials	12,546	1.2467
6. Household goods	0	.0000
7. Light ind. goods	20,275	2.0118
8. Heavy ind. goods	14,277	1.4167
9. Labor (Urban)	10,078	1.0000
10. Services	2,339	.2321
11. Luxury goods	7,324	.7267

Figure 8-9

6. Addition of Disposal and Defense Industries

Two more activities that are frequently deemed necessary for modern economies are pollution disposal and defense. These activities are also unprofitable in the input-output sense previously defined. In the case of the pollution disposal industries, we can add (compare Cremeans [17]) the requirement that each polluting industry require as an input some of the services of the disposal industry to the input coefficients of the various previously defined industries. As far as the defense industry goes, we will not have its outputs required in our initial model, although we will add such requirements in the model of the next section.

The new model, which contains the model of the previous section together with two new industries, disposal and defense, and two new goods, disposal services and defense goods, appears in Figure 8-10. The reader will note that we have inserted appropriate input and output coefficients in the new rows and columns.

The solution to the new model gives an expansion factor of $\alpha = 1.05464$, which means that the expansion rate has dropped still further from 6.96% to 5.46% due to the disposal activity requirements. The optimal intensity and price vectors, and the corresponding ratios, appear in Figures 8-11 and 8-12. Note that the defense industry, being extremely unprofitable, is not run at all, and the price of defense goods is zero. This could have been predicted in advance. Note also that although the disposal industry is run at a very low level, the price of disposal services is relatively high, reflecting the (input-output) unprofitability of this industry. Part of the cost of running unprofitable industries is reflected in the reduced expansion rate, and another part is in the high cost of the goods produced by unprofitable industries.

7. Addition of Defense Requirement

As the last variant of the previous models, we shall add an urban labor requirement for both disposal and defense. To do this we changed the input coefficients in the 12th and 13th columns of row 8 in Figure 8-10 each to $-\alpha$; that is, $a_{8,12} = a_{8,13} = 1$. This means that when the urban labor industry is run at unit intensity, it requires one unit each of disposal services and defense goods. With these input coefficients it is obvious that the defense industry must now be run with positive intensity for the whole economy to operate. This in turn means that the growth rate will go down further because of the requirement that an additional unprofitable industry must be operated.

The new solution, shown in Figures 8-13 and 8-14, bears out these

	1. Food	2. Labor (Rural)	3. Transp. (Rail)	4. Transp. (Auto)	5. Raw mat'ls	6. Household goods	7. L. Ind. goods	8. H.Ind goods	9. Labor (Urban)	10. Services	11. Luxury goods	12. Disposal	13. Defense goods
1. Food	$12-2\alpha$	-2α					$-\alpha$	$-\alpha$					
2. Labor (Rural)	-4α	14		$-\alpha$		$-\alpha$	$-\alpha$				-2α		
3. Transp. (Rail)			$23-\alpha$		-3α		-2α	-7α				$-\alpha$	
4. Transp. (Auto)				$43-\alpha$	-7α		-11α	-4α	-13α				
5. Raw mat'ls			-12α	-4α	45		-2α	-11α	-16α			$-\alpha$	
6. Ind. (Light)			-2α	-8α	-6α	8	$33-9\alpha$	-7α	-14α			-3α	
7. Ind. (Heavy)			-12α	-3α	-11α	6	-2α	$38-5\alpha$	-10α			-4α	
8. Labor (Urban)	-3α	-2α		-2α		-2α	$-\alpha$		12	-5α	-4α		
9. Servs. ind.				-3α			-5		-25α	180			
10. Lux. ind.				-4α	-9α		-8α		-19α		76		
11. Disp. ind.			-4α	-3α	-16α		-10α	-3α	-18α			147	
12. Def. ind.			-17α	-5α	-29α		-27α	-28α	-24α			-3α	62

Figure 8-10

remarks. The new expansion factor is $\alpha = 1.01124$, so the expansion rate has dropped from 5.46% to 1.12%. Note that in Figure 8-13 the defense industry is operated at a relatively low level, and that in Figure 8-14 the cost of defense goods is higher than any other good. These observations demonstrate the large cost of requiring the economy to operate, even at a relatively low level, unprofitable industries.

8. Comparisons Among the Solutions

Having worked out several variations of these models, it is interesting to compare their solutions. In Figures 8-15 and 8-16 we collected, for comparison purposes, the ratios of the intensities and prices for each of the models of Sections 4, 5, 6, and 7.

In Figure 8-15 we note that as activities and goods are added to the model, the intensities devoted to each industry relative to that of urban labor tend to go down. This is, in part, because the number of industries is increasing, and hence the relative effort on each is decreasing. It is also due to the decrease in the expansion rate.

Industries	Solution	Ratios
1. Food	15,783	.4105
2. Labor (Rural)	8,170	.2061
3. Transportation (Rail)	7,727	.2001
4. Transportation (Auto)	5,520	.1436
5. Raw materials	5,069	.1319
6. Industry (Light)	8,587	.2234
7. Industry (Heavy)	6,743	.1754
8. Labor (Urban)	38,445	1.0000
9. Services industry	1,126	.0293
10. Luxuries industry	2,361	.0614
11. Disposal industry	470	.0022
12. Defense industry	0	.0000

Figure 8-11

Prices	Solution	Ratios
1. Food	4,599	.4929
2. Labor (Rural)	4,828	.5175
3. Transportation (Rail)	9,431	1.0108
4. Transportation (Auto)	12,584	1.3488
5. Raw materials	11,963	1.2822
6. Household goods	0	0.0000
7. Light ind. goods	19,484	2.0883
8. Heavy ind. goods	13,988	1.4992
9. Labor (Urban)	9,330	1.0000
10. Services	2,159	.2314
11. Luxury goods	6,816	.7305
12. Disposal	4,819	.5165
13. Defense goods	0	.0000

Figure 8-12

Industries	Solution	Ratios
1. Food	14,869	.3852
2. Labor (Rural)	7,925	.2053
3. Transportation (Rail)	8,198	.2124
4. Transportation (Auto)	5,321	.1378
5. Raw materials	5,350	.1386
6. Industry (Light)	8,128	.2106
7. Industry (Heavy)	7,014	.1817
8. Labor (Urban)	38,603	1.0000
9. Services industry	1,169	.0303
10. Luxuries industry	2,260	.0585
11. Disposal industry	732	.0190
12. Defense industry	630	.0163

Figure 8-13

Prices	Solution	Ratios
1. Food	3,496	.3838
2. Labor (Rural)	3,719	.4082
3. Transportation (Rail)	7,443	.8170
4. Transportation (Auto)	10,269	1.1272
5. Raw materials	9,784	1.0740
6. Household goods	0	.0000
7. Light ind. goods	15,817	1.7362
8. Heavy ind. goods	11,242	1.2340
9. Labor (Urban)	9,110	1.0000
10. Services	1,897	.2082
11. Luxury goods	5,705	.6262
12. Disposal	3,942	.4327
13. Defense goods	17,576	1.9293

Figure 8-14

Industries	Sec. 4	Sec. 5	Sec. 6	Sec. 7
1. Food	.4707	.4195	.4105	.3852
2. Labor (Rural)	.2418	.2196	.2061	.2053
3. Transp. (Rail)	.2567	.2020	.2001	.2124
4. Transp. (Auto)	.1569	.1453	.1436	.1378
5. Raw materials	.1463	.1303	.1319	.1386
6. Industry (Light)	.2381	.2243	.2234	.2106
7. Industry (Heavy)	.2202	.1775	.1754	.1817
8. Labor (Urban)	1	1	1	1
9. Services industry		.0297	.0293	.0303
10. Luxuries industry		.0624	.0614	.0585
11. Disposal industry			.0022	.0190
12. Defense industry			0	.0163

Figure 8-15

Prices	Sec. 4	Sec. 5	Sec. 6	Sec. 7
1. Food	.7584	.4834	.4929	.3838
2. Labor (Rural)	.6525	.5142	.5175	.4082
3. Transp. (Rail)	1.4874	.9598	1.0108	.8170
4. Transp. (Auto)	1.9430	1.3312	1.3488	1.1272
5. Raw materials	1.8137	1.2467	1.2822	1.0740
6. Household goods	0	0	0	0
7. Light ind. goods	2.9618	2.0118	2.0883	1.7362
8. Heavy ind. goods	2.1253	1.4167	1.4992	1.2340
9. Labor (Urban)	1	1	1	1
10. Services		.2321	.2314	.2082
11. Luxury goods		.7267	.7305	.6262
12. Disposal			.5165	.4327
13. Defense goods			0	1.9293

Figure 8-16

Similarly, in Figure 8-16 we note that as goods are added to the model, the prices of all goods, relative to the price of urban labor, decreases. This is probably due to the decrease in the expansion rate which makes the (internal) demand for these goods go down. The most surprising thing is the relatively high prices attached to the goods produced by inefficient industries. However, since these prices measure the degree of inefficiency, perhaps their magnitude is best explained by their "drag" on the economy.

Exercises

1. Show that the rural model of Figure 8-1 has the solution claimed in (1).
2. Show that the solution to the agribusiness model of Figure 8-2 is given in (2).
3. Show that when $\delta = 1/2$ in Figure 8-3, there is a solution in which the agribusiness industry produces all the food, and the old rural economy is inefficient and not used.
4. In Figure 8-4, add a constraint to force household goods to have a positive price. Give an interpretation of this constraint in terms of exporting these goods.

Long-Term Planning Models

1. Introduction

In this chapter, we will refer to the open model of Chapter 4 as the *static or steady-state open model* to distinguish it from the *dynamic open model* we define in Sections 4 and 5. We discuss the problem of the determination of the control variables for the static model in Sections 2 and 3.

One might argue that the von Neumann model, whether closed or open, is already "dynamic." What it does is determine the conditions of uniform expansion, either for the economy as a whole, or for the subeconomies of which it is composed. This steady-state expansion is, of course, in some sense dynamic and thus different from a static case in which, period after period, exactly the same processes are run at the same intensities and where the same prices prevail.

However, in Sections 5 and 6 we are looking at an economy over many periods, and given the fact that control variables exist, we take into consideration that through planning, using these variables, the steady state may be changed deliberately from period to period. It is not unreasonable to call such sequences of expansions "dynamic" in the true sense. At any rate, there is a considerable extension of the applicability of the model.

The results of this chapter are indeed of an applied nature, since the linear programming models could actually be set up and be used for computations. The new model is much richer than the old one since it has numerous control variables which can be changed period by period and allows for the possibility of setting various goals (i.e., whether to prefer one type of activity over another). It also gives the interesting possibility of attaching a utility to having a particular expansion factor, or to having a mixture of imports and exports. We consider furthermore the costs of programmed changes incurred in going from one endowment vector over to another. In this manner, many of the elements required of a practical planning model are coming into their own.

2. Determination of the Control Variables for the Static Model

As shown in Chapter 4, the static model, defined by the axioms and

This chapter is based largely on our paper [95].

assumptions stated here together with the additional economically reasonable condition that $\alpha = \beta$, may be solved by considering the pair of dual linear programming problems whose initial tableau is shown in Figure 9-1. In that figure, blank entries are zero matrices and I stands for an identity matrix of the proper dimension. Solution techniques that involve binary search on the variable α and solving the resulting linear programs have been discussed in Chapter 3.

$$
\begin{array}{c}
\begin{array}{ccc}
\quad y & \quad z^p & \quad z^n
\end{array} \\
\begin{array}{c}
x \\
w^e \\
w^i
\end{array}
\left|
\begin{array}{ccc}
M_\alpha & -I & I \\
-I & & \\
I & &
\end{array}
\right|
\begin{array}{l}
= 0 \\
\leq -p^e \\
\leq p^i
\end{array} \\
\begin{array}{ccc}
= & \geq & \geq \\
0 & -t^p & t^n
\end{array}
\end{array}
$$

Figure 9-1

The question can be raised as to how the economy should determine the control variables t^p and t^n for the static open model. We shall sketch the answer to this question. First we give the dual variable interpretations of the variables in Figure 9-1.

As can be seen from Figure 9-1, z_k^n is the dual variable corresponding to the constraint $x_k \geq t_k^n$. Suppose that the units in which intensity x_k is measured are the number of hours per year that industry k is to be run. Then t_k^n gives the minimum number of hours per year that industry k must be run. It follows from this and from the definitions in Chapter 4 that the units of z_k^n are the *dollar increase in balance of trade per unit increase in the maximum number of hours that industry k can be operated*. Similarly, z_k^p is the dual variable corresponding to the constraint $x_k \geq t_k^p$ so that z_k^p can be interpreted as the *dollar decrease in balance of trade per unit increase in the minimum number of hours that industry k must be operated*.

Similar interpretations can be made for the variables w_k^e and w_k^i in terms of the export and import prices p_k^e and p_k^i when they are subject to change. (See Exercises 1 and 2.) Of course, these prices cannot be changed within the economy since they are determined externally. However, the dual variables indicate how the economy will react to such changes.

Suppose that we let $t^n(\delta)$ and $t^p(\delta)$ represent changed values of these variables and let $x(\delta)$, $y(\delta)$, and $\alpha(\delta)$ be the corresponding determined variables. Since to change the intensity levels of various industries involves effort and cost, we let $C(t^n(\delta),\ t^p(\delta))$ be the *cost* of making this change. Similarly, we let $U((x(\delta),\ y(\delta),\ \alpha(\delta))$ be the *utility* to the economy of the new solutions. The (nonlinear) problem that must be solved in making the decision is to

$$\text{Maximize}[U(x(\delta),\ y(\delta),\ \alpha(\delta)) - C(t^n(\delta),\ t^p(\delta))] \tag{1}$$

subject to any constraints that there may be on the choices of the variables.

Various rationale may be used in determining the form of the utility function such as:

(1) Increase the output of heavy industry.
(2) Increase the output of consumer goods.
(3) Consume more now at the expense of later consumption.
(4) Increase the expansion rate.
(5) Increase exports.
(6) Limit imports.

In a similar way, one can itemize factors that determine the costs of making changes in control variables.

3. Example for the Static Model

We illustrate by performing computations with Example 4-8. We assume, as we did there, that there are two industries that produce "essentials" and "inessentials" with input and output matrices as follows

$$
\begin{array}{c}
 & \begin{array}{cc} E & IE \end{array} & & \begin{array}{cc} E & IE \end{array} \\
\text{Essentials industry} & & & \\
& A = \begin{pmatrix} 1 & 0 \\ 1 & 1 \end{pmatrix}, & B = \begin{pmatrix} 4 & 0 \\ 0 & 2 \end{pmatrix} \\
\text{Inessentials industry} & & &
\end{array}
$$

The constraints to be satisfied are:

$$0 \le x_1 \le 1 - a = t_1^p \qquad p_1^e = 1/2 \le y_1 \le 1$$

$$t_2^n = a \le x_2 \le 1 \qquad 1/2 \le y_2 \le 1 = p_2^i$$

In other words, the total effort of the economy is divided between the essentials industry which is run at $1-a$ units of intensity and the inessentials industry which is run at a units of intensity. The optimal solution strategies, provided $0 < a \le 1/2$, are:

$$x = (1 - a,\ a) \quad \text{and} \quad y = \begin{pmatrix} 1/2 \\ 1 \end{pmatrix}$$

Given these, it can easily be shown (see Exercise 3) that

$$\alpha = \frac{4}{1 + 2a}$$

which follows, since $xM_\alpha y = 0$ at the optimum. Next the calculations of the export and import functions yield the following (see Exercise 4):

$$w_1^e = \alpha a(1-2a) \qquad w_1^i = 0$$

$$w_2^e = 0 \qquad w_2^i = (1/2)\alpha a(1 - 2a) = (1/2)w_1^e$$

In the same way the profits and losses are found to be:

$$z_1^p = a\alpha \qquad z_1^n = 0$$

$$z_2^p = 0 \qquad z_2^n = (1 - a)\alpha$$

Thus the solution shows that the economy must export two units of essentials in order to import one unit of inessentials. In this case, the essentials industry is profitable, and the inessentials industry is unprofitable. The graph of w_1^e as a function of the variable a is given in Figure 9-2. Note that the function is positive for a in the range $0 < a < 1/2$ and is zero at both endpoints. The export function rises to a unique maximum at the value $a = 0.207$, which can be found easily by elementary calculus.

Suppose that we adopt the utility function that tries to maximize the total quantity of exports. We then choose $a = 0.207$ which gives $w_1^e = 0.343$, the maximum possible export. The rest of the solution is as follows:

$$\alpha = 2.828, \quad x = (0.793, 0.207), \quad y = \begin{pmatrix} 0.5 \\ 1 \end{pmatrix}$$

$$w_1^e = 0.343, \quad w_2^e = 0, \quad w_1^i = 0, \quad w_2^i = 0.172$$

$$z_1^p = 0.586, \quad z_2^p = 0, \quad z_1^n = 0, \quad z_2^n = 2.242$$

The total amount of essentials produced is $4(0.793) = 3.1172$, of which 2.829 units remain in the country and 0.343 units are exported. The total amount of inessentials that is in the country each time period consists of the amount produced, 0.414, plus the amount imported, 0.172, for a total of 0.586. We have not explicitly introduced consumption into the model; if we did, this balance of essential and inessential goods would provide a more desirable consumption package than the solution which provides only essentials obtained by making $\alpha = 4$, the technologically maximum possible expansion factor.

We have thus illustrated an economy which, for its own reasons, wishes to be an important factor in the world export market. In order to do so, it

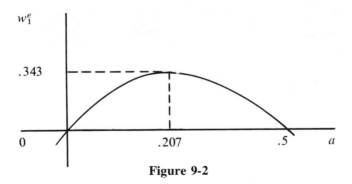

Figure 9-2

reduces its expansion rate below its maximum expansion rate so as to maximize its exports and to provide a desired balance of essential and inessential goods. It is not hard to alter this example to include a cost for changing the control parameter a or to change the utility function to other plausible forms, but we shall not carry this out here.

4. The One-Period Dynamic Open Model

The first "turnpike" questions connected with a multiperiod discrete-time version of the von Neumann expanding economy model were posed by Dorfman, Samuelson, and Solow in [20], and later proved rigorously and in more general settings by Radner [111], Morishima [99], and McKenzie [68].

Here we pose more general turnpike questions for the open model. Some of the original questions will not have meaning in the new setting unless certain additional requirements are added to the model.

We assume that we initially have an endowment vector R^1 whose components give the quantities of the various goods that are available as inputs for the first period. We pose the goal of achieving an endowment vector R^2 by the end of the period, where now R^1 need not be equal to R^2, as was true in the static model. We can also suppose that the export and import prices change from p^{e1}, p^{i1} during the first time period to p^{e2}, p^{i2} during the second time period. We want to choose the control vectors t^{p1} and t^{n1} so as to achieve endowment R^2 given R^1, and possibly to satisfy other criteria as given by utility and cost functions as in the previous section. The basic problem is given in the initial linear programming tableau of Figure 9-3. Clearly this tableau and the corresponding dual linear programming problems can be derived from Figure 9-1 by splitting M_α into its constituents B and $-\alpha A$ and making the other obvious changes.

	y^1	z^{p1}	z^{n1}	y^2	
x^1	$-\alpha A$	$-I$	I	B	$= 0$
w^{e1}	$-I$				$\leq -p^{e1}$
w^{i1}	I				$\leq p^{i1}$
w^{e2}				$-I$	$\leq -p^{e2}$
w^{i2}				I	$\leq p^{i2}$
	$-R^1$	$-t^{p1}$	t^{n1}	R^2	

Figure 9-3

With the problem as posed in Figure 9-3, we clearly need an additional assumption. Namely, we must assume that the beginning vector R^1 and the ending vector R^2 are such that a feasible solution exists for $\alpha > 1$, since otherwise the problem posed would have a solution only by running the economy down.

We can now pose the problem of determining the control variables t^{p1} and t^{n1} to maximize a utility function, similar to that in the previous section. That function measures the value to the economy of a given expansion rate, given terminal endowment R^2, given export and import quantities of each of the goods, etc. We may also have a cost function that measures the difficulty of changing the control variables from one setting to another. We shall call the above model the *dynamic open expanding economy model* since it poses the problem of how to go from one endowment vector to another, using the control variables of the open expanding economy model.

5. Numerical Example of the One-Period Open Dynamic Model

Let us extend the static model of Section 3 to a one-period open dynamic model by assuming that initial and final endowments are given by $R^1 = (1.7, 1.9)$ and $R^2 = (2, 2.5)$. We also assume the following import and export price vectors

$$p^{e1} = (0.4,\ 0.5) \qquad p^{i1} = (0.5,\ 0.6)$$
$$p^{e2} = (0.4,\ 0.3) \qquad p^{i2} = (0.5,\ 0.4)$$

	y_1^1	y_2^1	z_1^{p1}	z_1^{n1}	z_2^{p1}	z_2^{n1}	y_1^2	y_2^2	
$x_1 = 1$	-2.4	0	-1	0	1	0	4	0	$= 0$
$x_2 = .25$	-2.4	-2.4	0	-1	0	1	0	2	$= 0$
$w_1^{e1} = 0$	-1	0	0	0	0	0	0	0	$\leq -.4$
$w_2^{e1} = 1.3$	0	-1	0	0	0	0	0	0	$\leq -.5$
$w_1^{i1} = 1.3$	1	0	0	0	0	0	0	0	$\leq .5$
$w_2^{i1} = 0$	0	1	0	0	0	0	0	0	$\leq .6$
$w_1^{e2} = 2$	0	0	0	0	0	0	-1	0	$\leq -.4$
$w_2^{e2} = 0$	0	0	0	0	0	0	0	-1	$\leq -.3$
$w_1^{i2} = 0$	0	0	0	0	0	0	1	0	$\leq .5$
$w_2^{i2} = 2$	0	0	0	0	0	0	0	1	$\leq .4$
	-1.7	-1.9	-1	-1	$.5$	$.25$	2	2.5	

Figure 9-4

and we assume the production and constraints:

$$0.5 \leq x_1 \leq 1 \quad \text{and} \quad 0.25 \leq x_2 \leq 1$$

Solution of the problem gave $\alpha = 2.4$. See Exercise 8. The initial tableau with this value of α and the various solution values for the variables marked around the sides is given in Figure 9-4. Note that $x = (1, 0.25)$ means that we run the first industry at full intensity and the second at minimum intensity; also, we have $w_1^{i1} = 1.3$ and $w_1^{e2} = 2$, which means that we import good 1 in time period 1 and export it in time period 2. Similarly, $w_2^{e1} = 1.3$ and $w_2^{i2} = 2$, which means that we export good 2 in time period 1 and import it in time period 2. This kind of erratic behavior is due, in part, because of the requirement of the model that the balance of profits and payments conditions hold each time period. It may be possible to alleviate this somewhat by using the *balance of payments and balance of profits over time conditions,* discussed in the next section.

It should be remarked that the solution of even simple versions of this model seems to be difficult, in part because of the numerous parameters that can be varied. The complete treatment of the computational difficulties of this problem awaits further study.

6. The N-Period Dynamic Open Expanding Economy Model

It is possible to expand the model of Section 5 to an N-period model. Figure 9-5 gives the initial linear programming tableau for the extension. Note that we now have control vectors t^{pk} and t^{nk} for $k = 1, \ldots, N$. The corresponding variables for each of these terms are also defined on the left side and on the top of the tableau.

We must assume that the final endowment R^n is close enough to the initial endowment R^1 so that the model has a solution with $\alpha \geq 1$. Now we want to determine the expansion factor α and the control variables t^{pk} and t^{nk} so that the model achieves or exceeds the terminal endowment in N periods, while satisfying the axioms of the model at all intermediate steps. The difficult technical question of determining conditions (if any) for which a solution can be found has not yet been settled.

If we write the equality of primal and dual objective functions for the linear program of Figure 9-5, we obtain

$$-R^1 y^1 + \sum_{k=1}^{N-1} t^{nk} z^{nk} - \sum_{k=1}^{N-1} t^{pk} z^{pk} + R^N y^N$$

$$= \sum_{k=1}^{N} w^{ik} p^{ik} - \sum_{k=1}^{N} w^{ek} p^{ek} \tag{2}$$

If we use the period-by-period balance of trade and balance of profits conditions, namely,

$$t^{nk} z^{nk} = t^{pk} z^{pk} \quad \text{for } k = 1, \ldots, N-1 \tag{3}$$

and

$$w^{ik} p^{ik} = w^{ek} p^{ek} \quad \text{for } k = 1, \ldots, N \tag{4}$$

we can derive from (2)

$$R^1 y^1 = R^N y^N \tag{5}$$

In other words, the initial and terminal prices must put equality of values on the initial and terminal endowments.

Note that (5) can be derived from (2) by using the following conditions:

$$\sum_{k=1}^{n-1} t^{nk} z^{nk} = \sum_{k=1}^{n-1} t^{pk} z^{pk} \tag{6}$$

which can be called the *balance of trade over time* and *balance of profits over time conditions*. Clearly (3) and (4) imply (5) and (6), but not conversely. There may well be economic situations for which (5) and (6) provide

Figure 9-5

	y^1	z^{p1}	z^{n1}	y^2	z^{p2}	z^{n2}	$\cdots$	y^{n-1}	$z^{p,N-1}$	$z^{n,N-1}$	y^N	
x^1	$-\alpha A$	$-I$	I	B								$=0$
w^{e1}	$-I$											$\leqq -p^{e1}$
w^{i1}	I											$\leqq p^{i1}$
x^2				$-\alpha A$	$-I$	I						$=0$
w^{e2}				$-I$								$\leqq -p^{e2}$
w^{i2}				I								$\leqq p^{i2}$
$\vdots$							$\vdots$					
x^{n-1}								$-\alpha A$	$-I$	I	B	$=0$
$w^{e,N-1}$								$-I$				$\leqq -p^{e,N-1}$
$w^{i,N-1}$								I				$\leqq p^{i,N-1}$
x^N											$-\alpha A$	$=0$
w^{eN}											$-I$	$\leqq -p^{eN}$
w^{iN}											I	$\leqq p^N$
	$\geqq -R^1$	$\geqq -t^{p1}$	$\geqq t^{n1}$	> 0	$\geqq -t^{p2}$	$\geqq t^{n2}$		$\geqq 0$	$\geqq -t^{p,N-1}$	$\geqq t^{n,N-1}$	$\geqq R^N$	

more realistic conditions than (3) and (4). (We are indebted to G. Oroszel for this observation.)

Note here that the classical turnpike problem cannot be directly formulated, since we have control variables t^{pk} and t^{nk} whose values may change each time period; thus *there is no single "von Neumann ray" to act as a "turnpike,"* but rather a different ray in each period. However, if we add the condition that the control variables must not change from period to period, then a meaningful turnpike question could be posed as follows: given an initial endowment and a feasible final endowment and fixed control variables, solve the usual turnpike question for the resulting von Neumann ray; then choose among all these turnpike solutions the most desirable one, using some criterion.

Note that the dynamic open model is susceptible to a number of other changes. For instance, we could set or determine the expansion rate α^k for each time period. We can also pose very difficult questions for which the economy must determine a utility for a series of changes over time; e.g., suppose the economy wants to approach a zero growth situation, that is, with $\alpha = 1$. (In Section 3 of Chapter 10 we go further in the latter question.)

Exercises

1. In Figure 9-1, show that w_k^e evaluates the dollar decrease in balance of profits per unit decrease in the export price of good k.

2. In Figure 9-1, show that w_k^i evaluates the dollar decrease in balance of profits per unit increase in the import price of good k.

3. Consider the essentials-inessentials model of Section 3.

   (a) If $0 < a \le 1/2$, show that $x = (1-a,a)$ and $y = (1/2,1)'$ are optimal for M_α.

   (b) Use $xM_\alpha y = 0$ at optimality to show that $\alpha = 4/(1 + 2a)$.

4. For the strategies given in Exercise 3, use $xM_\alpha - w^e + w^i = 0$ to show that
$$w_1^e = \alpha a(1 - 2a), \ w_1^i = 0, \ w_2^e = 0, \ w_2^i = (1/2)w_1^e$$

5. For the optimal strategies in Exercise 3, use $M_\alpha y - z^p + z^n = 0$ to show that
$$z_1^p = a\alpha, \ z_1^n = 0, \ z_2^p = 0, \ z_2^n = (1 - a)\alpha$$

6. Show that $w_1^e = \alpha a(1 - 2a)$ has the graph shown in Figure 9-2, including the fact that the maximum is taken on at $\alpha = 0.207$.

7. Show that the tableau in Figure 9-3 is derived from that in Figure 9-1.

8. Verify that the solution to the problem in Figure 9-4 is correct. Include the following vectors.
$$y^1 = (0.5,0.5)' \quad \text{and} \quad y^2 = (0.4,0.6)'$$

10 Stationarity, Contraction, and Compression of Economies

1. Introduction

So far in this book we have treated expansion as a desirable characteristic of an economy. But in recent years it has become clear that natural resources such as some kinds of fossil energy and minerals may soon be close to exhaustion, that uncontrolled growth creates pollution leading to health hazards and degradation of quality of life, and that the finite size of the earth puts an absolute upper limit on the ultimate size and type of economic activities and hence of human population. Therefore a vitally important problem of the future is that of controlling economic growth, not simply by cutting it back indiscriminately, but in such a way as to achieve an economic system that provides a desirable way of life.

The classical von Neumann model, even as generalized in the KMT model of Chapter 2, embodies no forces to take these tasks into account. Consequently, control variables had to be introduced as in Chapter 4, which, by proper manipulation, will achieve a stationary economy or even one which is cut back in some manner should the economy have already expanded beyond a point where stationarity at that level cannot be maintained indefinitely. We do not investigate which political or administrative system is required to operate the control variables. The crucial point is that the underlying reality is largely independent of whatever political system might be functioning in a given country or in any composition of countries making up a world economy or subeconomy.

In Section 2 we review the numerous ways of controlling economic growth that we have discussed and illustrated in preceding chapters. We note that some kinds of control tend to decrease the expansion rate, while other kinds of control tend to increase it.

In Section 3 we discuss stationary economies and long-term planning, making use of the results given in Chapter 9. We show that it is possible to move from the current state of an expanding economy with expansion factor greater than one (expansion rate positive) to a stationary economy with expansion factor equal to one (expansion rate zero). This movement can be carried out gradually, in a series of small steps, so that there is no major disruption or distortion of the economy as the control variables of the economy are changed.

The idea of an economy contracting in equilibrium, which has only

161

rarely if ever been discussed in the literature, is considered in Section 4. Here it is obvious that contraction cannot be continued indefinitely without collapse, at least if we consider realistic economies in which activities have a finite minimum possible size.

In the last section of the chapter we consider the idea of economic compression. In compressing an economy, we act to suppress, or at least severely limit, the operation of an industry, or the production of a good. We investigate the effect on the economy of such suppressions.

We believe that the processes of contracting or compressing an economy, while they have not been important in the past, may become of primary importance in solving the economic problems to be faced in the future.

2. Controlling Economic Growth

Throughout this book we have given numerous methods with illustrations of controlling economies so that they are compatible with the economic, sociological, and political factors of the milieu in which they are embedded. In each of these cases the expansion rate obtained has been determined only after the constraints needed to achieve the required controls were imposed. However, such constraints may also be imposed with the independent objective of changing the expansion rate for whatever reasons. In this section we discuss our previous results from this point of view.

In a certain sense one can regard the profits of the profitable industries as being available to be "spent" by the economy on many different activities. Every "modern" economy supports governmental activities, which, in turn, provide in some degree essential services such as police and fire protection, public transportation, roads, health services, sanitation, control of foods and drugs that may be sold, power, communication, education, defense, etc. Each of these activities, while being unprofitable in the sense defined in Chapter 4 (i.e., the value of its outputs being less than the value of its inputs) is certainly necessary to have to some degree. In each economy there is a continuing debate and struggle as to what the proper mixture of these activities should be.

Every economy also has restrictions that prevent certain kinds of economic activities, such as production of certain drugs or poisons, criminal activities of various kinds, activities that pollute or destroy the environment excessively, etc. Again, the activities that are limited and the extent of the limitation varies from economy to economy.

The above kinds of economic variations can be achieved by means of control variables as discussed in Chapter 4. In addition, we discussed private and public consumption in the form of foreign aid given or received, and also private and public savings in Chapters 6 and 7. These activities too can be changed deliberately by society at will. These types of economic controls are achieved by changing input (or output) coefficients and consumption and savings coefficients.

Suppose that all the desired changes in patterns of consumption and production have been made so that the desired quality of life has been achieved by the economy. However, the growth rate of the economy is still higher than desired or needed to match the rate of population growth. In the next section we show that by making a simple proportional cutback in the profitable activities we can achieve any expansion less than the current one. This is easily done by means of the control variables of the open model.

We summarize the five principal methods of controlling economic growth discussed above as follows:

(1) Require more or less of the outputs of unprofitable industries.
(2) Limit or stimulate the outputs of profitable industries.
(3) Change the consumption (or savings) coefficients of labor or government.
(4) Change the amount of outside consumption or foreign aid the economy gives or receives.
(5) Make a proportional reduction in the intensities with which profitable industries are operated.

These changes will make changes in the expansion coefficient in the manners described in earlier chapters. If it is desired to change the expansion rate, then we can make appropriate changes in control variables or consumption coefficients of the model. We illustrate next some of these kinds of changes.

Recall that in Chapter 8, Section 4, we described an urban economy that could expand at a rate of 15.08% per year. When we added service and luxury industries (see Figure 8-7) which are unprofitable in our sense, and changed the input coefficients of labor so that some services and luxuries would be supplied to and consumed by the laborers, then the expansion rate went down from 15.08 to 6.96%. Note that this was a conscious decision to improve the "quality of life" for the worker, and the effect was achieved at the expense of a decreased expansion rate. Suppose that we wanted to increase the consumption of services and luxuries still further. Some numerical experimentation shows that if we increase $a_{2,11}$, $a_{8,10}$, $a_{8,11}$, from 2, 5, 4 to 3.925, 9.8125, 7.85, respectively, i.e., we increase these input coefficients by 96.25%, then the expansion rate $[a = 100(\alpha - 1)]$ goes to 0. In this case we would have "spent" all of the profits from the profitable industries on services and luxuries and, as a consequence, changed our economy from an expanding to a stationary economy.

Similarly, in Sections 8-6 and 8-7, we considered the addition of disposal and defense industries to the economy and changes in the various input coefficients so that these unprofitable industries are required to operate in the economy. The expansion rate drops still further to 5.46% when disposal, but not defense, is required and then to 1.12% when, in addition, defense is required. Again, by numerical experimentation it can be shown that if in the table of Figure 8-10, $a_{8,12} = a_{8,13} = 1$ are changed to $a_{8,12} = 1$ and $a_{8,13} = 1.34$, that is, if the input coefficient for defense is increased by 34%, then the expansion rate goes to 0. If we try to triple the defense coefficients, the expansion factor would drop to $\alpha = .952$, that is, the expansion rate would become negative ($a = -4.8\%$) and the economy would become contracting and eventually "run down." Here is a case in which the desire to consume "profits" of the profitable industries has lead to a deficit or overconsumption situation and the economy starts contracting. We say more about this possibility in Section 4.

It is interesting to see that the open model in its various versions as discussed above can be used to answer the question of controlling the rate of growth as well as answering the previously formulated questions.

3. Stationary Economies

In our previous models we have ignored the problem of population growth and simply made the implicit assumption—common to most if not all current growth models—that the rate of growth of the population will exactly match that of the economy. With current problems being faced by the countries of the world, it seems necessary to be able to control simultaneously the rate of growth of the population and the economy of a country. In the long run it will be necessary to reach a steady-state equilibrium rate, that is, $\alpha = 1$, for both. In the present section we discuss ways in which this kind of economic equilibrium can be achieved and maintained. We confine our discussion to a small example and consider principally the methods (3) and (5) of controlling economic growth listed in Section 2, since the other methods have been amply demonstrated previously.

Let us consider a chicken-and-eggs model whose input and output matrices are as follows:

		Chicken	Eggs	Labor	
Laying		1	0	1	
Hatching	$A =$	1	4	1	,
Labor		4	8	0	

		Chicken	Eggs	Labor	
Laying		1	12	0	
Hatching	$B =$	5	0	0	
Labor		0	0	4	

$$(1)$$

This model has an expansion factor of $\alpha = 1.303$ and optimal activity vector

$$x = (.377, .377, .246) \tag{2}$$

and an optimal price vector

$$y = (.318, .074, .608)' \tag{3}$$

The reader may recall that we discussed a model identical to this one in Example 2-4, except that $b_{33} = 2$ instead of 4, for which the expansion factor was $\alpha = 1$. In that model the consumption was twice as large as in our present model, that is 2 (instead of 4) people consumed 4 chickens and 8 eggs each time period. This added consumption was just enough to make the expansion rate fall to 0% ($\alpha = 1$) from 30.3% ($\alpha = 1.303$), and thus gives a good illustration of the third method of reducing the expansion rate discussed in the previous section.

Let us return to the example given in (1) and illustrate the fifth method of controlling economic expansion. Suppose we fix the intensity of the labor activity at $x_3 = .246$ and then see to what extent we can reduce the intensities of the laying and hatching activities, which are profitable industries, while keeping them at the same relative intensities as (2). To do this we set $x_1 = x_2 = z$ and try to see how much we can reduce z while keeping the intensity of labor constant so that the consumption of the workers is unchanged. It is easy to show that the smallest value of z for which this is true is $z = .246$ (see Exercise 2). Thus the economy could continue forever in this stationary ($\alpha = 1$) balanced production situation with the first two (productive) industries being run at less than their full intensity. This in turn means that the laborers would have less work to do in these industries and hence more leisure time, while maintaining constant their real goods consumption. We have thus illustrated still another way of "consuming" productive resources—that of increasing leisure time—once an adequate level of real goods consumption has been reached.

It can be shown (see Exercise 3) that for the model in (1) any expansion rate between $\alpha^* = 1$ and $\alpha^* = 1.303$ can also be achieved by suitably choosing z. Of course, as α^* is increased, more work time is required of—and hence less leisure time is available to—the laborers.

In any actual implementation of a plan for controlling economic growth it is obvious that one should not rapidly change from a growth rate of 30% to one of 0%. Rather, one should set a certain number of time periods during which the economic controls on productive activities would gradually be imposed. In this way the necessary social adjustments to increased leisure time and other changes in economic and personal activities can be made. In this respect the long term planning models of Chapter 9 can be used to advantage.

We could go on almost indefinitely illustrating such economic systems obtained by making various combinations of changes in consumption coefficients and/or production constraints that achieve either zero or very small growth rates. Each of these gives economic systems that have different kinds of "quality of life." Each requires large-scale economic planning, and a huge number of calculations, to determine its feasibility. Finally, in order to implement most of these plans, governmental control of economic activities on regional, national, and even international levels will be necessary.

Our purpose here is not to evaluate the desirability of zero or small economic growth rates, nor is it to evaluate the degree of desirability of governmental control needed to implement plans necessary to achieve these growth rates. Rather it is to show how the calculations needed to formulate such plans, which are well within the capability of current computers, can be made within the framework of the models discussed in this book.

4. Contracting Economies

In the preceding parts of this book we have considered expanding economies as having *balanced expansion,* that is, following a growth process in which the outputs of one time period are just adequate to supply the inputs of the next period—the latter being larger (by the expansion factor $\alpha > 1$) than the inputs required of the previous period.

We now want to consider *balanced contraction* of economies in which the outputs of a given time period are just adequate to supply the inputs of the next period—the latter being smaller (by the factor $\alpha < 1$) than the inputs of the preceding period.

Both of these ideas of balanced expansion and contraction are to be clearly distinguished from the well-known ideas of expansion and contraction of economies due to the effects of business cycles. In our models, such cyclic behavior is impossible. (However, if we were to introduce lags into the model they would become possible; see the remarks in Chapter 14.)

The balanced expansion that we have discussed leads to economic models that can go on forever, each time period being larger (by α) than they were in the previous period. Such models can apply to the real world for only a limited number of time periods because of the eventual exhaustion of natural resources. Long before this point of resource exhaustion is reached, alternative goods and processes must be introduced, that is, we must switch to another economic model that will again apply only for a limited number of time periods, and so on. As discussed in the preceding section, the growth rates of these successive models must tend to become smaller, at least if these models are to continue to fit real economies.

In the same way, an economy exhibiting balanced contraction can apply to a real world economy for only a finite number of time periods. In this case we observe that real goods and real productive processes have a minimum size, so that once an economy has contracted to the point at which there remains only one of the necessary goods or processes, further contraction leads to economic collapse. We illustrate this in the chicken-and-eggs economy described below.

Before doing that, let us note that a new difficulty arises in connection with the interpretation of the interest rate for contracting economies. We retain the equality $\alpha = \beta$ in the model so that $\alpha < 1$ means $\beta < 1$. Since the interest rate b satisfies $b = 100(\beta - 1)$, it follows that $\beta < 1$ implies that $b < 0$. A negative interest rate seems at first to be a very peculiar economic construct. However, if we keep the equality of interest factor and expansion factor ($\alpha = \beta$) in mind we can give a natural interpretation to $\beta < 1$. Suppose we think of "borrowing" a vector w of real goods and want to pay it back one period later. The lender could "purchase" an amount w of productive capacity now. In order for him to be able to purchase the same relative amount of the next period's productive capacity, the borrower must repay a vector βw of real goods after the one period. Thus if $\beta > 1$ he must repay more ($b > 0$) than he borrowed while if $\beta < 1$ he repays less ($b < 0$) than he borrowed. In either case the lender is satisfied since his wealth, relative to the whole economy, is unchanged. With this interpretation, negative interest rates offer no further difficulty.

To illustrate the ideas of contraction and collapse mentioned above, let us begin with the stationary model, first encountered in Example 2-4, Section 3 of Chapter 2, given by:

$$
\begin{array}{c}
\text{Chicken Eggs Labor} \\
\begin{array}{l}
\text{Laying} \\
\text{Hatching} \\
\text{Labor}
\end{array}
\quad A = \left(
\begin{array}{ccc}
1 & 0 & 1 \\
1 & 4 & 1 \\
4 & 8 & 0
\end{array}
\right),
\end{array}
$$

$$
\begin{array}{c}
\text{Chicken Eggs Labor} \\
\begin{array}{l}
\text{Laying} \\
\text{Hatching} \\
\text{Labor}
\end{array}
\quad B = \left(
\begin{array}{ccc}
1 & 12 & 0 \\
5 & 0 & 0 \\
0 & 0 & 4
\end{array}
\right)
\end{array}
\tag{1}
$$

The expansion factor for this model is $\alpha = 1$, and its (normalized) optimal activity and price vectors are

$$x = (1/3, 1/3, 1/3) \tag{5}$$

$$y = (4/17, 1/17, 12/17)' \tag{6}$$

In order to describe "lumpy" economic units that will lead to economic collapse, we change to the unnormalized form of the activity vector and assume that the economy is currently operating with an unnormalized activity vector

$$x = (4, 4, 4) \tag{7}$$

This, in turn, leads to a stock vector of

$$xA = (24, 48, 8) \tag{8}$$

That is, we have 24 chickens, 48 eggs, and 8 laborers on hand, and the laborers consume 16 chickens and 32 eggs each time period. However, we have 8 chickens and 16 eggs remaining to run the economy another time period, which then replenishes the stock of 24 chickens, 48 eggs, and 8 laborers.

Suppose now that the laborers insist on increased consumption by requiring the use of a new intensity vector $x = (x_1, x_2, x_3)$ in which $x_3 > x_1$ and $x_3 > x_2$. We treat this case by setting $x_1 = x_2 = z$, as we did in the previous section, and then require that $x_3 > z$. It is clear that this condition, together with the integrality condition for unnormalized intensities means that z must be reduced from 4 to 3. When this is done, x_3 can go up from 4 to 4.5. These intensities and the resulting stocks and consumption are indicated in the first column of Figure 10-1.

In Exercise 5 the reader is asked to show that the intensity z must go from 3 to 2 in the second time period, and from 2 to 1 in the third time period. The other quantities are as shown in the second and third columns of Figure 10-1. Finally, note that in period 4 the stocks have dropped to 6

Time Period		1	2	3	4
Activities (not normalized)	Laying	3	2	1	
	Hatching	3	2	1	
	Labor	4.5	3.5	2.5	
Stocks	Chickens	24	18	12	6
	Eggs	48	36	24	12
Consumption	Chickens	18	14	10	
	Eggs	36	28	20	

Figure 10-1

chickens and 12 eggs so that the only feasible intensity vector at which the economy can now operate is $x = (1, 1, 0)$, which does not satisfy the condition $x_3 > z$. At this point the economy must collapse, since the only way it can run further is for the laborers to consume nothing which is not an economically viable solution.

The general case of contracting economies is similar. As an economy contracts, it gradually consumes its stocks of productive resources until at some point the "lumpiness" of the economic goods and processes involved causes it to collapse completely.

We know of no historical examples of actual economies that have contracted to the point of collapse in this manner. For large complicated economies, a very large number of time periods would elapse before the collapse point would be reached. The only warning signal for such collapse is a steady decrease in the stock of productive resources. We note in passing that the GNP index does not measure the size of such productive stocks and hence would not give a warning of such contraction, or of the imminent collapse of an economy.

5. Compression of Economies

This section is based on Morgenstern's paper [87] in which the first discussion (as far as we know) of economic compression was given. We discuss the ideas of that paper only as they apply to the models of this book and refer to that paper for a more general discussion.

By the *compression* of an economy, we mean the deliberate elimination or cutting back of existing activities or goods. In the models of this book, such elimination can be carried out by crossing out rows and/or columns of the input and output matrices for those processes that are actually eliminated or by reducing the upper bounds on the control variables of those activities that are to be cut back.

In the preceding section, we considered a contracting economy which simply meant an economy whose growth rate was negative due to excessive consumption or extreme inefficiency of the industries involved. In this case all industries continue to run and all goods continue to be produced, for a while at least.

However, in the case of compression, we find that the expansion rate may go either up or down as industries and goods are eliminated. This can most clearly be seen by reviewing Chapter 8 in which we showed how a rural economy could be changed into an urban economy by adding transportation, raw materials, heavy and light industries, and urban labor. The result was an urban model that could expand to a rather high rate, 15.08%.

We then added the following industries and their corresponding goods: services, luxuries, disposal, and defense. As we added each of these industries, which are unprofitable, the resulting expansion rate decreased.

We can consider compression of the economy of Chapter 8 by merely reversing the process above and dropping these industries and goods. If we want to drop them in the order in which they were added, we need merely read Chapter 8 from the end backwards to the beginning.

It is, of course, not necessary to drop these industries and goods in the exact order outlined above. For instance, if we take the economy of Figure 8-10 and eliminate services, luxury goods, and disposal activity—that is rows 9, 10, and 11—as well as the outputs of these industries—that is columns 10, 11, and 12—while keeping row 12 and column 13, which is the defense industry and defense goods, then we obtain what might be called a "war-time" economy having a large expansion rate. In this new economy we can obviously greatly increase the production of defense goods because of the slack provided by the elimination of services, luxuries, and disposal. In order to obtain this increase in defense goods production we must increase the lower bound on the defense activity, and this in turn causes the resulting expansion rate to decrease. It is clear that the output of defense goods can be greatly increased while still keeping $\alpha > 1$.

The first 8 rows and first 9 columns of Figure 8-10 constitute the *kernel* of the economy in the sense of [87]. That is, the kernel consists of a minimal set of industries and goods such that further deletions of industries and/or goods would result in the collapse of the economy. Thus, in that figure, it is clear that elimination of the raw material industry would cause the immediate shutting down of light and heavy industries, and the eventual shutdown of the transportation and agricultural industries as the rolling stocks wore out. Certainly once food production is halted, it is clear that the economy can no longer be considered functional. At this point the rural agricultural economy in Section 2 of Chapter 8 could become reactivated, since its activities, which were previously inefficient, now become efficient.

The same kind of analysis applies to the elimination of any one of the other 8 activities listed in Figure 8-10. Of course, if we eliminate railroad transportation we may substitute, in part at least, automobile (truck) transportation, or even call out horse or mule drawn vehicles as appropriate. Many other kinds of substitutions or alternate technological solutions can be employed to attempt to keep a partially destroyed kernel of an economy running. Further elaborations of these ideas including their application to military target selection are given in [87].

It seems obvious to us that an area of profitable research is that of extending, elaborating, and numerically applying the ideas we sketched above.

Exercises

1. Verify that $\alpha = 1.303$ and the vectors in (2) and (3) solve the model given in (1).
2. Show that when $z = x_1 = x_2 = .246$, the production of the laying and hatching industries is just enough to provide the consumption of labor when $x_3 = .246$.
3. In the model given by the input-output matrices in (1), assume that a balanced expansion rate α^* satisfying $1 \le \alpha^* \le 1.303$ is required while keeping the labor activity at $x_3 = .246$ and the real good consumption of the workers constant.
   (a) Show that to keep the laborers per capita consumption of chickens constant, z must satisfy
   $$z(6 - 2\alpha^*) = 4\alpha^* (.246)$$
   (b) Show that the optimal activity strategy vector is given by
   $$\left(\frac{.492\alpha^*}{3-\alpha^*}, \quad \frac{.492\alpha^*}{3-\alpha^*}, \quad .246 \right)$$
   for any α^* in the range $1 \le \alpha^* \le 1.303$.
4. Show that $\alpha = 1$ and the vectors in (5) and (6) solve the model whose input and output matrices are given in (4).
5. Verify that the entries in Figure 10-1 are correct by carrying out the following steps:
   (a) For period 1 show that $x_3 > z$ gives $x = 3$ as the only integral solution for z. Then verify that the rest of the entries for period 1 are correct.
   (b) For period 2, show that, given the stocks remaining from period 1, the condition $x_3 > z$ leads to $z = 2$, and verify the rest of the entries for period 2.
   (c) For period 3, show that, given the stocks remaining from period 2, the condition $x_3 > z$ leads to $z = 1$, and verify the rest of the entries for period 3.
   (d) For period 4, show that, given the stocks remaining from period 3, there is no solution with $x_3 > z$, hence the economy (in its given form) must collapse.

11 The World Model

1. Introduction

In Chapter 4 the KMT model of Chapter 2 was made into an open model by assuming the existence of a "world market." It was then possible to export and import any commodity at given world prices. This is clearly the first approach that has to be chosen. Though the assumptions are simple, the consequences are considerable as has been shown. Nor is the situation completely unrealistic: it certainly fits the condition of a small country having limited amounts of export and import goods and dealing with a very large world market, whether in raw materials or finished goods.

The situation changes profoundly if we consider the interaction between two, three, or more countries of about the same size, each acting as one player in a corresponding game. Then we have a true game situation. However, there are many additional conditions: If there are only two countries, what is the payoff, since clearly both cannot have a trade surplus versus the other? Do they wish to have (or have to have) the same expansion rate, each trading at least one efficient good and if so, does the one with an initially larger rate pull the other up or does the opposite happen? Are the two countries isolated in the world or does there exist in addition a world market on which they can sell surplus goods? These and other questions will be examined in what follows. We also ask how our results compare with current international trade theory, even though the latter has not dealt with expansion, let alone with expansion as a policy goal. (See Chapter 12.) We limit ourselves to laying only the groundwork of this interesting and also practically important area, leaving it to the reader to build a more complete structure.

By a "world model" we mean a set of open economies which are tied together by a common expansion rate and which exchange physical goods at given world prices. We define a world KMT model that determines one way (but by no means the only way) of determining a suitable set of world prices. The solution of the world model is obtained via a large linear program in which each country is represented by a block on the main diagonal, and there is an additional set of constraints that accounts for the physical flow of goods among countries.

We see that there is an enormous variety of solutions possible in the world model, but this is perhaps not surprising when we view the rich variety of economic and political systems that exist at present in the countries currently engaging in international trade.

In the next chapter we will call these world models *trading blocks*. We will see that if the expansion rate of such a world model (trading block) is low, then many countries will be able to achieve that rate and engage in profitable international trade because they have comparative advantages in the production of a good at that expansion rate. The better endowed nations (that is, those having the "largest" comparative advantage at that rate) of the block will be able to enjoy tremendous excess consumption. But if the expansion rate is high, then only a few nations will be able to participate in this trading block. The others will have to join another trading block with lower expansion rate or remain isolated, engaging in trade on a sporadic basis.

It can also be seen, although we touch on it only lightly, that the excess consumption ideas of Chapters 6 and 7 and the technological innovation ideas in Chapter 8 can be extended to this model in order to permit the study of effects of foreign aid and new technologies on world models.

2. The World Expanding Economy Model

Our objective is to develop a world expanding economy model by putting together several open expanding economy models, one for each country. We assume that terms of trade, that is, real good exchange ratios, have been determined so that at least some of the countries will find it desirable to expand at the same rate and engage in international trade. In Section 3 we describe a way in which the exchange ratios can be determined, but for the present section, we assume that they are already determined. In Section 4 we give numerical examples of two-country and three-country world models.

Assume that we have a world economy with κ countries such that each country is represented by an open expanding economy model in the sense of Chapter 4. That is, we assume that the seven axioms of the open model given in that chapter hold for each of the κ countries. The easiest way to indicate this is to give the linear programming tableau in terms of its corresponding variables for the μth economy, $\mu = 1, \ldots, \kappa$, as shown in Figure 11-1. Note that we are using the Greek letter superscript μ to denote different countries. This should not be confused with the superscript k used in Chapter 9 to denote different times for the same economy.

In Exercise 6 of Chapter 4 we stated that an equivalent way of representing the problem is by means of the tableau given in Figure 11-2. Note that the tableau of Figure 11-2 has two more rows and two more columns than that of Figure 11-1, but the solutions to the two are mathematically equiva-

	y^μ	$z^{p\mu}$	$z^{n\mu}$	
x^μ	M_α	$-I$	I	$= 0$
$w^{e\mu}$	$-I$			$\leq -p^{e\mu}$
$w^{i\mu}$	I			$\leq p^{i\mu}$
	$= 0$	$\geq -t^{p\mu}$	$\geq t^{n\mu}$	

Figure 11-1

	y^μ	$z^{p\mu}$	$z^{n\mu}$	v^μ	v'^μ	
x^μ	M_α^μ	$-I$	I			$= 0$
$w^{e\mu}$	$-I$			$p^{e\mu}$		≤ 0
$w^{i\mu}$	I			$-p^{i\mu}$		≤ 0
u^μ		$t^{p\mu}$	$-t^{n\mu}$		1	$= 0$
u'^μ				1		≤ 1
	$= 0$	≥ 0	≥ 0	$= 0$	≥ 1	

Figure 11-2

lent. To see this, note that if α^μ, x^μ, $w^{e\mu}$, $w^{i\mu}$, y^μ, $z^{p\mu}$, and $z^{n\mu}$ are solutions to the problem in Figure 11-1, then these same quantities together with $u^\mu = v^\mu = 1$ and u'^μ, $v'^\mu = 0$ are also solutions to the open economy model in Figure 11-2, and conversely.

In order to combine several different open economy models for different countries, we find the second form of the tableau, as given in Figure 11-2, more convenient.

Suppose now that we have κ countries and each one has a tableau as in Figure 11-2 for $\mu = 1, 2, \ldots, \kappa$. In order to satisfy the seven axioms of the open model stated in Chapter 4 for each country, we must find a solution to each of the tableaus with primal and dual objective values equal to zero. Also, in order to have a viable κ-country economy, we must have the vector sum of physical exports of all goods from all countries greater than or equal to the vector sum of physical imports. We can write this requirement[a] in equation form as

---

[a] When we write vector inequalities such as (1), we mean that the inequality is to hold component by component. Note also that the units of each component of the vector may be different.

$$\sum_{\mu=1}^{\kappa} w^{e\mu} \geq \sum_{\mu=1}^{\kappa} w^{i\mu} \tag{1}$$

In other words, the κ-country model is *closed*, since there is no outside economy to affect it further. In the case that the sum of all exports is greater than the sum of all imports, the export price of the goods produced in excess is zero. This is similar to the excess production case in the KMT model, and can be handled by similar devices. The problem here is that, with joint production, we may not be able to satisfy all components of (1) as equalities. If there are more industries than goods, it will usually be easy to assure this condition, but this is not the usual situation.

As stated, the κ-country world model is *closed*. The constituent open models, each representing a country, are *open*; but these models are *not* identical to the subeconomies of a KMT economy since the latter have no balance of trade tasks to accomplish.

Our problem now is to find a way of simultaneously solving the linear programming problem in Figure 11-2 for $\mu = 1, \ldots \kappa$ and also satisfying (1). Before we can do that we must determine a suitable set of export and import prices $p^{e\mu}$, $p^{i\mu}$ for each country, $\mu = 1, \ldots, \kappa$. In the next section we indicate one way in which these prices can be determined, but for the present we assume that they have been chosen. Given that we now state in Figure 11-3 the linear program whose solution will provide the solutions to the κ-country expanding economy model.

Note in Figure 11-3 that the open economy of each country is represented by a block on the main diagonal of the tableau, and the equations in (1) are displayed in the last column of the tableau.

Note also that the expansion factor is γ, the world expansion factor for each country. This is needed because in order for all the countries to engage in international trade under equilibrium conditions for arbitrarily long periods of time, they must have exactly the same expansion factor. For if this were not so, then the country or countries with the largest factor would eventually become arbitrarily much larger than the other countries with lower expansion rates and the latter would, in the long run, thus have negligible effects on the world economy.

We have not said very much so far about the control variables $t^{p\mu}$ and $t^{n\mu}$, but it is clear that they too must be adjusted in order to get world model solutions. In particular, it must be possible to shut down an industry in a given country if the product produced by that industry can be imported more cheaply than it can be made at home. Thus

$$t^{n\mu} = 0 \tag{2}$$

is a reasonable condition to impose at least during the initial search for solutions. It is also reasonable to make $t^{p\mu}$ as large as possible consistent

	y^1	z^{p1}	z^{n1}	v^1	v'^1		y^κ	$z^{p\kappa}$	$z^{n\kappa}$	v^κ	v'^κ		
x^1	M_y^1	$-I$	I										$= 0$
w^{e1}	$-I$			p^{e1}								I	$\leqq 0$
w^{i1}	I			$-p^{i1}$								$-I$	$\leqq 0$
u^1		t^{p1}	$-t^{n1}$		1								$= 0$
u'^1				1									$\leqq 1$
						⋱						⋮	⋮
x^κ							M_γ^κ	$-I$	I				$= 0$
$w^{e\kappa}$							$-I$			$p^{e\kappa}$		I	$\leqq 0$
$w^{i\kappa}$							I			$-p^{i\kappa}$		$-I$	$\leqq 0$
u^κ								$t^{p\kappa}$	$-t^{n\kappa}$		1		$= 0$
u'^κ										1			$\leqq 1$
	$= 0$	$\geqq 0$	$\geqq 0$	$= 0$	$\geqq 1$		$= 0$	$\geqq 0$	$\geqq 0$	$= 0$	$\geqq 1$	$\geqq 0$	

Figure 11-3

with the sizes of the various industries in country μ. In Section 5 we discuss further how variations in the control variables will affect the world model solutions.

We are now in a position to state the formal equivalence between the world expanding economy which consists of κ countries with solution variables

$$\gamma, \; x^{\mu}, \; w^{e\mu}, \; w^{i\mu}, \; y^{\mu}, \; z^{p\mu}, \; z^{n\mu}, \; u^{\mu} = v^{\mu} = 1, \; u'^{\mu} = v'^{\mu} = 0 \qquad (3)$$

for $\mu = 1, \ldots, \kappa$ and the corresponding solutions to the linear programming problem stated in Figure 11-3.

Theorem 11-1: Given choices of $p^{e\mu}$, $p^{i\mu}$, $t^{p\mu}$, and $t^{n\mu}$, then the variables in (3) satisfy the individual linear programming problems of Figure 11-2 as well as the export-import constraints of (1) for $\mu = 1, 2, \ldots, \kappa$, if, and only if, these same variables solve with objective value 0 the linear programming problem whose tableau is given in Figure 11-3.

Proof: It is easy to see that variables (3), satisfying the tableau of Figure 11-2 as well as equations (1), will give primal and dual feasible and hence optimal solutions to the tableau with objective value 0 in Figure 11-3. For the converse, we note that if we have a solution to the tableau of Figure 11-3 with objective value 0, then, because each u'^{μ} and v'^{μ} variable is $\geqq$ 0, and the objective values are

$$\sum_{\mu=1}^{\kappa} u'^{\mu} = \sum_{\mu=1}^{\kappa} v'^{\mu} = 0$$

we conclude that $u' = v' = 0$ in each case. These in turn imply that $u^{\mu} = v^{\mu} = 1$, which gives the necessary conditions (3).

Because of Theorem 11-1, we can find the solution to the world expanding economy model by using a binary search technique, similar to that described in Chapter 3 for selecting a suitable value of γ, then solving the corresponding linear program of Figure 11-3, and using the objective value of the resulting solution to divide the search interval in half, etc. We shall not describe this problem further because of its similarity to the procedures of the earlier chapter.

In Chapter 13 we give a discussion of the connections between the von Neumann and the Leontief input-output models, including the expanding version. However, none of the results of those models are needed for the present purpose.

3. Existence of Natural World Transfer Prices

The problem of determining suitable world export and import prices, which we call for short *transfer prices*, is not one of proving their existence, but rather choosing, from among the enormous number of possible price structures, one to describe. We select for this purpose what we call *natural transfer prices*, determined by putting industries located in all countries together into a single closed model, which we call the world KMT model. The solution to that model gives a price vector that, with suitable modifications, becomes the world price vector which determines the import and export prices for each country. In terms of classical economics, these prices can be called the free trade prices, since they are determined under the assumption that, given a choice of expansion factor α, only the industries that are efficient for that α produce goods, regardless in which country they are located.

Let us consider a κ-country problem with the μth country having its own matrices A^μ and B^μ of input and output matrices. By the *world KMT model*, we mean the KMT model with input and output matrices:

$$
A = \begin{pmatrix} A^1 \\ A^2 \\ \vdots \\ A^\kappa \end{pmatrix} \quad \text{and} \quad B = \begin{pmatrix} B^1 \\ B^2 \\ \vdots \\ B^\kappa \end{pmatrix}
$$

Then the WKMT model is defined by the matrix

$$
M_\alpha = B - \alpha A \tag{4}
$$

As shown in Chapter 2, there are at most a finite number of economic expansion factors $\alpha_1, \ldots, \alpha_t$ for which the model with matrix (4) has solutions. These expansion factors correspond to (world) subeconomies which appear as the blocks on the main diagonal of Figure 5-1 and there are processes that are always inefficient and goods that are always overproduced corresponding to the I^* rows and J^* columns in that figure. As in Chapter 5, we can obtain a decomposition of the WKMT model as shown in Figure 5-1. The main difference is that the industries making up a given subeconomy may come from different countries. (We are considering a simplified case in which transportation, tariffs, etc., between pairs of countries are nonexistent, or so small that they can be neglected.)

Suppose now that we concentrate on one of the expansion rates, α_h, of the WKMT model. Then the industries corresponding to the expansion rates $\alpha_{h+1}, \ldots, \alpha_t$ in the decomposition of Figure 5-1 are *inefficient* for α_h. On the other hand, the industries corresponding to the expansion factors

$\alpha_1, \ldots, \alpha_h$ are *efficient* for α_h. We use these concepts to define an extension of the classical concept of comparative advantage.

Definition: Let α_h be an economic expansion factor for the WKMT model and y its corresponding price vector. Let α be any expansion rate satisfying $\alpha_{h+1} < \alpha \leq \alpha_h$. Then country μ has *a comparative advantage* (is efficient) *in the production of good j for expansion rate α* if country μ contains an industry, say industry i, efficient for the expansion factor α, which produces good j. The technical conditions that must hold for comparative advantage are:

$$(M_\alpha)_i y \geq 0 \tag{5}$$

$$b_{ij} > 0 \tag{6}$$

More generally, we can say that country μ has a *comparative advantage in the production of good j for any expansion rate α and any price vector y* if (5) and (6) hold for an industry i belonging to that country.

We note immediately that a country may have a comparative advantage for the production of good j for some expansion factor α_h, but not for others. Exercises 1 and 2 give examples of this phenomenon.

The reader may also note that the above analysis may be considered as a considerable elaboration of the classical Ricardian concept of comparative advantage. Ricardo, of course, did not include expansion in this treatment of comparative advantage. The connection between economic expansion and comparative advantage is made here for the first time in a rigorous manner.

As we saw in Chapters 2 and 5, the existence of multiple expansion rates leads to the phenomenon that overproduced goods are becoming free, and the same situation occurs here in the WKMT model. We use the constrained game technique for permitting overproduced goods to have positive prices by restraining production or prices, as developed in Chapter 5, to handle the same problem in the WKMT model. Hence by adding suitable production constraints to the WKMT model, we are able to assure that (except for the goods that are free goods in all solutions) if a good is produced in a positive amount, then it has a positive price in the equilibrium price vector of the constrained WKMT model. (See Exercise 3.)

Recall that in Chapter 5 we saw that the prices of goods produced by industries whose production is constrained in the constrained KMT model, possess a high degree of arbitrariness, because they are not determined from the solution of linear equations, but are set in an ad hoc manner. In the present case, or when there are constraints on prices, the price of the good is determined by the country in which the industry producing it belongs, and that country also imposes the production restriction. Hence the ad hoc price determination can, in the present instance, be interpreted as a political, rather than an economic, price choice. In that sense this is seen to be a game situation, in which considerations of power, national advantage, and the like, come to the fore.

As the result of the above discussion, we can state the following theorem on the existence of world transfer prices.

Theorem 11-2: For the κ-country world model with $t^{n\mu} = 0$ and $t^{p\mu} = M$ (where M is a large number, say $M = 10^{100}$), let α_h be an economic expansion factor and x and y be the corresponding solutions to the WKMT model; then the solution to the κ-country expanding economy model is given by the following quantities:

$$\gamma = \alpha_h \tag{7}$$

$$x^\mu \text{ is the } x \text{ vector restricted to country } \mu \tag{8}$$

$$y^\mu \text{ is the } y \text{ vector restricted to country } \mu \tag{9}$$

$$p_j^{e\mu} = y_j \text{ and } p_j^{i\mu} = M \tag{10}$$

if country μ is efficient in producing good j

$$p_j^{i\mu} = y_j \text{ and } p_j^{e\mu} = M \tag{11}$$

if country μ is not efficient in producing good j.

The WKMT prices y_j for $j = 1, \ldots, n$ are the *natural transfer prices* and the quantities $w^{e\mu}$, $w^{i\mu}$, $z^{p\mu}$, and $z^{n\mu}$ are determined from the usual equations:

$$x^\mu M_\gamma^\mu = w^{e\mu} - w^{i\mu} \tag{12}$$

$$M_\gamma^\mu y^\mu = z^{p\mu} - z^{n\mu} \tag{13}$$

Proof: We recall that in the KMT model of Chapter 2 the five conditions of that model are satisfied. These results imply that the conditions of the open model including the balance of trade and balance of payments conditions hold on an *industry-by-industry* basis. Since these conditions hold for each industry in a country economy, they hold *a fortiori* for the entire economy of that country.

Although Theorem 11-2 could, no doubt, be generalized, there does not seem to be much point in doing so since for any given assumption as to the value of t^{pk}, t^{nk}, p^{ek}, and p^{ik} we can determine whether solutions exist to the linear program whose initial tableau is given in Figure 11-3 by merely putting the data of the problem into a computer. Any one of a number of commercially available linear programming codes will then calculate and print out the solution to the problem, if there is one, or else print out the fact that no such solution exists.

Except in cases where there are inconsistent production and/or price constraints, the solution to the world model will exist and will be readily found by using existing mathematical programming procedures.

4. Examples

In this section we give several examples of solutions to the world model that make use of the results of Theorem 11-2, since these calculations are much easier to carry out than using the full tableau of Figure 11-3.

Example 11-1: Let us first consider two countries, both of which are engaged in the production of chickens and eggs. We assume that country 1 is relatively more efficient in egg production and country 2 is more efficient in chicken production. The data for each of the two countries with the KMT solution for each are given in Figure 11-4.

If we now put all the industries of both countries into the WKMT model, we note that the laying industry of Country 2 is inefficient relative to that of Country 1, while the hatching industry of Country 1 is inefficient relative to that of Country 2. Hence the WKMT model appears with its solution as in Figure 11-5. Note that by engaging in international trade, both countries have succeeded in raising their expansion rates, but at the expense of closing down completely one industry in each country. Note also that in each country the relative price of the good in which that country was most efficient in producing has gone up, while the *relative* price of the good it was least efficient in producing has gone *down* because of the import from the other country that is more efficient in that good. This is intuitively reasonable because in the world model the overall efficiency of production has gone up; therefore the relative price ratio has necessarily gone down.

To summarize exports and imports for the world model with expansion factor $\alpha = 3$, we indicate in Figure 11-6 the imports and exports of each country, given that Country 1 starts with 250 laying chickens and Country 2 starts with 250 chickens and 1000 eggs. In that figure a positive amount indicates an export, while a negative amount refers to an import.

Exercise 4 treats this same example with consumption added. In Example 11-5 (Section 5) we will reconsider this example for a case in which each of the countries has imposed lower bounds on the operation of its inefficient industries.

Example 11-2: Our next example in a 3-country, 3-good model that will illustrate the free-goods difficulty noted earlier. The three industries are wheat-farming, laying, and hatching and the three goods are wheat, chickens, and eggs. Figure 11-7 gives the input-output data and the KMT solutions for each country. Note that Country 1 is efficient in producing wheat,

	Chickens	Eggs
Laying	1	0
Hatching	1	3

$$A = \begin{pmatrix} 1 & 0 \\ 1 & 3 \end{pmatrix}, \quad B = \begin{pmatrix} 1 & 12 \\ 4 & 0 \end{pmatrix}$$

	Chickens	Eggs
	1	12
	4	0

$\alpha = 2.772, \quad x = (.409, .591), \quad y = (.871, .129)'$

Country 1

	Chickens	Eggs
Laying	1	0
Hatching	1	4

$$A = \begin{pmatrix} 1 & 0 \\ 1 & 4 \end{pmatrix}, \quad B = \begin{pmatrix} 1 & 10 \\ 5 & 0 \end{pmatrix}$$

$\alpha = 2.864, \quad x = (.534, .466), \quad y = (.843, .157)'$

Country 2

Figure 11-4

	Chickens	Eggs
Country 1, Laying	1	0
Country 2, Hatching	1	4

$$A = \begin{pmatrix} 1 & 0 \\ 1 & 4 \end{pmatrix}, \quad B = \begin{pmatrix} 1 & 12 \\ 5 & 0 \end{pmatrix}$$

$\alpha = 3 \quad x = (.500, .500), \quad y = (.857, .143)'$

WKMT Model

Figure 11-5

	Chickens	Eggs
Country 1, Laying	−500	3000
Country 2, Hatching	500	−3000

Figure 11-6

Country 2 is efficient in producing eggs, and Country 3 is efficient in producing chickens. Thus the WKMT model consists of only one efficient industry operating in each country. The solution to the WKMT model is presented in Figure 11-8. The corresponding export-import data, given intensities of 250 for each industry, for the WKMT solution appear in Figure 11-9.

		W	C	E			W	C	E	
Wheat		1	0	0			9	0	0	$\alpha = 2.61,$
Laying	A	1	1	0	,	B	0	1	9	$x = (.290, .330, .380),$
Hatching		1	1	3			0	4	0	$y = (0, .849, .151)'$

Country 1

		W	C	E			W	C	E	
Wheat		1	0	0			3	0	0	$\alpha = 2.772,$
Laying	A	1	1	0	,	B	0	1	12	$x = (.924, .031, .045),$
Hatching		1	1	3			0	4	0	$y = (0, .871, .129)'$

Country 2

		W	C	E			W	C	E	
Wheat		1	0	0			4	0	0	$\alpha = 2.864,$
Laying	A	1	1	0	,	B	0	1	10	$x = (.716, .152, .132),$
Hatching		1	1	4			0	5	0	$y = (0, .843, .157)'$

Country 3

Figure 11-7

		W	C	E			W	C	E	
Wheat #1		1	0	0			9	0	0	$\alpha = 3$
Laying #2	A	1	1	0	,	B	0	1	12	$x = (.333, .333, .333)$
Hatching #3		1	1	4			0	5	0	$y = (0, .857, .143)'$

WKMT Model

Figure 11-8

		Wheat	Chickens	Eggs
Country 1	Wheat	1500	0	0
Country 2	Laying	−750	−500	3000
Country 3	Hatching	−750	500	−3000

Figure 11-9

Note that the solution presented in Figure 11-9 is mathematically correct, but economically unacceptable (unless Country 1 is a colony of one of the other countries; see Chapter 12) because it requires Country 1 not only to accept a zero price for its exported wheat and a lower expansion rate for its wheat economy than it could obtain by itself, but it also does not give Country 1 any chickens or eggs as imports, since it has no export surplus with which to pay for them. In Example 3 we correct this deficiency by adding consumption directly, and in Example 4 we correct it by adding labor.

Example 11-3:   Let us add consumption to the models of Example 11-2. Specifically, let each country consume wheat, chickens, and eggs in the ratios 1, 1, 2. The new input-output coefficients and solutions for the country models and WKMT model (given industry intensities of 1000 each) are shown in Figures 11-10, 11-11, and 11-12.

Note that in their original solutions, Countries 2 and 3 were actually contracting, while Country 1 was expanding at about 8% per year. With the WKMT solutions, all countries expand at a rate of almost 26% per year and all enjoy a relative high rate of consumption. Here we find, as noted earlier in Chapters 6 and 7, that consumption and similarity of tastes tend to tie together otherwise disparate subeconomies even when they exist in different countries.

Example 11-4:   As a final example, we consider a three-country, four-good situation in which all three countries, by themselves, are capable only of steady-state contraction. However, by joining together in international trade, a world expansion factor of 1.101, that is, expansion rate of .101, is possible. To construct the example, we add labor as an industry which consumes goods and produces laborers as outputs. This represents another way of including consumption into Example 11-2. The original three-country models appear in Figure 11-13, the WKMT model in Figure 11-14, and the export-import table (given industry-intensities of 1,000) in Figure 11-15.

Note in Figure 11-15 that labor is a good and must be exported or imported as necessary between countries in order to achieve the given world expansion rate.

In the examples above we noted that the world economy *expands* when the countries engage in international trade, but when each is operating as a closed economy, then each individual economy faces only contraction. This result is intuitively plausible, but it has not been observed before in the theory of international trade as far as we know.

A further observation is that the addition of labor is equivalent to an increase in consumption. Another kind of consumption is foreign aid as

$$
\begin{array}{c}
\begin{array}{ccc} W & C & E \end{array} \\
\begin{array}{l} \text{Wheat} \\ \text{Laying} \\ \text{Hatching} \end{array}
\; A
\begin{pmatrix} 2 & 1 & 2 \\ 2 & 2 & 2 \\ 2 & 2 & 5 \end{pmatrix},
\end{array}
\quad
B
\begin{pmatrix} 9 & 0 & 0 \\ 0 & 1 & 9 \\ 0 & 4 & 0 \end{pmatrix}
\quad
\begin{array}{l}
\alpha = 1.082, \\
x = (.241, .378, .381), \\
y = (.159, .675, .165)'
\end{array}
$$

Country 1

$$
\begin{array}{c}
\begin{array}{ccc} W & C & E \end{array} \\
\begin{array}{l} \text{Wheat} \\ \text{Laying} \\ \text{Hatching} \end{array}
\; A
\begin{pmatrix} 2 & 1 & 2 \\ 2 & 2 & 2 \\ 2 & 2 & 5 \end{pmatrix},
\end{array}
\quad
B
\begin{pmatrix} 3 & 0 & 0 \\ 0 & 1 & 12 \\ 0 & 4 & 0 \end{pmatrix}
\quad
\begin{array}{l}
\alpha = .839, \\
x = (.556, .192, .252), \\
y = (.422, .479, .099)'
\end{array}
$$

Country 2

$$
\begin{array}{c}
\begin{array}{ccc} W & C & E \end{array} \\
\begin{array}{l} \text{Wheat} \\ \text{Laying} \\ \text{Hatching} \end{array}
\; A
\begin{pmatrix} 2 & 1 & 2 \\ 2 & 2 & 2 \\ 2 & 2 & 6 \end{pmatrix},
\end{array}
\quad
B
\begin{pmatrix} 4 & 0 & 0 \\ 0 & 1 & 10 \\ 0 & 5 & 0 \end{pmatrix}
\quad
\begin{array}{l}
\alpha = .962, \\
x = (.481, .283, .236), \\
y = (.362, .495, .143)'
\end{array}
$$

Country 3

Figure 11-10

$$
\begin{array}{c}
\begin{array}{ccc} W & C & E \end{array} \\
\begin{array}{l} \text{Wheat \#1} \\ \text{Laying \#2} \\ \text{Hatching \#3} \end{array}
\; A
\begin{pmatrix} 2 & 1 & 2 \\ 2 & 2 & 2 \\ 2 & 2 & 6 \end{pmatrix},
\end{array}
\quad
B
\begin{pmatrix} 9 & 0 & 0 \\ 0 & 1 & 12 \\ 0 & 5 & 0 \end{pmatrix}
\quad
\begin{array}{l}
\alpha = 1.257, \\
x = (.280, .360, .360), \\
y = (.187, .658, .155)
\end{array}
$$

WKMT Model

Figure 11-11

		Wheat	Chickens	Eggs
Country 1	Wheat	1812	−342	−703
Country 2	Laying	−906	−544	3416
Country 2	Hatching	−906	896	−2713

Figure 11-12

Country 1

A

	W	C	E	L
Wheat	1	0	0	1
Laying	1	1	0	1
Hatching	1	1	3	1
Labor	2	2	6	0

B

	W	C	E	L
Wheat	9	0	0	0
Laying	0	1	9	0
Hatching	0	4	0	0
Labor	0	0	0	2

$\alpha = .99,$
$x = (.146, .292, .220, .331),$
$y = (.071, .283, .071, .566)'$

Country 2

A

	W	C	E	L
Wheat	1	0	0	1
Laying	1	1	0	1
Hatching	1	1	3	1
Labor	2	2	6	0

B

	W	C	E	L
Wheat	2	0	0	0
Laying	0	1	12	0
Hatching	0	4	0	0
Labor	0	0	0	2

$\alpha = .756,$
$x = (.482, .126, .118, .274),$
$y = (.284, .205, .043, .468)'$

Country 3

A

	W	C	E	L
Wheat	1	0	0	1
Laying	1	1	0	1
Hatching	1	1	4	1
Labor	2	2	6	0

B

	W	C	E	L
Wheat	3	0	0	0
Laying	0	1	10	0
Hatching	0	5	0	0
Labor	0	0	0	2

$\alpha = .869,$
$x = (.377, .200, .121, .303),$
$y = (.212, .206, .061, .522)'$

Figure 11-13

$$
A \begin{pmatrix} & W & C & E & L \\ \text{Wheat} & 1 & 0 & 0 & 1 \\ \text{Laying} & 1 & 1 & 0 & 1 \\ \text{Hatching} & 1 & 1 & 4 & 1 \\ \text{Labor} & 2 & 2 & 6 & 0 \end{pmatrix} \quad B \begin{pmatrix} & W & C & E & L \\ & 9 & 0 & 0 & 0 \\ & 0 & 1 & 12 & 0 \\ & 0 & 5 & 0 & 0 \\ & 0 & 0 & 0 & 2 \end{pmatrix}
$$

$\alpha = 1.101,$
$x = (.166, .271,$
$\quad .208, .355),$
$y = (.082, .262,$
$\quad .064, .591)'$

WKMT Model

Figure 11-14

	W	C	E	L
Country 1, Wheat	1311	0	0	−183
Country 2, Laying	−298	−27	3255	−298
Country 3, Hatching	−229	811	−914	−229
Countries 1, 2, 3 Labor	−782	−782	−2343	710

Figure 11-15

noted earlier. Thus foreign aid, such as the Marshall Plan, did help the recipient countries but had, indirectly, an equally great beneficial effect on the United States economy. The difference between help to other countries—which is equivalent to an increase in U.S. consumption—and war goods production is this: the former will strengthen another economy that may begin to increase trade with the United States, thus enlarging the U.S. economy. But war goods production—irrespective of whether war goods are merely produced and stored or used in an active war—merely consumes resources: there is no corresponding feedback upon the own economy.

While these relationships can be observed directly, there was still a need for rigorous theory as is established here.

5. Effects on the World Model Solution of Changes in Control Variables

Once a solution to the world model has been found with one set of control variables, it is interesting to ask how the solution might change if these control variables were changed. Given the existence of large electronic computers, perhaps the easiest way to answer such a question is to make the necessary changes in the data of the control variables of the linear programming problem and to resolve it on the computer. Indeed, if we change very many of these control variables at the same time, there is virtually no other way to answer the question.

On the other hand, for simple changes in control variables, it is possible to give some theoretical results. We indicate two such results here, and then conclude the section with an example.

Suppose that we have a world for which the corresponding WKMT model has no subeconomies. Examples 11-3 and 11-5 (Section 4) have this property. For such a model, the following results are clear:

(1) If $t^{n\mu}$ are increased or $t^{p\mu}$ are decreased for any country μ, then the world expansion rate γ must go down or stay the same.

(2) If $p^{i\mu}$ is decreased or $p^{e\mu}$ is increased for any country μ, the world expansion rate γ must go up or stay the same.

These results are obvious if we use our game-theoretic intuition, for the changes in (1) cause the row player to have his strategy space diminished, and hence the expansion rate must (in general) be reduced to permit the game to be fair. On the other hand, the changes indicated in (2) cause the column player to have his strategy space reduced, and hence the expansion rate must (in general) be increased in order for the resulting game to be fair.

Doubtless other theoretical results can be derived, but we leave those for future research. We conclude with an example which illustrates (1) above.

Example 11-5. Let us return to Example 11-1 and assume that each country wishes to keep its less efficient industry operating, and does so by putting a positive lower bound on the intensity of operation of that industry. The WKMT model becomes as shown in Figure 11-16.

$$\begin{pmatrix} 1-\alpha & 12 \\ 4-\alpha & -3\alpha \\ 1-\alpha & 10 \\ 5-\alpha & -4\alpha \end{pmatrix}$$

Figure 11-16

Let x_2, x_2, x_3, and x_4 be the intensities with which each industry is operated. Let us assume that the following constraints have been imposed on these intensities:

$$x_2 \geq .1 \tag{14}$$

$$x_3 \geq .2 \tag{15}$$

$$x_1 + x_2 = 1 \tag{16}$$

Thus (14) is imposed by Country 1 to keep its hatching industry active and (15) is imposed by Country 2 to keeps its laying industry active. Condition (16) is imposed to make the solution determinant. The method of solving this example is sketched in Exercise 6. Its solution is indicated in (17).

$$\alpha = 2.932, \quad x = (.4471, .1, .2, .5529), \quad y = (.8557, .1443)' \quad (17)$$

By comparing it with the solution given in Example 11-1, we see that the expansion factor decreases from 3 to 2.932, in accordance with the prediction in (1). Note also that the relative price changes of the two goods in each country change in the same direction as, but to a lesser extent than, the corresponding changes in Example 11-1.

We have illustrated only a few of the possible effects of control variable changes on the solutions to world models. The reader may wish to construct examples for himself that illustrate other phenomena.

In Exercise 5, the reader is asked to show that an increase in consumption for either country in Example 11-1 and Exercise 4 has the effect of decreasing the world expansion rate. The reader should also show that a decrease in consumption has the opposite effect.

Exercises

1. Consider a country that can produce two goods and whose input and output matrices are:

$$A = \begin{pmatrix} 1 & 0 \\ 1 & 1 \end{pmatrix}, \quad B = \begin{pmatrix} 3 & 0 \\ 0 & 2 \end{pmatrix}$$

Assume that the world transfer price vector for these goods is $y = (1/2, 1/2)'$.

(a) Show that the country has comparative advantage in the production of both goods for this price vector and any α satisfying $0 \le \alpha \le 1$.

(b) Show that the country has comparative advantage in the production of good 1 but not good 2 for α satisfying $1 < \alpha \le 3$.

(c) If $\alpha > 3$, show that the country does not have comparative advantage in the production of either good for $\alpha > 3$ and *any* price vector y.

2. Consider the chicken and eggs farm example:

$$A = \begin{pmatrix} 1 & 0 \\ 1 & 4 \end{pmatrix}, \qquad B = \begin{pmatrix} 1 & 12 \\ 5 & 0 \end{pmatrix}$$

Assume the world transfer price vector for chickens and eggs is $y = (6/7, 1/7)'$ which is the same as the KMT prices of this model.

(a) Show that the farm has a comparative advantage in the production of chickens and eggs for this price vector and any α satisfying $0 \le \alpha \le 3$.

(b) Show that the farm does not have a comparative advantage in the production of either chickens or eggs for $\alpha > 3$.

3. Suppose that the WKMT model has the A and B matrices of Exercise 1. Show that by adding the constraint $x_1 \le 2x_2$ we can assure that the natural transfer price of good 1 can be chosen to be positive when $\alpha = 2$.

4. In Example 11-1, assume that each country wishes to consume a vector $d = (1, 4)$, that is, the consumption ratio is four eggs to one chicken. Show that the world expansion rate is now

$$\alpha = (-9 + \sqrt{201})/4 = 1.2944$$

Show also that

$$x = (.6028, .3972) \quad \text{and} \quad y = (.8111, .1889)'$$

5. (a) If Country 1 has a consumption vector $d^{(1)} = (1, 6)$ while Country 2 has the consumption vector $d^{(2)} = (1, 4)$, show that the expansion rate of the world model is less than that in Exercise 4.

(b) If Country 1 has a consumption vector of $d^{(1)} = (1, 2)$ while Country 2 has the consumption vector $d^{(2)} = (1, 4)$, show that the expansion rate of the world model is greater than that in Exercise 4.

(c) Comment on the results in (a) and (b).

6. Show that the following steps will solve the problem in Figure 11-16 subject to constraints (14), (15), and (16).

(a) Show that the vector

$$x = (x_1, .1, .2, 1 - x_1)$$

satisfies (14), (15), and (16).

(b) Multiply the vector in (a) by the matrix in Figure 11-16 and equate the two marginal expectations to each other. From that derive the following condition

$$-x(16 + 4\alpha) + 3\alpha + 3.6 = 0$$

(c) Set the second term of the marginal expectation computed in (a) to 0 and derive the following:

$$x(12 + 4\alpha) - 4.3\alpha + 2 = 0$$

(d) Solve the equations in (b) and (c) simultaneously to obtain the values shown in (17).

12 International Transactions

1. Trading Blocks

In the preceding analysis, we saw that countries (economies) in their expansion can be open or closed. We saw further that as a consequence of being "open," economies must be trading with each other. Thereby their expansion rates are tied to each other (cf. chapter 11).

Now the question arises whether the world is expanding at a uniform rate or whether, for example, political differences or technological or developmental differences tie some countries more closely together than others. For example, there may be sanctions against trading, or there may be special tariffs, or special market arrangements aimed at producing or preserving such groupings. Examples are offered by the "Common Market" and the "Eastern block." There are also sometimes commitments by countries vis-à-vis others such that they will be treated not less favorably than any other (the "most favored nation" clause in some international trade treaties).

In trying to formalize these facts, we speak of trading blocks, which we define formally as follows.

Definition: Consider a set $S = 1, 2, \ldots, k$ of k different countries and a partition of S into subsets $B_1, B_2, \ldots, B_t$ satisfying the following conditions:

(a) B_i is not empty and $B_i \subseteq S$, for $i=1, \ldots, t$.
(b) $B_i \cap B_j = \phi$ if $i \neq j$, for all $i, j=1, \ldots, t$.
(c) $B_1 \cup \ldots \cup B_t = S$.
(d) The countries in B_i form a world model in the sense of Chapter 11 with a unique expansion rate α_i.
(e) The expansion rate (holding its consumption fixed) of every country in B_i considered by itself is at most α_i.

Then by *trading blocks* we mean the sets $B_1, \ldots, B_t$.

To give interpretations of these conditions, observe that (a), (b), and (c) are simply the well-known conditions that are satisfied by any partition. Conditions (d) and (e) are added so that the countries in block B_i have incentives to trade with each other. Specifically, condition (e) means that no country in B_i has an incentive to leave the trading block and form a trading block by itself.

193

Of course it is possible that one country in trading block B_i might be tempted to leave that trading block and join another one having a higher expansion rate, a different political ideology, etc.

Questions concerning the formation and stability of trading blocks are difficult, and we only begin to state some of the problems connected with them here. We note, however, that trading blocks may form partly because of political or ideological reasons and partly because of economic considerations. However, even if there were absolutely no political, ideological, or monetary restrictions on trade (i.e., completely "free trade") we *predict* that trading blocks as defined would form simply from economic considerations. The main advantage of a trading block is that its members enjoy larger expansion rates than they could achieve singly. Thus some countries may, because of technological (subeconomy) considerations, fit into a trading block and help increase its expansion rate; hence they may be able to join. Other countries may be unable to make such a contribution to the expansion of the trading block and not be able to join. The question of attractiveness of a country to a trading block may depend on the state of technology. Thus the invention of a new source of power requiring a given mineral (e.g., uranium) may cause a previously unattractive country, having large supplies of that mineral, to be welcomed by the trading block.

Let us sketch a theory of trading-block formation. Assume that each country has included its desired consumption in its input matrix and that this consumption is temporarily held constant. Now, for each subset of countries, calculate the resulting expansion rate if they form a trading block, and eliminate any countries that do not possess an efficient industry at this rate. If we now carry out this calculation for each possible consumption level for each country, we can obtain the characteristic function of the resulting n-person (country) noncooperative game in which the imputation to each country in a coalition is its consumption. The resulting game is clearly decomposable in the sense of the Theory of Games ([106] Sections 41-46). The different subgames correspond to trading blocks as defined earlier. Interestingly enough, the idea of excess ([106] Section 44.5) can be directly related to an exchange ("tribute") between trading blocks which may represent an arbitrarily determined price for a raw material (e.g., oil) or foreign aid (e.g., the Marshall Plan).

The above references to game theory refer to an important area of that theory that has, as yet, not been studied by economists. But even our brief treatment indicates that there are significant phenomena here worthy of further exploration. Some games are decomposable, others are not. But both such types of games correspond to economic activities and the consequences of decomposability or not are serious for an understanding of—especially international—economic systems. Furthermore, it has been shown in [106] that if transfers of gifts, aid, etc., exceed certain limits, they will exercise disruptive influences upon the receiving party. All this can and must be related to the expansion rates of the different units, in our case, trading blocks.

Clearly the above ideas as sketched are worthy of further study in the game theory context. Both empirical and theoretical studies of these problems are indicated.

Suppose that the trading blocks are listed in order of decreasing expansion rates, i.e.,

$$\alpha_1 \geq \alpha_2 \geq \ldots \geq \alpha_t \qquad (1)$$

Clearly, for a given trading block to maintain its growth rate, it must have few or no transactions with trading blocks having lower expansion rates. On the other hand, if a trading block is able, for whatever reason, to trade with a block having a larger expansion rate, then it will find it beneficial to do so.

One common example of transactions between trading blocks is when a block produces a physical excess of a good (e.g., oil, food, gold) and sells it to a trading block with a different expansion rate. As indicated earlier, such exchanges between trading blocks can be only temporary, unless they are to be joined into a single new trading block with a new common expansion rate.

2. Classes of International Transactions

There are essentially three categories of international transactions: private, governmental, and those of multinational corporations, the latter representing a fairly new type of economic organization.

They shall at least be briefly listed where our interest is primarily how they relate to expansion or contraction.

(1) *Trade between companies, private and public*: Trade of this kind constitutes the bulk of international transactions regarding both the physical movements of goods and loans which can be private or public (i.e., a government may float a loan on the private capital market of another country). This trade has a very complex nature, but the principles which govern it are the usual ones of profit.

(2) *Government Transactions*: Here transactions are carried out qua governments. This would typically be the case for the eastern block while they are rare in the west. However, in the west, private transactions sometimes require special government approval, as, for example, private U.S. grain sales to the Soviet Union.

We now list the principal types of intergovernmental transactions:

(a) *Foreign aid, credits, and loans*: These are equivalent to increased home demand but cause goods and services to leave the country.

(b) *Indemnities paid*: Extraction of goods and services by a foreign state. Again equivalent to the (home) consumption of physical goods and services.

(c) *Subsidies*: These are likely to be government activities. They may be outright money grants to exporters, or remission of taxes, etc. Their effect on international transactions is that they work indirectly via the private sector.

(d) *Sanctions, blockades, tributes*: There are various means a government may use to prevent, or at least impede, various international transactions. These means can be directed against other governments, singly or in combinations, against specific goods wherever their origin. To enforce the measures, any variety of devices can be used, from mere prohibitions to naval blockade, etc.

Clearly, the study of the effects of all four of these kinds of intergovernmental transactions leads directly to game-theoretic considerations. For instance, the size of a subsidy or foreign aid grant would deserve special study. It is not only the amount the donor country can afford to give, but also how much the beneficiary country can receive. Also, the donor may receive indirect benefits from its largesse. Again, in the case of a tribute, too high a demand by a trading block can lead to an excess (Theory of Games [106], p. 366) which has a dissoluting effect on the block. It is easy to see that these lead to questions of which might be the proper kinds of grants and contributions in international relationships. However, we shall not pursue this matter any further at this juncture.

It must be emphasized that all possible transactions that may occur under any of the above listed categories ultimately involve physical balances (or their disturbance, as the case may be). These are the movements of goods and services across borders. When credits are given, then it is the subsequent movement of goods purchased with these credits that matters. If a more complete account is desired, then lags in such movements become important (see Truchon [129]).

(3) *Multinational Companies*. A multinational company is an organization that organizes and operates a subeconomy consisting of various activities in different countries, without being required to contribute anything to the balance of payments or balance of profits conditions in any of these countries. As a whole, it can and frequently does contribute to the overall efficiency of the world economy. However, in the process it may exploit one country and aid another. It must obey the laws of the countries in which it operates, and constantly runs the risk of being taken over by one of its respective host countries. Our main contribution is in recognizing that it

operates, efficiently, a subeconomy of the world and thus performs a useful function, at least during its existence.

(4) *Cartels*. A cartel is a national or international organization of industries that again form a subeconomy. In some cases (e.g., oil, gold) the cartel has (for a time at least) a virtual monopoly on the output of a commodity. In this case (compare Example 11-3) the technological price structure breaks down and the cartel can charge (within limits) any price it wishes. Thus, in effect, it is exacting a *tribute* in the sense of the theory of games ([106], p. 401). However, as noted (op. cit. p. 366), too large a tribute can cause a disorganizing effect on the cartel members.

(5) *Country-colony relationships*. Although becoming rare, the relationship of a "mother country" to a colony has been important in the historical past. Here the colony is regarded as a subpart of the mother country. It usually contributes a vital raw material, that is, it operates a subeconomy with large expansion rate, and receives in return an arbitrary payment, in terms of consumer goods, from the mother country. Again the price structure breaks down (compare Example 11-3). The country-colony pair must satisfy the balance of payments condition as a whole, but not on an individual basis. This relationship is now regarded as *exploitation*, even though it was not necessarily bad for the colony.

3. Causes of International Transactions

It is easy to enumerate the causes of international transactions and we list them here only briefly:

(1) Need for *consumers' goods* specific to some country, either finished industrial goods or food, etc.

(2) Need for *raw materials*: This may apply to oil, minerals, and other factors, specific to some single country or region.

(3) Need for *labor*: Shifts in labor barely across borders have occurred for a long time. International trade theory has not only neglected them—presumably because of their possibly quantitative insignificance—but has on the contrary always assumed that labor is immovable as is land. This assumption is no longer valid as the mass movements of labor, especially in Europe since the end of World War II, demonstrate.

(4) Need for *technical expertise*: While always somewhat of a factor, "technology transfer" has become one of the most striking developments in the last two decades or so. The manner in which it occurs need not concern us here. It suffices to refer to nuclear energy (origin in the United States), to outer space related technology (largely a U.S. development), to the transistor, to the laser, to computers (origins in the U.S.), etc. in order to indicate the importance and the speed of these matters.

Technology transfer in some manner makes countries more equal to each other, though as a rule the "mother country" will stay ahead at least for some time. It is frequently believed that similarity is adverse to trade, but the facts show the opposite to be the case. Indeed, our definition of trading blocks puts no requirements of dissimilarity on the countries in a trading block. We merely require that the countries in a trading block form an economic unit in which each country possesses at least one activity that is efficient at the stated expansion rate. Whether the efficiency of that industry is due to the natural resources of the country (e.g., Arabian oil) or to an arbitrary specialization of the country in producing a given good (e.g., Swiss watches) is irrelevant. The important point is the ability to achieve a given expansion rate, and this can happen with similar as well as dissimilar countries.

(5) Formation of *subeconomies*: In Chapter 5 the role of subeconomies was shown; they can exist in both closed and open models. It is natural to extend this concept to the world economy. If the latter is an entity of its own, all countries and trading blocks are tied to each other by virtue of the relation of their expansion rates as already discussed briefly in (1) above. It is clear, however, that a subeconomy in a closed economy has no balance of trade problems. A subeconomy of the world at large does, however, have to solve such problems. Thus there are two types of subeconomies in that respect.

(6) To complete this list, we mention the classical idea of *comparative advantage* as one of the principal causes why international trade is supposed to occur. Curiously, the chief, original illustration, given by Ricardo, was that Portugal had a comparative advantage over England in producing wine, and England had one in making cloth. In fact, drinkable wine cannot be made in England at all. But, of course, better illustrations have since been found to express this very simple idea. It is, of course, questionable whether comparative advantage in production between two countries is a sufficient condition for explaining trade among nations. It certainly is not a necessary condition as is obvious even when merely looking at some of the points enumerated above. The fraction of all international transactions for specific countries that are principally due to comparative advantage (when properly defined) varies undoubtedly greatly. Apparently there are no empirical and historical studies.

4. Benefits from International Trade

It is obvious that (voluntary) trade would not occur unless *both* parties consider that thereby they obtain an advantage. This excludes tributes, indemnities, sanctions, and country-colony relationships, i.e., all forms of imposed transfers. Aid, voluntarily offered, may be viewed either way. Much of what went on—and presumably still goes on—in the trade between some developed and some underdeveloped countries falls under the category of exploitation, the latter term used in a common sense meaning only, for want of a rigorous, truly scientific concept.[a] Exploitation in that sense need, however, not be restricted to differences in the stage of development of countries. "Exploitation" has, of course, been discussed variously in economic theory. But the results are practically nil. What has emerged are descriptions of some intuitively acceptable nature, though they are mostly dependent on political, religious, and other value judgments. There are no quantitative measurements, but such could now be made within the framework described above. The attempt by Marx to discover and describe economic exploitation by means of a labor value theory was, of course, ineffective due to the invalidity of the labor value theory itself and therefore need not be considered. The lack of applicability of labor value theory to international trade attempted by Ricardo is equally obvious, although his formulation of comparative advantage, couched in such terms, has dominated the theory of international trade for generations.

Technological discoveries can suddenly influence the situation of countries or whole regions. For example, oil was of minor interest before the development of the automobile and jet engines. Now it is a crucial, almost monopolistically controlled factor having great influence upon the development of widely different nations. The formation of a cartel is an event outside the normal considerations of international trade theory. The formation of trading blocks with their own expansion rates—completely neglected in the theory on international trade—is, however, a fundamental characteristic of the world!

If we could say that before the rise in oil prices the oil producers did not get their fair share, they are now possibly exploiting their customers by virtue of having created a near monopoly.

On the other hand, we have seen in Chapter 9 that when an economy is confronted with exhaustible supplies of raw materials, the question arises at which rate these materials should be used up. This means that the economy must somehow decide on a rate of expansion and interest: to consume more for a shorter period per time unit, or less per time unit for a longer period. We have shown in Chapter 10 how control variables can be used to determine the rate of expansion.[b] The proper choice of the variables

[a]In game theory, however, there are sharp concepts for partial, incomplete exploitation, discrimination, etc., as they arise first in zero-sum four person games. These concepts are free of value judgments, political attitudes, etc., as they should be. See von Neumann-Morgenstern [106] Sect. 38.3 pp. 328-329.

[b]We refer to the interesting paper on oil pricing by D. Fischer-D. Gately-J. Kyle: "The Prospects for OPEC: A critical survey of models of the world oil market," *Journal of Development Economies*, vol. 2, (1976)(in press).

would then be governed by the role of the exhaustible material in the complex of production patterns, the supply of the material, and the expansion rates of the various economies at that time.

5. International Trade Theory and Expansion

We limit ourselves to a few comments only. A restatement by us of the presently held theory is unnecessary in view of the two ample and competent accounts given by Chipman [16] and Haberler [33]. The very origins of economic theory are intrinsically tied to international trade. But it is safe to say that the latter theory has not yet reached the state of development of general equilibrium theory as represented by the work of Wald and his successors. This is in part a reflection of the difficulty of constructing mathematical models in this area, which is moreover visibly dominated by policy decisions using tools of great variety and sometimes of great scope (as mentioned above). An ordinary general equilibrium approach is under such circumstances far too simplistic to satisfy even very modest demands to be put on a scientific theory.

Common to all versions of international trade theory except ours is the complete lack of consideration of *expansion*. This is perhaps the more surprising, because from the outset economists were concerned with trying to show the possibility of *advantage* for each of two countries if they were to trade and specialize, use their comparative advantage, etc. It is clear from our results that such trade brings a larger expansion in each country concerned. But the concept of expansion was not developed; there was only a study of particular cases of comparative advantage. However, it was not translated into larger expansion.

6. Summary

We now list our contributions to international trade theory as briefly sketched in this chapter.

(a) Expansion included in definition of comparative advantage.

(b) Existence of trading blocks, tributes, or foreign aid exchanged among them.

(c) Game theory analysis of trading block formation, stability, inter-block transactions, etc.

(d) Formal characterization of international subeconomies, cartels, etc.

(e) Observation that technological prices break down in the case of cartels, country-colony and trading block relationships. Game theory provides an analysis of the possible resulting price solutions, but only historical, psychological, or political considerations suffice to determine the exact solution that results.

13

Relationships Between Von Neumann-KMT Models, Leontief Models, and Eigensystems

1. Introduction

Although the Leontief input-output model [38, 61, 84] was proposed somewhat later than and is less sophisticated than the von Neumann expanding economy model, it has been much more widely used in practice. Many countries, including the United States, gather data with which to compute the coefficients of the input-output matrix. Also, the volume of published work on the Leontief model up to now (1975) is much greater than that for the von Neumann model. (This may change in the future.) It is therefore of interest to state the similarities and differences between the two models. It is the purpose of this chapter to make such comparisons.

In Section 2 we define the basic Leontief model and a related von Neumann-Leontief expanding model. In Section 3 we show that if the input-output matrix is indecomposable, the ordinary Leontief model is solvable if, and only if, the expanding von Neumann-Leontief model has an expansion factor greater than one. In Section 4 we discuss consistent aggregation and show that under the same assumptions, the von Neumann price vector provides a consistent aggregation vector. In Section 5 we discuss the expanding von Neumann-Leontief model with outside demand and again give a theorem on consistent aggregation for this model.

Because of the close connection between expansion factors and eigenvalues for the Leontief model, it seems reasonable that there should be a similar connection between the general KMT model and generalized eigenvalues of matrix pencils. Such a connection has been investigated in depth by Thompson and Weil. An outline of some of their results appears in Section 6.

2. Solutions of Ordinary and Expanding Leontief Models

Consider an economy in which there are n processes, each one of which produces a unique good. Let x_i be the intensity with which the ith process is to be run, and let a_{ij} be the amount of the jth good needed to make one unit of good i. Clearly, $A \geq 0$ and is $n \times n$. Suppose that the economy must produce d_i units of good i for consumption. We call the vector d the *outside demand vector* or *bill of goods*. The basic equation to be satisfied is

$$x = xA + d \qquad (1)$$

That is, production x must be just enough to satisfy internal demand plus outside demand. Rewriting (1) yields

$$x(I - A) = d \qquad (2)$$

We also have the non-negativity conditions

$$x \geq 0 \qquad (3)$$

Expressions (2) and (3) are the basic conditions of the *Leontief input-output model*. It is easy to see that (2) and (3) have solutions for arbitrary $d \geq 0$ only if the matrix $(I - A)$ has an inverse $(I - A)^{-1}$, all of whose entries are non-negative (see Exercise 1). Hence we explore conditions under which such a non-negative inverse exists.

In most expositions of this model, e.g., Wong [143], Woodbury [146], Gale [24], Nikaido [107], etc., the transpose of system (2) and (3) is considered. We choose the present notation to conform to the earlier parts of this book.

The close connection of (2) to the well-known eigenvalue problem of matrix algebra makes inevitable (see Wong [143]) the replacement of (2) by the equation

$$x(\rho I - A) = d \qquad (4)$$

where ρ is a fixed parameter. Again, for consistency with earlier parts of this book and for a technical reason that will appear later, we prefer to consider the equation

$$x(I - \lambda A) = d \qquad (5)$$

It is easy to see that if $\rho > 0$ and $\lambda > 0$, then (4) and (5) are equivalent by replacing λ by $1/\rho$, x by $(1/\rho)x$, and d by $(1/\rho)d$.

Given the generalized Leontief system (3) and (5), we can easily define (see KMT [48]) the *expanding von Neumann-Leontief model* given by

$$\xi(I - \lambda A) \geq 0 \qquad (6)$$

$$(I - \lambda A)\eta \leq 0 \qquad (7)$$

$$\xi\eta > 0 \qquad (8)$$

$$\xi, \eta \geq 0 \qquad (9)$$

where ξ and η are probability vectors, that is, $\xi f = e\eta = 1$.

Clearly, (6) through (9) determine a special case of a KMT expanding economy model with $m = n$ and $B = I$. In this model the ith industry has a unique good as output and requires a_{ij} units of good j when run at unit intensity. Since $v(B) = v(I) = 1/n > 0$, the only assumption needed to insure that at least one solution exists to the KMT model (6) through (9) is

$$v(-A) < 0 \qquad (10)$$

which holds if, and only if, every industry requires a positive input of some good. The existence theorem of Chapter 2 shows that if (10) holds, then there are $r(\geq 1)$ expansion factors

$$0 < \lambda_r < \lambda_{r-1} < \ldots < \lambda_1 \qquad (11)$$

such that for each λ_k there are economic solutions $\xi^{(k)}$ and $\eta^{(k)}$ to (6) through (9).

In the next section we show how the existence of solutions to the expanding Leontief model relate to the existence of solution to the ordinary Leontief input-output model.

3. Solvability of the Leontief Input-Output Model

We now want to consider conditions under which there are economic solutions to (2) and (3). Throughout this section, we assume that (10) holds in order to rule out the possibility of a process that produces something from nothing.

Let us call the ith process *profitable* if

$$a_{i1} + \ldots + a_{in} < 1 \qquad (12)$$

We call it *profitless* if

$$a_{i1} + \ldots + a_{in} = 1 \qquad (13)$$

and call it *unprofitable* if

$$a_{i1} + \ldots + a_{in} > 1 \qquad (14)$$

These names follow from the interpretation of the sum of the left-hand sides of expressions (12), (13), and (14) as the value of the inputs to the ith process and the 1 on the right-hand sides of the same expressions as the value of the output.

One result that is easy to prove is the following: If all processes are profitable, then there is a solution to the Leontief input-output model (2) and (3). An outline of the proof of this result is given in Exercise 2.

A more difficult and more general existence condition is the following: If all processes are profitable or profitless, and if every profitless process orders either directly or indirectly from a profitable industry, then a solution to the Leontief input-output model, (2) and (3), exists. This result was discovered by Wong (see Morgenstern and Wong [145]) and later, independently, by Kemeny, Snell, and Thompson [49, 50]. We do not go further into this result, but it can be found in the above references.

Still another more general existence result can be obtained from the classical Perron-Frobenius theorem which is stated as follows: *If A is a square non-negative matrix, then A has a real positive eigenvalue ρ^* of maximum modulus, and an associated positive eigenvector; moreover the matrix $(\rho I - A)$ is non-negatively invertible if, and only if, $\rho > \rho^*$.* Applying this result to (2) and (3), we see that the Leontief input-output model is solvable for arbitrary $d \geq 0$ if, and only if, $1 > \rho^*$ (see Exercise 3). We refer the reader to Nikaido's book [107] where a very readable explanation of this result is given.

We devote the rest of this section to explaining the connection between the expanding von Neumann-Leontief model, (6) through (10), and the ordinary input-output model, (2) and (3). In so doing, we provide a (new) proof for the Perron-Frobenius theorem. We follow the exposition of Thompson [122], but we will give only part of the results contained in that paper.

We begin by proving a lemma that characterizes the solutions to the expanding Leontief model when A is indecomposable.

Lemma 13-1: Input matrix A is indecomposable if, and only if, all the solutions to the expanding von Neumann-Leontief model (6) through (10), have no free goods and no inefficient industries.

Proof: It is easy to show (see Exercise 4) that A is indecomposable if, and only if, every industry orders inputs either directly or indirectly from every other industry. We make use of that fact in what follows.

Assume that A is indecomposable and that $\xi_i = 0$, that is, the ith good is not produced. Since $\xi f = 1$, there is some good, say the kth good, with $\xi_k > 0$. By the above remark, industry k must use directly or indirectly a positive amount of good i, but since none of good i is produced, this is a contradiction. Hence $\xi > 0$, that is, there are no inefficient industries. Assume now that $\eta_j = 0$, that is, the jth good is free. Since $I - \lambda A$ is a fair game and $\xi > 0$, it follows that $(I - \lambda A)\eta = 0$. Hence, if $a_{jk} > 0$, that is, if industry j orders an input directly from industry k, then $\eta_k = 0$ also. In the same way we can show that each industry that produces a free good can order directly or indirectly *only* from industries that also produce free goods. Since $e\eta = 1$, there is at least one nonfree good. Therefore if we list the free good industries first and then the nonfree good industries, we will have A decomposed with a block of zeros in the upper right-hand corner, contradicting the fact that A is indecomposable. Hence $\eta > 0$ and there are no free goods.

If A is decomposable, then by a simultaneous reordering of rows and columns, it can be written as

$$A = \begin{pmatrix} A^{11} & 0 \\ A^{21} & A^{22} \end{pmatrix} \tag{15}$$

where both A^{11} and A^{22} contain at least one row and column and A^{11} is indecomposable. If we now solve the smaller expanding Leontief model A^{11}, we obtain solutions $\xi^{(1)}$ and $\eta^{(1)}$. These solutions can be extended by adding 0 components to the vectors:

$$\xi = (\xi^1, 0) \qquad \text{and} \qquad \eta = \begin{pmatrix} \eta^{(1)} \\ 0 \end{pmatrix} \tag{16}$$

which solve the expanding von Neumann-Leontief model A given in (15). Clearly, in these solutions we have both free goods and inefficient industries.

Theorem 13-1: If A is indecomposable, then the generalized Leontief model (3), (5) is solvable for arbitrary $d \geq 0$ if, and only if, the solution to the expanding von Neumann-Leontief model (6) through (10) has $\lambda_1 > \lambda$.

Proof: Since A is indecomposable, it follows from the decomposition results of Chapter 2 that for the solutions to the expanding model (6) through (10), $r = 1$, and hence we call $\lambda_r = \lambda_1$. Because of (10) we know that $\lambda_1 > 0$. Lemma 13-1 shows that the corresponding solutions satisfy $\xi > 0$ and $\eta > 0$.

Assume that $\lambda > \lambda_1$. Then $v(M_\lambda) \leq 0$ so that $\xi(I - \lambda A) \leq 0$ for all probability vectors ξ, and hence $x(I - \lambda A) \leq 0$ for all $x \geq 0$. Hence (5) cannot be solved for arbitrary $d \geq 0$.

Assume that $\lambda_1 > \lambda$, where λ is given as in (5). Define a vector K by

$$K = (I - \lambda A)\eta \qquad (17)$$

We assert that $K > 0$. To prove this, observe that

$$K = (I - \lambda A)\eta = [(I - \lambda_1 A) + (\lambda_1 - \lambda)A]\eta \geq (\lambda_1 - \lambda)A\eta \qquad (18)$$

because $\xi > 0$ implies that $(I - \lambda_1 A)\eta = 0$. The latter equation also yields $\lambda_1 A\eta = \eta > 0$. Thus $A\eta = (1/\lambda_1)\,\eta > 0$, and this fact together with $\lambda_1 > \lambda$ shows that $K > 0$.

The preceding paragraph has established that $\eta > 0$ solves (17), where $K > 0$. From this and the structure of A, we must now show that the inverse of $I - \lambda A$ exists and $(I - \lambda A)^{-1} \geq 0$. We use mathematical induction to prove it: *If $A \geq 0$ is $n \times n$, $K > 0$ and $\eta > 0$ are $n \times 1$ and solve (17), then the inverse of $(1 - \lambda A)$ exists and $(I - \lambda A)^{-1} \geq 0$.*

When $n = 1$, (17) becomes merely

$$(1 - \lambda a_{11})\eta_1 = K_1 \qquad (19)$$

If there is a positive solution $\eta_2 > 0$ to (19), then since $K_1 > 0$ we must have $1 - \lambda a_{11} > 0$ or $\lambda a_{11} < 1$. Hence $A = 1 - \lambda a_{11}$ has an inverse $A^{-1} = 1/(1 - \lambda a_{11}) > 0$ as claimed.

Assume that the above statement holds for systems (17) of size $n - 1$; we must show that it holds for size n. Writing out equation (17) for a system of size n gives (in detached coefficient form)

η_1	η_2	$\cdots$	η_n	
$1 - \lambda a_{11}$	$-\lambda a_{12}$	$\cdots$	$-\lambda a_{1n}$	K_1
$-\lambda a_{21}$	$1 - \lambda a_{22}$	$\cdots$	$-\lambda a_{2n}$	K_2
$\vdots$	$\vdots$	$\cdots$	$\vdots$	$\vdots$
$-\lambda a_{n1}$	$-\lambda a_{n2}$	$\cdots$	$1 - \lambda a_{nn}$	K_n

$$(20)$$

Note that the only (possibly) positive coefficients on the left-hand side of (20) are on the main diagonal; moreover, they must all be positive (that is, $\lambda a_{ii} < 1$) or else (17) cannot have solutions with $\eta > 0$. If we pivot on the $1 - \lambda a_{11}$ entry in (20), we get the tableau in (21).

$$
\begin{array}{cccc}
\eta_1 & \eta_1 & \cdots & \eta_n
\end{array}
$$

$$
\left[\begin{array}{cccc}
1 & -\lambda a_{12} & \cdots & -\lambda a_{1n} \\
0 & 1 - \lambda a_{22}^* & \cdots & -\lambda a_{2n}^* \\
\vdots & \vdots & \cdots & \vdots \\
0 & -\lambda a_{n2}^* & \cdots & 1 - \lambda a_{nn}^*
\end{array}\right.
\left.\begin{array}{c}
K_1^* \\
K_2^* \\
\vdots \\
K_n^*
\end{array}\right] \tag{21}
$$

where

$$
a_{ij}^* = a_{ij} + \frac{\lambda a_{i1} a_{1j}}{1 - \lambda a_{11}} \geq a_{ij} \geq 0 \quad \text{for} \quad 2 \leq i, j \leq n \tag{22}
$$

$$
K_i^* = K_i + \frac{\lambda a_{i1}}{1 - \lambda a_{11}} \geq K_i > 0 \quad \text{for} \quad 2 \leq i \leq n \tag{23}
$$

Clearly, $\eta_2, \ldots, \eta_n$ satisfies the $(n-1) \times (n-1)$ system in the lower right-hand corner of (21). By the same argument as before, the main diagonal entries of this system must be positive; also (22) and (23) imply that $A^* \geq 0$ and $K^* > 0$. Hence, by the induction hypothesis, $(I_{n-1} - \lambda A_{n-1})^{-1} \geq 0$. From this we can construct (see Exercise 5) the inverse of $1 - \lambda A$ and show that it is non-negative by using elementary matrix theory. This completes the proof of the theorem.

With the exception of assumption (10), Theorem 13-1 is equivalent to the Perron-Frobenius theorem if we merely replace the eigenvalue ρ by $1/\lambda_1$. However, if A is indecomposable, assumption (10) necessarily holds since if A violates (10), then it has a zero row and hence A is automatically decomposable. Hence Theorem 13-1 is, in fact, equivalent to the Perron-Frobenius theorem and its proof gives a new proof of this well-known theorem.

Corollary: The ordinary Leontief model (2), (3) has a solution if, and only if, $\lambda_1 > 1$.

In [122] Thompson proved much stronger and more detailed versions of these theorems in which the indecomposability assumption is dropped.

4. Consistent Aggregation in the Leontief Model

In 1956 McManus [70] introduced the idea of consistent aggregation for the

Leontief model, which was closely related to earlier ideas of Hotelling, Stone, and Tintner (see Tintner [127] for a discussion.) We first define the concept and then relate it to the prices in the expanding von Neumann-Leontief model.

Definition. A *consistent* aggregation $(1 \times n)$ column vector η for the Leontief model (2), (3) is a probability vector ($\eta \geq 0$ and $e\eta = 1$, where e is a row vector of ones) that defines quantities x^* and d^* satisfying

$$x^* = x\eta \tag{24}$$

$$d^* = d\eta \tag{25}$$

$$x^* = Cd^* \tag{26}$$

where C is a positive number.

In 1974 Tintner [127] showed that η had to be a real non-negative eigenvector associated with a real positive eigenvalue of A. Since Gale [24] had remarked that in the indecomposable case the expansion rate to the expanding von Neumann-Leontief model was the reciprocal of the largest real eigenvalue, Tintner could have noted (but did not note) that connection. We make the connection explicit in the next theorem.

Theorem 13-2: If A is indecomposable and $\lambda_1 > \lambda$, then the price vector η of the expanding von Neumann-Leontief model (6) through (10) provides a positive consistent aggregation vector for the generalized Leontief model (3) and (5).

Proof: Since A is indecomposable and $\lambda_1 > \lambda$, the Leontief model (2) and (3) is solvable for arbitrary $d \geq 0$ by Theorem 13-1. By Lemma 13-1, both $\xi > 0$ and $\eta > 0$ for the expanding von Neumann-Leontief model. The fact that $\xi > 0$ implies $(I - \lambda_1 A)\eta = 0$ so that $A\eta = (1/\lambda_1)\eta$, and hence η is an eigenvalue associated with eigenvalue $\rho_1 = (1/\lambda_1)$. Let us define x^* and d^* as in (24) and (25). Now multiplying (5) on the right by η and using the eigenvector properties we obtain

$$x(I - \lambda A)\eta = d\eta$$

or

$$x\eta(1 - \lambda\rho_1) = d\eta$$

Using definitions (24) and (25), we obtain

$$x^* (1 - \lambda\rho_1) = d^*$$

which gives (26) if we divide by $(1 - \lambda\rho_1)$ and set

$$C = 1/(1 - \lambda\rho_1) = \lambda_1/(\lambda_1 - \lambda).$$

This Theorem is capable of considerable generalization, see Tintner [127] and Thompson [122]. (For an example of consistent aggregation, see Exercise 6.)

5. Expanding Models with Outside Demand

Various writers including Gale [23], Wong [143], and Woodbury [146] have discussed an expanding von Neumann-Leontief model in which, at each time period, the goal is to produce not just enough to satisfy the internal demand plus the given external demand, but at least an amount α' times the total demand. The expressions to be satisfied for this model are

$$x = \alpha'(xA + d) \tag{27}$$

$$x \geq 0, \quad xf = 1 \tag{28}$$

We can easily rewrite (27) as

$$x[I - \alpha'(A + fd)] = 0 \tag{29}$$

where f if a column vector of all ones. As already noted in the KMT paper [48] and above in Chapter 2, this model can be imbedded in the KMT expanding model with outside demand, using the ideas of Section 8 of Chapter 2. The matrix game to be solved is

$$M_{\alpha'} = I - \alpha'(A + fd) \tag{30}$$

This is, of course, a special case of the von Neumann model with $B = I$. If $d > 0$, that is, there is positive demand to consume each good, then $I + A + fd > 0$ so the original von Neumann assumption (AO) of Chapter 2 holds, and there is a unique expansion factor α' and solution vectors $x > 0$ and $y > 0$. We also consider the model without the outside demand vector d whose matrix is

$$M_\alpha = I - \alpha A \tag{31}$$

If A is indecomposable it will have a unique expansion factor $\alpha > 0$ and solution vectors $\xi > 0$ and $\eta > 0$.

With these quantities in mind, we can now state the next theorem whose results appear hear for the first time.

Theorem 13-3: Assume that A is indecomposable, $d > 0$, the solutions to (30) are α', x, and y, and the solutions to (31) are α, ξ, and η;

(a) α' and x give the unique solution to the expanding Leontief model with outside demand given by (27) and (28).

(b) $\alpha' < \alpha$

(c) The price vector η is a consistent aggregation vector for the model of (27) and (28).

Proof: (a) Since $d > 0$, there is a unique α' solving (30) and corresponding $x > 0$ and $y > 0$. But then $y > 0$ implies that $x[I - \alpha A] = \alpha d$ can be solved with $x > 0$. By an argument similar to that of Theorem 13-2, $(I - \alpha A)^{-1} > 0$ so that x is unique.

(b) Since $d > 0$, it is obvious that $\alpha' < \alpha$.

(c) Since A is indecomposable, the solutions α, ξ, η to (31) are unique. Since $\xi > 0$, we have $[I - \alpha A]\eta = 0$ so that $A\eta = (1/\alpha)\eta$ and $\eta > 0$ is an eigenvalue of A. Since x and α' solve (27), we have

$$x (I - \alpha'A) = \alpha'd \qquad (32)$$

Multiplying (32) on the right by η gives

$$x(I - \alpha'A)\eta = \alpha'd\eta$$

Using the fact that η is an eigenvector, we have

$$x\eta(1 - \alpha'/\alpha) = \alpha'd\eta$$

Using the abbreviations $x^* = x\eta$ and $d^* = d\eta$, we now have

$$x^* = \frac{\alpha\alpha'}{\alpha - \alpha'}d^* = Cd^* \qquad (33)$$

where $C = \alpha\alpha'/(\alpha - \alpha') > 0$, so that, by the definition of the previous section, η provides a consistent aggregation vector for the model.

This result is also capable of considerable generalizations; see Thompson [122].

6. Generalized Eigensystems

In a series of papers [123, 124, 125, 126] Thompson and Weil have investigated the connections between game theory and generalized eigensystems. Most of this work was inspired by an attempt to relate expansion factors in the von Neumann-KMT model to ordinary and generalized eigenvalues. Many of the results in these papers are of peripheral interest to the theme of this book and so will not be discussed here. We content ourselves with a brief summary of the primarily economic results contained in [125].

Recall from Chapter 2 that in the KMT model an *economic solution* is a triple (α, x, y) where α is a positive number and x and y are probability vectors satisfying

$$x(B - \alpha A) \geq 0 \tag{34}$$

$$(B - \alpha A)y \leq 0 \tag{35}$$

$$xBy > 0 \tag{36}$$

We know that there are a finite number of expansion factors $\alpha_1, \ldots,$ α_r for which there are vectors $x^{(i)}, y^{(i)}$ such that $(\alpha_i, x^{(i)}, y^{(i)})$ are *economic solution triples*.

By a *central* economic solution triple, we mean a triple $(\alpha_i, x^{(i)}, y^{(i)})$ in which $x^{(i)}$ and $y^{(i)}$ are central solutions, that is, chosen to be in the interior of their respective solution sets.

We shall define $\hat{A}$ and $\hat{B}$ to be *coordinated submatrices* of A and B if they are constructed by striking out the same rows and columns from A and B. We also define $\hat{x}$ to be obtained from x by striking from x components corresponding to rows struck in constructing $\hat{A}$ and $\hat{B}$; also, $\hat{y}$ is obtained from y by striking components corresponding to columns struck in constructing $\hat{A}$ and $\hat{B}$. Then Thompson and Weil define the economic solution triple (α, x, y) to be a *generalized eigensystem triple* if

$$\hat{x}(\hat{B} - \alpha\hat{A}) = 0 \tag{37}$$

$$(\hat{B} - \alpha\hat{A})\hat{y} = 0 \tag{38}$$

Note that α plays the role of an eigenvalue, $\hat{x}$ plays the role of a left eigenvector, and $\hat{y}$ the role of a right eigenvector.

In [124, 126] Thompson and Weil showed that generalized eigenvalue problems for rectangular matrices can be solved by first pivoting and then applying ordinary eigenvalue routines. In the present case, we have the constructive method of Chapter 3 for obtaining the economic triples, and we are merely interpreting those results in a new way.

We now quote two results from [125].

Theorem 13-4: ([125], p. 143). Let (α, x, y) be a central economic solution triple to the von Neumann model. Let $\hat{M}_\alpha$ be the (possibly rectangular) submatrix of $M_\alpha = B - \alpha A$ on which $x_i > 0$ and $y_j > 0$. Then $(\alpha, \hat{x}, \hat{y})$ is a generalized eigensystem triple of $\hat{M}_\alpha$.

Proof: By the complementary slackness theorem of linear programming, if $x_i > 0$, then $M_\alpha^{(i)}y = 0$, where $M_\alpha^{(i)}$ is the ith row of M_α. Similarly, if $y_j > 0$, then $xM_\alpha^j = 0$, where M_α^j is the jth column of M_α. Hence the triple $(\alpha, \hat{x}, \hat{y})$ satisfies (37) and (38).

We can enlarge the matrix $\hat{M}_\alpha$ and still get a similar result. To do this, let $\bar{M}_\alpha$ be the (possibly rectangular) submatrix of M_α, given $v(M_\alpha) = 0$, which includes all columns j of M_α such that $xM_\alpha^{(j)} = 0$ for all optimal strategies x, and it includes all rows i such that $M_\alpha^{(i)} = 0$ for all optimal strategies y. Define the corresponding coordinated strategies x and y. Clearly, $\hat{M}_\alpha \subseteq \bar{M}_\alpha$. It is easy to see that the following theorem is true.

Theorem 13-5: If α is an economic expansion rate, $v(M_\alpha) = 0$, then the triple (α, x, y) is a generalized eigensystem of $\bar{M}_\alpha$.

Many other results, including numerous examples, are given in the papers referred to. However, since they are rather detailed in nature, it seems best to stop here and refer the interested reader to the papers cited for further details.

7. Final Observations

The preceding sections have established the mathematical properties of the Leontief system and have shown how it compares with the von Neumann and the KMT model when made into an expanding system.

It remains to add a few further observations to complement and interpret the purely formal characteristics. The following five remarks are in order:

(1) Leontief's coefficients are not technological-physical quantities as are those of the KMT model. Rather, they are obtained by dividing price sums by other price sums. That is, the value of the output of one industry is the numerator and the value of the output of another industry is the denominator; thus each coefficient is obtained.

It is clear that at whatever time the coefficients are calculated, their values are strongly influenced by the price situation of the economy *as of that moment*. That is to say that if there has occurred in the preceding period a big price movement (e.g., inflation, increase in oil prices, good or bad harvest, etc.) the coefficients may be affected. While they reflect technology to some extent, they can be grossly distorted too.

(2) The Leontief system does not account for (technological) *prices* as the von Neumann-KMT model does. This is a severe restriction.

(3) There is *no joint production*: another severely restrictive characteristic. Joint production is one of the most fundamental facts of *any* production system. It is particularly obvious in modern times.

(4) The original input-output model is entirely *static*: it has no expansion factor. It was shown above how expansion can be introduced

into the model, but the latter does not thereby lose its other restrictive properties.

(5) The input-output model—whether static or expanding—describes an economy of singular *vulnerability*. That is to say, if one single cell in the matrix is "destroyed," the whole economic system described by that coefficient matrix collapses. Neither does the model allow for compression without causing a similar collapse. In this there is a fundamental difference with the KMT model. If this were a true description of an economy, then it would be easy to destroy the economy of a whole country in war. We know that this is not the case.

The total interdependence of the (indecomposable) Leontief system can also be expressed differently by stating that there are no *subeconomies*, that there is no way of distinguishing between essential and nonessential industries and services. As a further consequence, there is no choice of different mixtures of goods that can be produced.

From all this it is seen that the Leontief input-output system, even when transformed into an expanding von Neumann-Leontief model, is but a very special case of the KMT model, let alone its further development.

Finally, we refer back to the opening paragraph of this chapter: Many countries have made an effort to collect input-output data in conformity with the needs of the Leontief scheme. A corresponding effort to implement the KMT model is desirable. It would prove very fruitful in view of the vastly greater analytical power of the KMT model and its extensions.

Exercises

1. (a) If the inverse of $I - A$ exists, show that the solution to (2) is $x = d(I - A)^{-1}$.
   (b) If $(I - A)^{-1}$ has a negative entry in row i, show that by choosing d to have $d_i > 0$ and $d_j = 0$ for $j \neq i$, that the corresponding x does not satisfy (3).
   (c) Use (a) and (b) to show that a necessary condition for an x to exist solving (2) and (3) is that $(I - A)^{-1} \geq 0$.
   (d) Show that the condition in (c) is also sufficient.
2. Let A be an $n \times n$ matrix with $A \geq 0$ and $eA < e$, where e is a row vector of all ones.
   (a) Let k be the smallest number so that $eA \leq ke$. Show that $0 < k < 1$.
   (b) Show that $eA^2 \leq keA \leq k^2e$.

(c) Show that $eA^n \leq k^n e$.

(d) Use (c) to show that $A^n \to 0$.

(e) By multiplying out the terms, show that
$$(I - A)(I + A + \ldots + A^{n-1}) = I - A^n$$

(f) Use (d) and (e) to show that
$$(I - A)^{-1} = I + A + \ldots + A^n + \ldots$$

(g) Use (f) to show that
$$(I - A)^{-1} \geq 0.$$

3. Let A be a square non-negative matrix and let ρ^* be its positive eigenvalue given by the Perron-Frobenius theorem (see text). Show that (2) and (3) are solvable if, and only if, $1 > \rho^*$.

4. Let A be a square non-negative matrix of a Leontief model.

(a) Show that the entries of A^2 give the two stage orders from each industry to each other industry; show similarly that the entries of A^n give the n-stage orders.

(b) Use the result of Exercise 2(f) to show that if industry i does not order directly or indirectly from industry j, then the (i, j)th entry of $(I - A)^{-1}$ is zero.

(c) By reordering industries, show that if the condition in (b) holds, then A is decomposable.

(d) If A is indecomposable, show that every industry orders directly or indirectly from every other industry.

5. Let $T^{(1)}$ be the tableau in (20) and let $T^{(2)}$ be the tableau in (21).

(a) Show that $PT^{(1)} = T^{(2)}$, where P is the non-negative pivot matrix

$$P = \begin{pmatrix} \dfrac{1}{1 - \lambda a_{11}} & 0 & \ldots & 0 \\[2mm] \dfrac{\lambda a_{21}}{1 - \lambda a_{11}} & 1 & \ldots & 0 \\[2mm] \vdots & \vdots & & \vdots \\[2mm] \dfrac{\lambda a_{n1}}{1 - \lambda a_{11}} & 0 & \ldots & 1 \end{pmatrix}$$

(b) Let $u - (\lambda a_{12}^*, \ldots, \lambda a_{1n}^*)$; Let $I_{n-1} - \lambda A_{n-1}$ be the $n \times n$ matrix in the lower right-hand corner of (21). Let Q be the matrix

$$Q = \begin{pmatrix} 1 & (I_{n-1} - \lambda A_{n-1})^{-1}u \\ 0 & (I_{n-1} - \lambda A_{n-1})^{-1} \end{pmatrix}$$

Now show that $QPT^{(1)} = QT^{(2)} = I$.

(c) Show that $QP = (I - \lambda A)^{-1} \geq 0$.

6. Consider the Leontief economy whose input matrix is

$$A = \begin{pmatrix} 0 & 1/3 \\ 1/3 & 0 \end{pmatrix}$$

(a) Show that for the corresponding expanding von Neumann-Leontief economy, the unique expansion factor is $\alpha = 3$.

(b) Show that the optimal price vector for $\alpha = 3$ in (a) is $\eta = (1/2, 1/2)'$.

(c) Show that η provides a consistent aggregation vector for the generalized Leontief model (3) and (5), provided that $\lambda < 3$.

14 Conclusion and Outlook

1. Review of New Concepts and Results Obtained

Our theory is based on the von Neumann model of an expanding economy. The first step was to generalize it with John G. Kemeny to the KMT model which gave rise to subeconomies. Further generalizations by us allowed the introduction of private and public savings and consumption. Constructive computational techniques and algorithms were developed that permitted the determination of all economically significant solutions. A further step was to reconcile the simultaneous existence of "profitable" and "unprofitable" activities and at the same time to introduce control variables. Adding the possibility of exporting to, and importing from, the outside world the model became open. In the new model we were able to include both theoretically and quantitatively the phenomenon of technological change, the operation of private and government services, the control of economic growth, contraction, compression and long term planning.

We believe that the introduction of control variables into an equilibrium growth model is an important step towards making them applicable to the description of existing economies. For it seems to us that many economic decisions (however made and in whatever political setting) are imposed on real economies as constraints which place definite upper and/or lower limits on the operation of activities. It *might* be possible to construct a community utility function that would have exactly the same effect when added to the model, but we find it difficult to do so, especially for decisions that have an arbitrary character such as the example given in Section 5 of Chapter 6. We have taken the same stand in regard to demand and supply functions. Our models have explicitly stated linear supply functions and demand coefficients. We have indicated how these latter coefficients can be varied to apply to different kinds of economies.

By combining the several open single country models we obtained an expanding world model. For that model we discussed the existence of trading blocks which are a set of separate economies each one of which has a comparative advantage in the production of one or more goods relative to other members of the same trading block. We have further shown that the concept of subeconomies carries over to the world model. The use of these concepts explained the multiple types of international transactions that can be observed and give insight into the workings of multinational corporations.

The concepts used in this anlaysis arose from a rigorous but accessible theory developed to analyze models of economic growth. Many of these ideas are novel and will require time to become assimilated into economic literature. Besides offering an abstract theory which we believe adds to the understanding of economic phenomena we also provide constructive, computational methods for calculating actual economic programs for large economic entities.

2. The Next Steps

Having come to the end of this study it is proper to ask: What next? Where should further research go?

This is clearly an exceedingly difficult matter. As a rule neither the direction or nor the speed of scientific progress can be predicted. There are, of course, at any one moment, concrete questions that should be properly formulated and answered. We have tried to do this in the various research problems listed below in Section 4. Each one of these problems is one that deserves attention; its solution would advance the present theory. In addition there is the empirical problem of whether or not the phenomena which our theory describes occur as formulated in existing or historical economies. Our expectation is that every new result would fit into the framework we have established.

Whatever the concrete state of science may be, science is always unfinished, regardless of the framework. Elaboration is always possible. But it may be elaboration that later on turns out to have been in the wrong direction. If we knew that to be the case, then the resolution of our research problems would be a waste of effort. But, obviously we have no such knowledge. On the contrary, we are convinced that the present theory rests on a firm basis so as to make the resolution of these problems fruitful and imperative.

It is, of course, conceivable that some day a very different approach to economic phenomena may be undertaken, similar to the appearance of the von Neumann model itself. While such an event cannot be excluded from possible developments, there is no way of anticipating it and it would be remiss not to develop the present theory further. It has, after all, led to novel and important insights into the working of an economy under most varied conditions.

We realize that it is not customary in economic writings—unfortunately—to indicate unsolved problems, to formulate them carefully wherever possible. There is far too often (especially in textbooks!) the impression given that what is presented is the last and final word. We take an entirely different attitude.

In Sections 3 and 4, therefore, we enumerate some directions into which further work might profitably go. Section 3 discusses some questions for empirical investigation while Section 4 lists theoretical questions.

Some of those questions, as well as others, will doubtless be investigated in the near future. However there are two immediate practical steps which should be taken in order that it should be possible to make use of the concepts and results of this book.

First, a *technological data bank* should be created that will collect the technological coefficients required by the model. It is an indispensible step to establish this bank because of the great possibilities the theory offers for concrete applications. Before any important policy decision based on the theory can be made, the right data must exist.

Second, the necessary *computer programs* for solving large closed, open, and world models must be developed and tested. Fortunately this step is made easier by the existence of many codes developed to solve problems in operations research and management science. In these areas it is a routine matter to formulate and solve problems having thousands— even hundreds of thousands or millions—of variables, and a similar number of constraints. The problems we state here are not identical to those, but many, if not most of the techniques employed in the operations research literature can be profitably applied, if necessary in a modified form.

One difficulty in the latter is that most economists are usually not acquainted with the operations research literature. We hope that the present book will stimulate them to investigate further such references as [15, 18, 28].

3. Empirical Research Questions

Whenever a scientific theory produces new concepts and results concerning a model of reality, it is natural to try to observe the corresponding concepts and results in reality. Examples of this procedure abound in physics, chemistry, astronomy, etc. We wish to list here several lines of empirical economic investigations suggested by the results we have obtained earlier in this book. We do not claim completeness in our list, and encourage the reader to add to it. We hope that at least some of these problems will be investigated empirically in the near future.

(1) *Identification of national subeconomies.* Once the technological data bank for a given country has been established it is desirable to use the methods of chapters 3 to 5 to identify the technological sub-economies within the country.

(2) *Identification of international subeconomies.* Whenever technological data banks for several countries have been collected, particularly if they are in the same trading block, it is natural to extend the questions in (1) to the determination of international subeconomies.

(3) *Contracting Economies.* Are there any contemporary economies that are contracting? Have any historical economies (e.g., the Roman Empire) been in the contracting state?

(4) *Compressed Economies.* Without question war-time economies are compressed versions of peace-time economies. But a careful, complete analysis—including the corresponding technological data and setting of control variables—is lacking for any such economy.

(5) *Technological Change.* In Chapter 8 a method was suggested for handling technological change by gradually increasing a control variable to permit the introduction of a new technology. It would be interesting to try to do this for a specific new technology (e.g., computer, laser, space, etc. technologies).

(6) *Lags.* In this book we have assumed that production of every good could take place in one period. In reality there are many goods that require several periods for their production. An empirical investigation to determine what kinds of goods have lags in their production is in order to see how significant the problem is. We are convinced that the theory is powerful enough to be able to accommodate lags.

(7) *Identification of Control Variables.* The magnitudes of many production processes are controlled in many different ways in any given economy. In many cases such controls are set by legal, political, or other rules. A complete identification of control variables and how they are controlled for a given economy would be of great interest. This might establish an interesting relation to political science.

(8) *Trading Blocks.* As we saw in Chapter 12, our theory predicts the existence of trading blocks, with each block having its own expansion rate. The identification of such trading blocks at a given point of time would provide verification of this prediction.

(9) *Uncertainty.* In this book we have left uncertainty out of our models. Yet it is obviously important. An empirical investigation should be made to find out where and how important the uncertainty is relevant for our models.

(10) *Comparative advantage and expansion rates.* In Chapter 11 we showed that a country having a comparative advantage in the production of a good depends on the world expansion rate. We can now pose the question of finding actual historical instances in which a country has gained or lost its comparative advantage due to a change in the expansion rate.

4. Theoretical Research Questions

Here we shall collect together several theoretical research questions, some of which were noted in earlier places in the text, whose answers would extend the theory. The list is not complete and the reader may wish to add further problems to the list.

(1) *The linearity assumption.* The models we have presented are linear, but the world is non-linear. The only non-linear expanding economy model presented to date is that of Morishima and Thompson [103]. However, the results of that—and most other—nonlinear models are likely to be non-constructive, and are not necessarily computable or if so, only with great difficulty. Perhaps a more fruitful approach would be to approximate nonlinear functions by piecewise linear methods. Extensions of linear programming to mixed integer programming have been developed to accomplish the same extension in other areas, a field of research that is in a state of active development.

(2) *Exhaustible Resources.* By extending the linear programming tableaus of long range planning models to include constraints on exhaustible resources, it would be possible to make a study of how the economy can adjust to this problem by determining the various time spans over which the resources could be used up.

(3) *Feasibility of Economic Programs.* When many different, separately operating agencies are responsible for setting different sets of control variables of an economy, it is quite likely that the resulting problem is totally unfeasible. Methods should be found for quickly finding this out, communicating that fact to the control agencies, such as a planning board, the Congress, etc.

(4) *Technological Innovation and Change.* The discussion in Section 3 of Chapter 8 should be further elaborated to include improvement in old processes as well as to the introduction of new processes.

(5) *Computation of Long-term Planning Models.* Some of the theoretical difficulties of computing solutions to the long-term planning models of Chapter 9 were discussed in Section 6 of that chapter. Clearly further work on this problem is needed.

(6) *Trading Blocks.* One of the results of Chapter 12, surprising in terms of current international trade theory, was that even in a so-called "free trade" situation, countries will form into trading blocks in ways best understood by using n-person game theory. Such an analysis will lead to interesting theoretical problems and new insights.

(7) *Sanctions, Blockades, Cartels, and Tributes.* In the same way in Chapter 12 it was noted that a game theory analysis of intergovernmental actions such as sanctions, blockades, cartels and tributes would be perhaps difficult but of great value.

(8) *Lags*. In [128, 129] Truchon has given a discussion of the effects and importance of lags in expanding economy models. Doubtless further work is possible in this direction.

(9) *Money*. Without question the introduction of money in the model would be a great step forward. Money also brings uncertainty, because of the many ways in which it can be spent once an individual has achieved more than a subsistence level of living. The introduction of money would be difficult, but would probably not make radical changes in the model. We are quite aware of the far-reaching implications of this statement.

While far from wanting to draw a parallel, one must note that the classical theory of mechanics did not account for light, but was not invalidated when the theory of light was finally developed and both theories were fitted together.

(10) *Uncertainty*. We have not discussed uncertainty in the model but it is obviously important. The linear programming literature offers some clues as to how to handle uncertainty in the technological coefficients of the model, so that a first step would be to ascertain to what extent those methods would work in the present case.

This list of research problems is not necessarily complete but we feel that they are sufficiently clearly formulated so that there is a reasonable expectation that they can be solved in the near future.

We find it gratifying that we are not expounding a completed theory but rather one which is capable of being further developed in many directions. This is based on the belief that our theory is built upon a firm foundation. We hope that our readers agree and that some will make their own contributions.

We would like to indicate the existence of important contributions to growth models by other authors that we have been unable for lack of space to discuss: Afriat [1], Förstner [21], Henn [41,42,43], Morishima [100,101,102], and Steinmetz [116].

Appendix 1
Matrix Game Theory

1. Definitions, Concepts, and Basic Results

We give here a very brief discussion of matrix games, which are the two-person zero-sum games in normalized form described in [106]. We list only the important results that we need for purposes of this book, and give references to places where more extensive expositions with proofs can be found. The material presented here is quite elementary, and readers are encouraged to take the time to work through the solution details of several numerical examples of matrix games if he or she has not already done so before trying to solve some of the expanding economy models in the text. Reference [50, third edition, pp. 370-410] gives an elementary exposition of matrix game theory.

Definition 1: Consider two players called R and C who play the following game: R chooses an integer $i = 1, 2, \ldots, m$; and simultaneously C chooses an integer $j = 1, 2, \ldots, n$; then the outcome of the game is the entry g_{ij} in a real-valued $m \times n$ matrix G; if $g_{ij} \geq 0$, then C pays R the amount g_{ij}, but if $g_{ij} < 0$, then R pays C the amount $|g_{ij}| = -g_{ij}$. The game just defined is called a *matrix game* and the $m \times n$ real-valued matrix G is the *payoff* matrix. The choices $i = 1, \ldots, m$ are called *pure strategies* for (the row) player R and the choices $j = 1, \ldots, n$ are called pure strategies for (the column) player C.

Definition 2: Let G be an $m \times n$ payoff matrix. A *mixed strategy* for player R in G is an m-component probability row vector x; that is, x satisfies

$$xf = 1, \qquad x \geq 0 \tag{1}$$

where f is an $m \times 1$ vector, all of whose components are ones. Similarly, a mixed strategy for player C in G is an n-component column vector y; that is, y satisfies

$$ey = 1, \qquad y \geq 0 \tag{2}$$

where e is a $1 \times n$ vector, all of whose components are ones.

Definition 3: A *solution* to the $m \times n$ matrix game G consists of a number v, called the *value of the game* and denoted by $v(G) = v$, and mixed strategies vectors x^0 for R and y^0 for C satisfying

$$x^0 G \geq ve' = \underbrace{(v, \ldots, v)}_{n \text{ components}} \tag{3}$$

$$Gy^o \leq vf' = \left. \begin{pmatrix} v \\ \vdots \\ v \end{pmatrix} \right\} \quad m \text{ components} \tag{4}$$

Game G is said to be *fair* if, and only if, $v = 0$.

The following facts are needed; proofs of these statements will be found in the above reference.

(i) Every matrix game has a solution; the solution can be found by using the simplex method to solve an equivalent linear programming problem.

(ii) The value of the game is unique and $v = x^o G y^o$.

(iii) The set X^o of all optimal solutions x^o for R and the set Y^o of all optimal solutions y^o for C are each bounded, polyhedral, nonempty, convex sets. (A set S is convex if it has the following property: for any elements u, v in S it is true that $w = au + (1-a)v$ is also in S for all a satisfying $0 \leq a \leq 1$.)

(iv) The *extreme points* of the sets X^o and Y^o are called *basic solutions*. Each set has a finite number of such extreme points.

(v) Let G be an $m \times n$ matrix game and E be an $m \times n$ matrix, all of whose entries are ones. Consider both of the games G and $G + kE$, where k is any real number. It is easy to show the following: $v(G + kE) = v(G) + k$, and the two games have exactly the *same* sets of optimal strategies X^o and Y^o.

(vi) The solution by the simplex method of the linear program described in (i) produces a pair x^o, y^o of basic optimal solutions.

Definition 4: An $m \times n$ matrix game G is said to be *strictly determined* if it can be solved in *pure strategies*; i.e., it has an optimum solution x^o for R and y^o for C such that exactly one component of each of these strategies is one and the rest are zero.

(vii) Matrix game G is strictly determined if, and only if, it contains an entry $g_{ij} = v$, called a *saddle value*, such that g_{ij} is equal to the smallest entry in row i and also equal to the largest entry in column j.

We concentrate on 2×2 games for the rest of this section. Let G be the 2×2 game with payoff matrix

$$G = \begin{pmatrix} a & b \\ c & d \end{pmatrix} \tag{5}$$

(vii) The 2×2 game G is *nonstrictly determined* if a and d are *both larger than* or *both smaller than* both b and c.

Consider the examples in Figure A1-1. Using the result in (vii) we see that the game in Figure A1-1(a) is strictly determined with solution

$$v = 2, \quad x = (1,0), \quad y = (1,0)' \tag{6}$$

$$\begin{pmatrix} 2 & 3 \\ 1 & -10 \end{pmatrix} \quad \begin{pmatrix} 2 & 0 \\ 1 & 4 \end{pmatrix} \quad \begin{pmatrix} -1 & 3 \\ 0 & 1 \end{pmatrix} \quad \begin{pmatrix} -1 & 4 \\ 1/2 & -2 \end{pmatrix}$$

(a)   (b)   (c)   (d)

Figure A1-1

The games in Figures A1-1(b) and (d) are not strictly determined.
The game in Figure A1-1(c) is strictly determined with solution

$$v = 0, \quad x = (0,1), \quad y = (1,0)' \tag{7}$$

Since $v = 0$, this game is *fair*.

For nonstrictly determined 2×2 games, the following formulas provide the solution:

$$v = \frac{ad - bc}{a + d - b - c} \tag{8}$$

$$x_1^o = \frac{d - c}{a + d - b - c} \tag{9}$$

$$x_2^o = \frac{a - b}{a + d - b - c} \tag{10}$$

$$y_1^o = \frac{d - b}{a + d - b - c} \tag{11}$$

$$y_2^o = \frac{a - c}{a + d - b - c} \tag{12}$$

The reader can check by matrix multiplication that formulas (8) through (12) solve the game in (5).

Using these formulas, we find the solution to the game in Figure A1-1(b) to be

$$v = \frac{8}{5}, \quad x = \left(\frac{3}{5}, \frac{2}{5}\right), \quad y = \left(\frac{4}{5}, \frac{1}{5}\right)' \tag{13}$$

as the reader can easily check.

Similarly, the solution to the game in Figure A1-1(d) is

$$v = 0, \quad x = \left(\frac{1}{3}, \frac{2}{3}\right), \quad y = \left(\frac{4}{5}, \frac{1}{5}\right)' \tag{14}$$

as can also be checked. This is a fair game.

2. Solving Economic Games

In Chapter 2 it is necessary to solve games of the form $M_\alpha = B - \alpha A$, where A and B are non-negative $m \times n$ matrices and α is chosen so that $v(M_\alpha) = 0$. Chapter 3 gives a general solution method for such games. Here we discuss in detail how to solve 2×2 games of this form, using the 2×2 results obtained as the end of the last section.

Consider the following non-negative matrices:

$$A = \begin{pmatrix} a_{11} & a_{12} \\ a_{21} & a_{22} \end{pmatrix}, \qquad B = \begin{pmatrix} b_{11} & b_{12} \\ b_{21} & b_{22} \end{pmatrix} \tag{15}$$

From these and a parameter α, we form the matrix game M_α as

$$M_\alpha = B - \alpha A = \begin{pmatrix} b_{11} - \alpha a_{11} & b_{12} - \alpha a_{12} \\ b_{21} - \alpha a_{21} & b_{22} - \alpha a_{22} \end{pmatrix} \tag{16}$$

We want the solution to M_α only for values of α such that $v(M_\alpha) = 0$, and we also want solutions satisfying $xBy > 0$. The following procedure will suffice to do this. There are two cases, depending on whether M_α is strictly determined or not.

Case 1: *An α exists such that $v(M_\alpha) = 0$ and M_α is strictly determined.* It is easy to see that this case can happen only if α is chosen to make one of the matrix entries in (16) equal to zero; that is,

$$b_{ij} - \alpha a_{ij} = 0 \tag{17}$$

for some pair i,j, with $i = 1,2$ and $j = 1,2$. As examples, consider the two games in Figure A1-2. In Figure A1-2(a), it is clear that there are two strictly determined solutions such that $xBy > 0$, namely,

$$\alpha = 2, \quad x = (1,0), \quad y = (a, 1-a)', \quad \text{where } 0 < a \le 1 \tag{18}$$

$$\alpha = 1, \quad x = (a, 1-a), \quad y = (0,1)', \quad \text{where } 0 \le a < 1 \tag{19}$$

$$\begin{pmatrix} 2-\alpha & 0 \\ 1-\alpha & 1-\alpha \end{pmatrix} \qquad \begin{pmatrix} 2-\alpha & 3-\alpha \\ 1-\alpha & 5-6\alpha \end{pmatrix}$$

$$\text{(a)} \qquad\qquad\qquad \text{(b)}$$

Figure A1-2

On the other hand, the game in Figure A1(b) has only the following solution:

$$\alpha = 2, \quad x = (1,0), \quad y = (1,0)' \tag{20}$$

The reader should show that the other three ways of satisfying (17) for this example do not lead to fair games.

Case 2: *An α exists such that $v(M_\alpha) = 0$ and M_α is not strictly determined.* Here the formulas (8) through (12) apply. From (8) it follows, since the denominator of (8) is never zero for a nonstrictly determined game, that the α which makes $v(M_\alpha) = 0$ must satisfy

$$\begin{vmatrix} b_{11} - \alpha a_{11} & b_{12} - \alpha a_{12} \\ b_{21} - \alpha a_{21} & b_{22} - \alpha a_{22} \end{vmatrix} \tag{21}$$

where the vertical bars represent the determinant. From (21) it follows upon expanding the left hand side that α satisfies the following quadratic equation.

$$\alpha^2 \begin{vmatrix} a_{11} & a_{12} \\ a_{21} & a_{22} \end{vmatrix} - \alpha \left(\begin{vmatrix} a_{11} & b_{12} \\ a_{21} & b_{22} \end{vmatrix} + \begin{vmatrix} b_{11} & a_{12} \\ b_{12} & a_{22} \end{vmatrix} \right) + \begin{vmatrix} b_{11} & b_{12} \\ b_{21} & b_{22} \end{vmatrix} = 0 \tag{22}$$

Once α is determined, the rest of the solution can be obtained by substitution into the formulas in (9) through (12).

As an example, let us solve the chicken-and-eggs example given in Example 2-1. We had

$$A = \begin{pmatrix} 1 & 0 \\ 1 & 4 \end{pmatrix}, \quad B = \begin{pmatrix} 1 & 12 \\ 5 & 0 \end{pmatrix} \tag{23}$$

so that equation (22) is

$$\alpha^2 \begin{vmatrix} 1 & 0 \\ 1 & 4 \end{vmatrix} - \alpha \left(\begin{vmatrix} 1 & 12 \\ 1 & 0 \end{vmatrix} + \begin{vmatrix} 1 & 0 \\ 5 & 4 \end{vmatrix} \right) + \begin{vmatrix} 1 & 12 \\ 5 & 0 \end{vmatrix} = 0 \tag{24}$$

which gives

$$4\alpha^2 + 8\alpha - 60 = 0 \tag{25}$$

which factors into

$$4(\alpha - 3)(\alpha + 5) = 0 \tag{26}$$

Here there are two roots $\alpha = 3$ and $\alpha = -5$. The second one has no economic significance and is discarded. For $\alpha = 3$, we have

$$v(M_3) = \begin{pmatrix} -2 & 12 \\ 2 & -12 \end{pmatrix} \tag{27}$$

Using formulas (9) through (12), we obtain

$$x = (1/2, 1/2) \quad y = (6/7, 1/7)' \tag{28}$$

as optimal solutions to (27). These were described in Chapter 2.

3. Theorem of the Alternative: Central Solutions

Another important theoretical result about solutions to matrix games is the theorem of the alternative, which can be stated as follows.

(ix) *Theorem of the Alternative*. Let G be an $m \times n$ matrix game, $v = v(G)$ its value, and x^o and y^o any pair of optimal solutions; then the following statements are true

(a) $x_i^o > 0$ implies that

$$\sum_{j=1}^{n} g_{ij} y_j^o = v$$

(b) $y_j^o > 0$ implies that

$$\sum_{i=1}^{m} x_i^o g_{ij} = v.$$

In words, the theorem of the alternative states that if component x_i^o of x^o is positive, then the y^o strategy must satisfy the ith constraint of (3) as an equality; and if component y_j^o of y^o is positive, then the x^o strategy must satisfy the jth constraint of (4) as an equality.

Note that the theorem of the alternative says nothing when $x_i^o = 0$ or $y_j^o = 0$. Then all we know is that the corresponding inequalities in (3) and (4) hold. We can strengthen these results by going to the concept of a *central* (optimal) *solution* to a matrix game.

Definition 5: Let G be an $m \times n$ matrix game, let $x^{(1)}, \ldots, x^{(h)}$ be the extreme points of X^o [see (v)], and let $y^{(1)}, \ldots, y^{(k)}$ be the extreme points of Y^o. Then *central solutions* to G are of the form

$$x^* = \sum_{i=1}^{h} c_i x^{(i)}, \quad c_i > 0, \quad \sum_{i=1}^{h} c_i = 1 \tag{27}$$

and

$$y^* = \sum_{j=1}^{k} d_j y^{(j)}, \quad d_j > 0, \quad \sum_{j=1}^{k} d_j = 1 \tag{28}$$

In other words, a central solution for either player is obtained by taking a positive convex combination of the extreme points of the corresponding set of optimal solutions.

Intuitively, a central solution for a player corresponds to an interior point of the convex set of optimal strategies. In order to construct such a central solution it is necessary to be able to compute all extreme points of X^o and Y^o. A method for doing this by using the simplex method of linear programming is described in [119], but is too detailed to include here. The reader who does not want to consult that reference may instead merely accept the statement that a computationally efficient method exists for constructing a central solution to games.

The importance of the concept of central solutions is that statements (a) and (b) of (ix) can be strengthened.

(x) *Strong Theorem of the Alternative*. Let G be an $m \times n$ matrix game, $v = v(G)$ its value, and let x^* and y^* be any pair of *central solutions*; then the following statements are true:

(a) $x_i^* > 0$ if, and only if

$$\sum_{j=1}^{n} g_{ij} y_j^* = v$$

we may also state this equivalently as $x_i^* = 0$ if, and only if

$$\sum_{j=1}^{n} g_{ij} y_j^* < v$$

(b) $y_j^* > 0$ if, and only if

$$\sum_{i=1}^{m} x_i^* g_{ij} = 0;$$

we may also state this equivalently as $y_j^* = 0$ if, and only if

$$\sum_{i=1}^{m} x_i^* g_{ij} > 0.$$

For a proof of this result see Tucker [131].

The computational method used in Chapter 3 depends crucially on the strong theorem of the alternative.

4. Continuity of the Economic Game Value

The value function $v(M_\alpha)$ of the game $M_\alpha = B - \alpha A$ is a continuous function of α. In [141] R. Weil gave a proof of a slightly more general result. We specialize his proof for our case.

Let x and y solve M_α and set $v = v(M_\alpha)$; similarly, let x^o and y^o solve M_{α^o} and set $v^o = v(M_{\alpha^o})$. Then we have

$$
\begin{aligned}
v = xM_\alpha y &\leq xM_\alpha y^o \\
&= xM_{\alpha^o}y^o + (\alpha - \alpha^o)xAy^o \\
&\leq x^o M_{\alpha^o}y^o + (\alpha - \alpha^o)xAy^o \\
&\leq x^o M_{\alpha^o}y^o + (\alpha - \alpha^o)a \\
&= v_0 + (\alpha - \alpha^o)a
\end{aligned}
$$

where a is the largest element of A. Hence $v - v_0 \leq |\alpha - \alpha^o|a$. A similar calculation starting with $x^o M_\alpha^o y^o$ shows that $v_0 - v \leq |\alpha - \alpha^o|a$. Hence $|v - v_0| \leq |\alpha - \alpha^o|a$, and the continuity of $v(M_\alpha)$ follows.

Appendix 2
Linear Programming

1. Definitions, Concepts, and Basic Results

The theory and practice of linear programming is very well known and fully described in many references, e.g., [15, 18, 28]. Hence we content ourselves with a brief exposition of the basic facts without proofs, and then move on to the less emphasized topic of goal programming.

Let us take as the standard form of a pair of primal and dual linear programming problem the following:

$$
\begin{cases}
\text{Minimize} & xb = g \\
\text{Subject to } xM \geq c \\
\quad x \geq 0
\end{cases}
\qquad
\begin{cases}
\text{Maximize} & cy = h \\
\text{Subject to } My \leq b \\
\quad y \geq 0
\end{cases}
\tag{1}
$$

where M is an $m \times n$ matrix, x is $1 \times m$, y is $n \times 1$, c is $1 \times n$, b is $m \times 1$, and g and h are scalars. Vectors x and y will be said to be *feasible* if they satisfy their respective sets of constraints. The standard linear programming tableau of this problem is shown in Figure A2-1.

$$
\begin{array}{cc}
 & y \\
x & \boxed{M} \quad \leq b \\
 & \geq c
\end{array}
$$

Figure A2-1

Note that the inequality constraints $x \geq 0$ and $y \geq 0$ of (1) do not appear in Figure A2-1. They are automatically imposed by the steps of the simplex method.

However, we can impose the constraints $x \geq 0$ explicitly as in the following equivalent pair of primal-dual problems:

$$
\begin{cases}
\text{Minimize} & xb = g \\
\text{Subject to} & xM \geq c \\
\quad x \geq 0
\end{cases}
\qquad
\begin{cases}
\text{Maximize} & cy = h \\
\text{Subject to} & My + z = b \\
\quad y, z \geq 0
\end{cases}
\tag{2}
$$

where z is an $m \times 1$ vector of "slack" variables. The standard linear programming tableau of (2) is given in Figure A2-2. This is the tableau that is used in many explanations of the simplex method. The reader should show that linear programming problems (1) and (2) are equivalent.

233

$$\begin{array}{cc} y & z \end{array}$$

$$x \quad \boxed{\begin{array}{cc} M & I \end{array}} = b$$

$$\begin{array}{cc} \geq c & \geq 0 \end{array}$$

Figure A2-2

We can further impose the constraints $y \geq 0$ explicitly as in the following equivalent pair of primal-dual problems:

$$\left\{\begin{array}{lll} \text{Minimize} & xb = g \\ \text{Subject to} & xM - w = c \\ & w \geq 0 \end{array}\right. \qquad \left\{\begin{array}{lll} \text{Maximize} & cy = h \\ \text{Subject to} & My + z = b \quad (3) \\ & z \geq 0 \end{array}\right.$$

where w is a $1 \times n$ vector of slack variables. The standard linear programming tableau of (3) is given in Figure A2-3. The reader should show that (2) and (3) [hence (1) and (3)] are equivalent problems.

$$\begin{array}{cc} y & z \end{array}$$

$$\begin{array}{cc} x & \boxed{\begin{array}{cc} M & I \end{array}} = b \\ w & \boxed{\begin{array}{cc} -I & \end{array}} \leq 0 \end{array}$$

$$\begin{array}{cc} = c & \geq 0 \end{array}$$

Figure A2-3

Further information on the construction of primal-dual pairs of linear programs are given in Chapter 4 of [28].

We now quote some important results of linear programming.

(i) *Tucker's Duality Equation*. Using the third formulation (3) of our linear programming problem, we easily derive

$$g - h = xb - cy$$

$$= x(My + z) - (xM - w)y$$

After simplifying the right-hand side, we get

$$g - h = xz + wy \qquad (4)$$

which is called *Tucker's duality equation*. We will use this deceptively simple result to derive other results.

(ii) *Bounds on Objective Values*. Let $x, y, w,$ and z be feasible solutions to (3), that is, they satisfy the constraints of both problems. Let x^o, y^o, w^o, and x^o be *optimal* solutions to these problems, and let $g^o = x^o b$ and $h^o = c y^o$. Then direct application of (4) yields

$$g^o = x^o b \geq h = cy \tag{5}$$

because $g^o - h = x^o z + w^o y \geq 0$. In a similar manner, one can show that

$$h^o = c y^o \leq g = xb \tag{6}$$

Stated in words, (5) says that any feasible solution to the minimizing problem gives an upper bound to the optimum value of the maximizing problem, and (6) says that any feasible solution to the maximizing problem provides a lower bound to the optimum value of the minimizing problem.

(iii) *The Duality Theorem.* The theorem is the keystone of linear programming. Proofs may be found in [15, 18, 28]. It can be shown to be essentially equivalent to the minimax theorem of the theory of games [106]. We state it for problem (1).

Duality Theorem: The maximum problem of (1) has a feasible vector y^o such that $c y^o = \text{Max } cy$, if, and only if, the minimum problem has a solution that is feasible vector x^o such that $x^o b = \text{Min } xb$. Moreover, the equality $c y^o = x^o b$ holds if, and only if, y^o and x^o are solutions to their respective problems.

Note that the duality theorem states that one of the problems in (1) has a (finite) optimum solution if, and only if, the other one also does, and also that both of these problems have solutions, and their respective objective values are equal.

The reader will note that we use the duality theorem in proving the existence results for the open model of Chapter 4. The following theorem follows easily from the duality theorem.

Existence Theorem: Both of the dual programs (1) have optimal solutions x^o and y^o if, and only if, they both have feasible solutions x and y.

2. Goal Programming

Let us assume that our two linear programming problems in (1) have $b = 0$ and $c = 0$. Then, since both of the objective functions are identically zero, we are searching for two feasible vectors, x for the minimizing problem, and y for the maximizing problem. Any such pair will be optimal for these problems.

However, it is possible that either the set of primal constraints or the set of dual constraints, or both sets, may be infeasible. It is desirable to be able to test whether this happens or not. By solving the following pair of primal and dual *goal programming* problems in (7), we can test to see if any infeasibilities occur and, at the same time, come as "close as possible" to feasible solutions for infeasible constraint sets when they occur:

$$\text{Minimize} \quad -w^e p^e + w^i p^i \qquad \text{Maximize} \quad -t^p z^p + t^n z^n \tag{7}$$

$$\left\{ \begin{array}{l} \text{Subject to} \ \ xM - w^e + w^i = 0 \\[4pt] \qquad\qquad -x \qquad\qquad\quad \geq -t^p \\[4pt] \qquad\qquad\ x \qquad\qquad\quad\ \geq t^n \\[4pt] \qquad\qquad\qquad w^e, w^i \geq 0 \end{array} \right. \qquad \left\{ \begin{array}{l} \text{Subject to} \ \ M^y - z^p + z^n = 0 \\[4pt] \qquad\qquad -y \qquad\qquad\quad \leq -p^e \\[4pt] \qquad\qquad\ y \qquad\qquad\quad\ \leq p^i \\[4pt] \qquad\qquad\qquad z^p, z^n \geq 0 \end{array} \right.$$

where p^e and p^i are $n \times 1$ constant, non-negative "penalty" vectors and t^p and t^n are $1 \times m$ constant non-negative "penalty" vectors. Note that the constraints of (7) impose the following constraints on the x and y vectors

$$t^n \leq x \leq t^p \tag{8}$$

$$p^e \leq y \leq p^i \tag{9}$$

It is obvious that in order for (8) and (9) to have feasible solutions, we must assume that $t^n \leq t^p$ and $p^e \leq p^i$; from now on we assume that these inequalities hold. Given that assumption, both primal and dual solution sets in (7) are feasible because, having both positive and negative unbounded slack variables, we can always satisfy each equality constraint.

To explain (7) further, consider the constraint

$$xM - w^e + w^i = 0 \tag{10}$$

If there is a feasible x such that $xM = 0$, then we can set $w^e = 0$ and $w^i = 0$ and achieve 0 objective value for the minimizing problem in (7). If there is an x such that $xM \leq 0$, we can choose $w^i = -xM \geq 0$ so that $xM + w^i = 0$; in so doing, we incur the penalty $w^i p^i$ in the objective function. Similarly, if there is an x such that $xM \geq 0$, we can choose $w^e = xM \geq 0$ so that $xM - w^e = 0$; and we incur the "penalty" $-w^e p^e$ in the objective function. In general, some components of w^i must be chosen to be positive and some components of w^e must be chosen positive in order to satisfy (8). But the important fact is that we can *always choose* x, w^e, and w^i so that (8) is satisfied.

The linear programming tableau of (7) is shown in Figure A2-4. Note that it is a slight extension of the tableau in Figure A2-3. Also both primal and dual problems of (7) appear in Figure A2-4.

Of course, to optimize the minimizing problem in (7), we must choose

	y	z^p	z^n	
x	M	$-I$	I	$= 0$
w^e	$-I$			$\leq -p^e$
w^i	I			$\leq p^n$
	$= 0$	$\geq -t^p$	$\geq t^n$	

Figure A2-4

w^e and w^i so that the total penalty is made as small as possible. That is what was meant by "coming as close as possible" to feasibility.

Similar remarks can be made concerning the maximizing problem of (7). Hence the primal and dual problems of (7) both have optimal solutions. There are two important remarks to be made about the optimal solutions to the problems in (7).

(iv) For *basic optimal solutions* x^o, w^{eo}, w^{io} and y^o, z^{po}, z^{io} to (7), we always have

$$w_k^{eo} \, w_k^{io} = 0 \tag{11}$$

and

$$z_k^{po} \, z_k^{io} = 0 \tag{12}$$

Equation (11) follows because the column vectors in Figure A2-4 corresponding to the vectors w_k^{eo} and w_k^{io} are linearly dependent, and hence cannot both be in the basis at the same time. Hence necessarily either $w_k^{eo} = 0$ or $w_k^{io} = 0$, so that (11) holds. Equation (12) can be shown to hold by similar remarks concerning linearly dependent rows of Figure A2-4.

(v) If x^o, w^{eo}, w^{io} and y^o, z^{po}, z^{no} are optimal solutions to the pair of problems in (7), then we have

$$-w^e p^e + w^i p^i = -t^p z^p + t^n z^n \tag{13}$$

This fact follows immediately from the duality theorem (iii).

3. Complementary Slackness

As in the case of matrix games, treated in Appendix 1, there is a connection between positive components of solution vectors and the equality of the corresponding constraint. This has been given a different name in the linear programming literature.

(vi) *Complementary Slackness Condition*. From Tucker's duality relation (4), we can derive the following. Let x^o, w^o, y^o, z^o be optimal solutions to (3). By the duality theorem, $t^o = x^o b = h^o = c y^o$ so that (4) implies

$$x^o z^o + w^o y^o = 0 \tag{14}$$

Since all vectors are non-negative, we have

$$x^o z^o = 0 \tag{15}$$

$$w^o y^o = 0 \tag{16}$$

From (15) and non-negativity, we can derive the *first complementary slackness condition*:

$$x_i^o > 0 \quad \text{implies that} \quad z_i^o = b_i - \sum_{j=1}^{n} m_{ij} y_j^o = 0 \tag{17}$$

Similarly, from (16) and non-negativity, we can derive the *second complementary slackness condition*

$$y_j^o > 0 \quad \text{implies that} \quad w_j^o = \sum_{i=1}^{m} x_i^o m_{ij} - c_j = 0 \tag{18}$$

These conditions can be strengthened to if, and only if, statements by going to the concept of central solutions to linear programming problems. We refrain from doing that here, since it would only parallel the treatment of central solutions for matrix games given in Appendix 1, and we only need the latter, already developed, theory.

Appendix 3
A Model of General
Economic Equilibrium[1]

by John von Neumann

The subject of this paper is the solution of a typical economic equation system. The system has the following properties:

(1) Goods are produced not only from "natural factors of production," but in the first place from each other. These processes of production may be circular, i.e., good G_1 is produced with the aid of good G_2, and G_2 with the aid of G_1.

(2) There may be more technically possible processes of production than goods and for this reason "counting equations" is of no avail. The problem is rather to establish which processes will actually be used and which not (being "unprofitable").

In order to be able to discuss (1), (2) quite freely we shall idealize other elements of the situation (see paragraphs 1 and 2). Most of these idealizations are irrelevant, but this question will not be discussed here.

The way in which our questions are put leads of necessity to a system of inequalities (3)-(8') in paragraph 3 the possibility of a solution of which is not evident, i.e., *it cannot be proved by any qualitative argument*. The mathematical proof is possible only by means of a generalization of Brouwer's Fix-Point Theorem, i.e., by the use of very fundamental *topological* facts. This generalized fix-point theorem (the "lemma" of paragraph 7) is also interesting in itself.

The connection with topology may be very surprising at first, but the author thinks that it is natural in problems of this kind. The immediate reason for this is the occurrence of a certain "minimum-maximum" problem, familiar from the calculus of variations. In our present question, the minimum-maximum problem has been formulated in paragraph 5. It is closely related to another problem occurring in the theory of games (see footnote 2 in paragraph 6).

A direct interpretation of the function $\phi(X, Y)$ would be highly desirable. Its role appears to be similar to that of thermodynamic potentials in phenomenological thermodynamics; it can be surmised that the similarity will persist in its full phenomenological generality (independently of our restrictive idealizations).

[1] This paper was first published in German, under the title *Über ein Ökonomisches Gleichungssystem und eine Verallgemeinerung des Brouwerschen Fixpunktsatzes* in the volume entitled *Ergebnisse eines Mathematischen Seminars*, vol. 8, edited by K. Menger (Vienna, 1937). It was translated into English by G. Morton.

Another feature of our theory, so far without interpretation, is the remarkable duality (symmetry) of the monetary variables (prices y_j, interest factor β) and the technical variables (intensities of production x_i, coefficient of expansion of the economy α). This is brought out very clearly in paragraph 3 (3)-(8') as well as in the minimum-maximum formulation of paragraph 5 (7**)-(8**).

Lastly, attention is drawn to the results of paragraph 11 from which it follows, among other things, that the normal price mechanism brings about—if our assumptions are valid—the technically most efficient intensities of production. This seems not unreasonable since we have eliminated all monetary complications.

The present paper was read for the first time in the winter of 1932 at the mathematical seminar of Princeton University. The reason for its publication was an invitation from Mr. K. Menger, to whom the author wishes to express his thanks.

1. Consider the following problem: there are n goods $G_1, \ldots, G_n$ which can be produced by m processes $P_1, \ldots, P_m$. Which processes will be used (as "profitable") and what prices of the goods will obtain? The problem is evidently non-trivial since either of its parts can be answered only after the other one has been answered, i.e., its solution is implicit. We observe in particular:

(a) Since it is possible that $m > n$ it cannot be solved through the usual counting of equations.

In order to avoid further complications we assume:

(b) That there are constant returns (to scale);

(c) That the natural factors of production, including labour, can be expanded in unlimited quantities.

The essential phenomenon that we wish to grasp is this: goods are produced from each other (see equation (7) below) and we want to determine (i) which processes will be used; (ii) what the relative velocity will be with which the total quantity of goods increases; (iii) what prices will obtain; (iv) what the rate of interest will be. In order to isolate this phenomenon completely we assume furthermore:

(d) Consumption of goods takes place only through the processes of production which include necessities of life consumed by workers and employees.

In other words we assume that all income in excess of necessities of life will be reinvested.

It is obvious to what kind of theoretical models the above assumptions correspond.

2. In each process $P_i(i = 1, \ldots, m)$ quantities α_{ij} (expressed in some units) are used up, and quantities b_{ij} are produced, of the respective goods G_j $(j = 1, \ldots, n)$. The process can be symbolized in the following way:

$$P_i: \sum_{j=1}^{n} \alpha_{ij} G_j \rightarrow \sum_{j=1}^{n} b_{ij} G_j. \tag{1}$$

It is to be noted:

(e) Capital goods are to be inserted on both sides of (1); wear and tear of capital goods are to be described by introducing different stages of wear as different goods, using a separate P_i for each of these.

(f) Each process to be of unit time duration. Processes of longer duration to be broken down into single processes of unit duration introducing, if necessary, intermediate products as additional goods.

(g) (1) can describe the special case where good G_j can be produced only jointly with certain others, viz. its permanent joint products.

In the actual economy, these processes P_i, $i = 1, \ldots, m$, will be used with certain *intensities* x_i, $i = 1, \ldots, m$. That means that for the total production the quantities of equations (1) must be multiplied by x_i. We write symbolically:

$$E = \sum_{i=1}^{m} x_i P_i \tag{2}$$

$x_i = 0$ means that process P_i is not used.

We are interested in those states where the whole economy expands without change of structure, i.e., where the ratios of the intensities $x_1: \ldots : x_m$ remain unchanged, although $x_1, \ldots, x_m$ themselves may change. In such a case they are multiplied by a common factor α per unit of time. This factor is the *coefficient of expansion of the whole economy*.

3. The numerical unknowns of our problem are: *(i)* the *intensities* x_1, $\ldots, x_m$ of the processes $P_1, \ldots, P_m$; *(ii)* the *coefficient of expansion* of the whole economy α; *(iii)* the *prices* $y_1, \ldots, y_n$ of goods $G_1, \ldots, G_n$; *(iv)* the interest factor $\beta = 1 + z/100$, z being the rate of interest in per cent unit of time.

Obviously:

$$x_i \geqq 0, \tag{3}$$

$$y_j \geqq 0, \tag{4}$$

and since a solution with $x_1 = \ldots = x_m = 0$, or $y_1 = \ldots = y_n = 0$ would be meaningless:

$$\sum_{i=1}^{m} x_i > 0, \tag{5}$$

$$\sum_{j=1}^{m} y_j > 0. \tag{6}$$

The economic equations are now:

$$\alpha \sum_{i=1}^{m} a_{ij}x_i \leqq \sum_{i=1}^{m} b_{ij}x_i, \tag{7}$$

and if in (7) $<$ applies,

$$y_j = 0 \tag{7'}$$

$$\beta \sum_{j=1}^{n} a_{ij}y_j \geqq \sum_{j=1}^{n} b_{ij}y_j, \tag{8}$$

and if in (8) $>$ applies,

$$x_i = 0. \tag{8'}$$

The meaning of (7), (7') is: it is impossible to consume more of a good G_j in the total process (2) than is being produced. If, however, less is consumed, i.e., if there is excess production of G_j, G_j becomes a free good and its price $y_j = 0$.

The meaning of (8), (8') is: in equilibrium no profit can be made on any process P_i (or else prices or the rate of interest would rise—it is clear how this abstraction is to be understood). If there is a loss, however, i.e., if P_i is unprofitable, then P_i will not be used and its intensity $x_i = 0$.

The quantities a_{ij}, b_{ij} are to be taken as given, whereas the x_i, y_j, α, β are unknown. There are, then, $m + n + 2$ unknowns, but since in the case of x_i, y_j only the ratios $x_1 : \ldots : x_m$, $y_1 : \ldots : y_n$ are essential, they are reduced to $m + n$. Against this, there are $m + n$ conditions (7) + (7') and (8) + (8'). As these, however, are not equations, but rather complicated inequalities, the fact that the number of conditions is equal to the number of unknowns does not constitute a guarantee that the system can be solved.

The dual symmetry of equations (3), (5), (7), (7') of the variables x_i, α and of the concept "unused process" on the one hand, and of equations (4), (6), (8), (8') of the variables y_j, β and of the concept "free good" on the other hand seems remarkable.

4. Our task is to solve (3)-(8'). We shall proceed to show:

Solutions of (3)-(8') *always exist,* although there may be several solutions with different $x_1 : \ldots : x_m$ or with different $y_1 : \ldots : y_n$. The first is possible since we have not even excluded the case where several P_i describe the same process or where several P_i describe the same process or where several P_i combine to form another. The second is possible since some goods G_j may enter into each process P_i only in a fixed ratio with some others. But even apart from these trivial possibilities there may exist—for less obvious reasons—several solutions $x_1: \ldots : x_m, y_1: \ldots : y_n$. Against this it is of importance that α, β should have the same value for all solutions; i.e., α, β *are uniquely determined*.

We shall even find that α and β can be directly characterized in a simple manner (see paragraphs 10 and 11).

To simplify our considerations we shall assume that always:

$$a_{ij} + b_{ij} > 0 \qquad (9)$$

(a_{ij}, b_{ij} are clearly always ≥ 0). Since the a_{ij}, b_{ij} may be arbitrarily small this restriction is not very far-reaching, although it must be imposed in order to assure uniqueness of α, β as otherwise W might break up into disconnected parts.

Consider now a hypothetical solution x_i, α, y_j, β of (3)-(8'). If we had in (7) always $<$, then we should have always $y_j = 0$ (because of (7')) in contradiction to (6). If we had in (8) always $>$, we should have always $x_i = 0$ (because of (8')) in contradiction to (5). Therefore, in (7) $\leq$ always applies, but $=$ at least once; in (8) $\geq$ always applies, but $=$ at least once.

In consequence:

$$\alpha = \min_{j=1,\ldots,n} \left(\frac{\sum_{i=1}^{n} b_{ij} x_i}{\sum_{i=1}^{m} a_{ij} x_i} \right), \qquad (10)$$

$$\beta = \max_{i=1,\ldots,m} \left(\frac{\sum_{j=1}^{n} b_{ij} y_j}{\sum_{j=1}^{n} a_{ij} y_j} \right). \qquad (11)$$

Therefore the x_i, y_j determine uniquely α, β. (The right-hand side of (10), (11) can never assume the meaningless form 0/0 because of (3)-(6) and (9).) We can therefore state (7) + (7') and (8) + (8') as conditions for x_i, y_j only: $y_j = 0$ for each $j = 1, \ldots, n$, for which:

$$\frac{\sum_{i=1}^{m} b_{ij} x_i}{\sum_{i=1}^{m} a_{ij} x_i}$$

does not assume its minimum value (for all $j = 1, \ldots, n$) $\ldots$ (7*).

$x_i = 0$ for each $i = 1, \ldots, m$, for which:

$$\frac{\sum\limits_{j=1}^{n} b_{ij} y_j}{\sum\limits_{j=1}^{n} a_{ij} y_j}$$

does not assume its maximum value (for all $i = 1, \ldots, m$) . . . (8*).

The $x_1, \ldots, x_m$ in (7*) and the $y_1, \ldots, y_n$ in (8*) are to be considered as given. We have, therefore, to solve (3)-(6), (7) and (8) for x_i, y_j.

5. Let X' be a set of variables $(x_1', \ldots, x_m')$ fulfilling the analog of (3), (5):

$$x_i' \geqq 0, \tag{3'}$$

$$\sum_{i=1}^{m} x_i' > 0, \tag{5'}$$

and let Y' be a series of variables $(y_i', \ldots, y_n')$ fulfilling the analog of (4), (6):

$$y_j' \geqq 0, \tag{4'}$$

$$\sum_{j=1}^{n} y_j' > 0. \tag{6'}$$

Let, furthermore,

$$\phi(X', Y') = \frac{\sum\limits_{i=1}^{m} \sum\limits_{j=1}^{n} b_{ij} x_i' y_j'}{\sum\limits_{i=1}^{m} \sum\limits_{j=1}^{n} a_{ij} x_i' y_j'} \tag{12}$$

Let $X = (x_1, \ldots, x_m)$, $Y = (y_1, \ldots, y_n)$ be the (hypothetical) solution, $X' = (x_i', \ldots, x_m')$, $Y' = (y_1', \ldots, y_n')$ be freely variable, but in such a way that (3)-(6) and (3')-(6') respectively are fulfilled; then it is easy to verify that (7*) and (8*) can be formulated as follows:

$\phi(X, Y')$ assumes its minimum value for Y' if $Y' = Y$. (7**)

$\phi(X', Y)$ assumes its maximum value for X' if $X' = X$. (8**)

The question of a solution of (3)-(8') becomes a question of a solution of (7**), (8**) and can be formulated as follows:

(*) *Consider $\phi(X', Y')$ in the domain bounded by (3')-(6'). To find a saddle point $X' = X$, $Y' = Y$, i.e., where $\phi(X, Y')$ assumes its minimum value for Y', and at the same time $\phi(X', Y)$ its maximum value for X'.*

From (7), (7*), (10) and (8), (8*), (11) respectively, it follows that:

$$\alpha = \frac{\sum\limits_{j=1}^{n}\left[\sum\limits_{i=1}^{m} b_{ij}x_i\right]y_j}{\sum\limits_{j=1}^{n}\left[\sum\limits_{i=1}^{m} a_{ij}x_i\right]y_j} = \phi(X,\,Y) \text{ and } \beta = \frac{\sum\limits_{i=1}^{m}\left[\sum\limits_{j=1}^{n} b_{ij}y_j\right]x_i}{\sum\limits_{i=1}^{m}\left[\sum\limits_{j=1}^{n} a_{ij}y_j\right]x_i} = \phi(X,\,Y)$$

respectively.

Therefore:

(**) *If our problem can be solved, i.e., if $\phi(X',\,Y')$ has a saddle point $X' = X$, $Y' = Y$ (see above), then*:

$$\alpha = \beta = \phi(X,\,Y) = \textit{the value at the saddle point.} \qquad (13)$$

6. Because of the homogeneity of $\phi(X',\,Y')$ (in X', Y', i.e., in x_1', ..., x_m' and y_1', ... , y_n') our problem remains unaffected if we substitute the normalizations

$$\sum_{i=1}^{m} x_i' = 1\,, \qquad (5^*)$$

$$\sum_{j=1}^{n} y_j' = 1\,, \qquad (6^*)$$

for (5'), (6') and correspondingly for (5), (6). Let S be the X set described by:

$$x_i' \geqq 0\,, \qquad (3')$$

$$\sum_{i=1}^{m} x_i' = 1\,, \qquad (5^*)$$

and let T be the Y' set described by:

$$y_j' \geqq 0\,, \qquad (4')$$

$$\sum_{j=1}^{n} y_j' = 1\,, \qquad (6^*)$$

(S, T are simplices of, respectively, $m - 1$ and $n - 1$ dimensions).

In order to solve[2] (*) we make use of the simpler formulation (7*),

---

[2] The question whether our problem has a solution is oddly connected with that of a problem occurring in the Theory of Games dealt with elsewhere. (Math. Annalen, 100, 1928, pp. 295-320, particularly pp. 305 and 307-311). The problem there is a special case of (*) and is solved here in a new way through our solution of (*) (see below). In fact, if $a_{ij} \equiv 1$, then $\Sigma_{i=1}^{m} \Sigma_{j=1}^{n} a_{ij}x_i'y_j' = 1$ because of (5*), (6*). Therefore $\phi(X',\,Y') = \Sigma_{i=1}^{m} \Sigma_{j=1}^{n} b_{ij}x_i'y_j'$, and thus our (*) coincides with *loc. cit.*, p. 307. (Our $\phi(X',\,Y')$, b_{ij}, x_i', y_j', m, n here correspond to $h(\xi,\,\eta)$, a_{pq}, ξ_p, η_q, $M + 1$, $N + 1$ there.)

It is, incidentally, remarkable that (*) does not lead—as usual—to a simple maximum or minimum problem, the possibility of a solution of which would be evident, but to a problem of the saddle point or minimum-maximum type, where the question of a possible solution is far more profound.

(8*) and combine these with (3), (4), (5*), (6*) expressing the fact that $X = (x_1, \ldots, x_m)$ is in S and $Y = (y_1, \ldots, y_n)$ in T.

7. We shall prove a slightly more general lemma: Let R_m be the m-dimensional space of all points $X = (x_1, \ldots, x_m)$, R_n the n-dimensional space of all points $Y = (y_1, \ldots, y_n)$, R_{m+n} the $m + n$ dimensional space of all points $(X, Y) = (x_1, \ldots, x_m, y_1, \ldots, y_n)$.

A set (in R_m or R_n or R_{m+n}) which is *not empty, convex, closed, and bounded* we call a set C.

Let S^0, T^0 be sets C in R_m and R_n respectively and let $S^0 \times T^0$, be the set of all (X, Y) (in R_{m+n}) where the range of X is S^0 and the range of Y is T^0. Let V, W be two closed subsets of $S^0 \times T^0$. For every X in S^0 let the set $Q(X)$ of all Y with (X, Y) in V be a set C; for each Y in T^0 of all X with (X, Y) in W be a set C. Then the following lemma applies.

Under the above assumptions, V, W have (at least) one point in common.

Our problem follows by putting $S^0 = S$, $T^0 = T$ and $V =$ the set of all $(X, Y) = (x_1, \ldots, x_m, y_1, \ldots, y_n)$ fulfilling (7*), $W =$ the set of all $(X, Y) = (x_1, \ldots, x_m, y_1, \ldots, y_n)$ fulfilling (8*). It can be easily seen that V and W are closed and that the sets $S^0 = S$, $T^0 = T$, $Q(X)$, $P(Y)$ are all simplices, i.e., sets C. The common points of these V, W are, of course, our required solutions $(X, Y) = (x_1, \ldots, x_m, y_1, \ldots, y_n)$.

8. To prove the above lemma let S^0, T^0, V, W be as described before the lemma.

First, consider V. For each X of S^0 we choose a point $Y^0(X)$ out of $Q(X)$ (e.g., the center of gravity of this set). It will not be possible, generally, to choose $Y^0(X)$ as a continuous function of X. Let $\varepsilon > 0$; we define:

$$w^\varepsilon(X, X') = \max \left(0, 1 - \frac{1}{\varepsilon} \text{ distance } (X, X') \right). \tag{14}$$

Now let $Y^\varepsilon(X)$ be the centre of gravity of the $Y^0(X')$ with (relative) weight function $w^\varepsilon(X, X')$ where the range of X' is S^0. I.e., if $Y^0(X) = (y_1^0(X), \ldots, y_n^0(X))$, $Y^\varepsilon(X) = (y_1^\varepsilon(X), \ldots, y_n^\varepsilon(X))$, then:

$$y_j^\varepsilon(X) = \int_{S^0} w^\varepsilon(X, X') y_j^0(X') \, dX' \Big/ \int_{S^0} w^\varepsilon(X, X') \, dX'. \tag{15}$$

We derive now a number of properties of $Y^\varepsilon(X)$ (valid for all $\varepsilon > 0$):

(i) $Y^\varepsilon(X)$ is in T^0. Proof: $Y^0(X')$ is in $Q(X')$ and therefore in T^0, and since $Y^\varepsilon(X)$ is a centre of gravity of points $Y^0(X')$ and T^0 is convex, $Y^\varepsilon(X)$ also is in T^0.

(ii) $Y^\varepsilon(X)$ is a continuous function of X (for the whole range of S^0). Proof: it is sufficient to prove this for each $y_j^\varepsilon(X)$. Now $w^\varepsilon(X, X')$ is a continuous function of X, X' throughout; $\int_{S^0} w^\varepsilon(X, X') \, dX'$ is always $>$

0, and all $y_j^0(X)$ are bounded (being co-ordinates of the bounded set S^0). The continuity of the $y_j^\epsilon(X)$ follows, therefore, from (15).

(iii) For each $\delta > 0$ there exists an $\epsilon_0 = \epsilon_0(\delta) > 0$ such that for $0 < \epsilon < \epsilon_0$ the distance of each point $(X, Y^{\epsilon 0}(X))$ from V is $< \delta$. Proof: assume the contrary. Then there must exist a $\delta > 0$ and a sequence of $\epsilon_\nu > 0$ with $\lim_{\nu \to \infty} \epsilon_\nu = 0$ such that for every $\nu = 1, 2, \ldots$, there exists a X_ν in S^0 for which the distance $(X_\nu, Y^{\epsilon\nu}(X_\nu))$ would be $\geqq \delta$. A fortiori $Y^{\epsilon\nu}(X_\nu)$ is at a distance $\geqq \delta/2$ from every $Q(X')'$ with a distance $(X_\nu, X') \leqq \delta/2$.

All X_ν, $\nu = 1, 2, \ldots$, are in S^0 and have therefore a point of accumulation X^* in S^0; from which follows that there exists a subsequence of X_ν, $\nu = 1, 2, \ldots$, converging towards X^* for which distance $(X_\nu, X^*) \leqq \delta/2$ always applies. Substituting this subsequence for the ϵ_ν, X_ν, we see that we are justified in assuming: $\lim X_\nu = X^*$, distance $(X_\nu, X^*) \leqq \delta/2$. Therefore we may put $X' = X^*$ for every $\nu = 1, 2, \ldots$, and in consequence we have always $Y^{\epsilon\nu}(X_\nu)$ at a distance $\geqq \delta/2$ from $Q(X^*)$.

$Q(X^*)$ being convex, the set of all points with a distance $< \delta/2$ from $Q(X^*)$ is also convex. Since $Y^{\epsilon\nu}(X_\nu)$ does not belong to this set, and since it is a centre of gravity of points $Y^0(X')$ with distance $(X_\nu, X') \leqq \epsilon_\nu$ (because for distance $(X_\nu, X') > \epsilon_\nu$, $w^{\epsilon\nu}(X_\nu, X') = 0$ according to (14)), not all of these points belong to the set under discussion. Therefore: there exists a $X' = X'_\nu$ for which the distance $(X_\nu, X'_\nu) \leqq \epsilon_\nu$ and where the distance between $Y^0(X'_\nu)$ and $Q(X^*)$ is $\geqq \delta/2$.

Lim $X'_\nu = X^*$, lim distance $(X_\nu, X'_\nu) = 0$, and therefore lim $X'_\nu = X^*$. All $Y^0(X'_\nu)$ belong to T^0 and have therefore a point of accumulation Y^*. In consequence, (X^*, Y^*) is a point of accumulation of the $(X'_\nu, Y^0(X'_\nu))$ and since they all belong to V, (X^*, Y^*) belongs to V too. Y^* is therefore in $Q(X^*)$. Now the distance of every $Y^0(X'_\nu)$ including from $Q(X^*)$ is $\geqq \delta/2$. This is a contradiction, and the proof is complete.

(i)-(iii) together assert: for every $\delta > 0$ there exists a continuous mapping $Y_\delta(X)$ of S^0 on to a subset of T^0 where the distance of every point $(X, Y_\delta(X))$ from V is $< \delta$. (Put $Y_\delta(X) = Y^\epsilon(X)$ with $\epsilon = \epsilon_0 = \epsilon_0(\delta)$).

9. Interchanging S^0 and T^0, and V and W we obtain now: for every $\delta > 0$ there exists a continuous mapping $X_\delta(Y)$ of T^0 on to a subset of S^0 where the distance of every point $(X_\delta(Y), Y)$ from W is $< \delta$.

On putting $f_\delta(X) = X_\delta(Y_\delta(X))$, $f_\delta(X)$ is a continuous mapping of S^0 on to a subset of S^0. Since S^0 is a set C, and therefore topologically a simplex[3], we can use L.F.J. Brouwer's Fix-point Theorem[4]; $f_\delta(X)$ has a fix-point. I.e., there exists a X^δ in S^0 for which $X^\delta = f_\delta(X^\delta) = X_\delta(Y_\delta(X^\delta))$. Let $Y^\delta = Y_\delta(X^\delta)$, then we have $X^\delta = X_\delta(Y^\delta)$. Consequently,

---

[3] Regarding these as well as other properties of convex sets used in this paper, cf., e.g., Alexandroff and H. Hopf, *Topologie*, vol. I, J. Springer, Berlin, 1935, pp. 598-609.

[4] Cf., e.g., l.c., footnote 1, p. 480.

the distances of the point (X^δ, Y^δ) in R_{m+n} both from V and from W are $< \delta$. The distance of V from W is therefore $<2\delta$. Since this is valid for every $\delta > 0$, the distance between V and W is $= 0$. Since V, W are closed and bounded, they must have at least one common point. This proves our lemma completely.

10. We have solved (7*), (8*) of paragraph 4 as well as the equivalent problem (*) of paragraph 5 and the original task of paragraph 3: the solution of (3)-(8'). If the x_i, y_j (which were called X, Y in paragraphs 7-9) are determined, α, β follow from (13) in (**) of paragraph 5. In particular, $\alpha = \beta$.

We have emphasized in paragraph 4 already that there may be several solutions x_i, y_j (i.e., X, Y); we shall proceed to show that there exists only one value of α (i.e., of β). In fact, let X_1, Y_1, α_1, β_1 and X_2, Y_2, α_2, β_2 be two solutions. From (7**), (8**) and (13) it follows that:

$$\alpha_1 = \beta_1 = \phi(X_1, Y_1) \leqq \phi(X_1, Y_2),$$

$$\alpha_2 = \beta_2 = \phi(X_2, Y_2) \geqq \phi(X_1, Y_2),$$

therefore $\alpha_1 = \beta_1 \leqq \alpha_2 = \beta_2$. For reasons of symmetry $\alpha_2 = \beta_2 \leqq \alpha_1 = \beta_1$, therefore $\alpha_1 = \beta_1 = \alpha_2 = \beta_2$.

We have shown:

At least one solution X, Y, α, β exists. For all solutions:

$$\alpha = \beta = \phi(X, Y) \tag{13}$$

and these have the same numerical value for all solutions. In other words: the interest factor and the coefficient of expansion of the economy are equal and uniquely determined by the technically possible processes $P_1, \ldots, P_m$.

Because of (13), $\alpha > 0$, but may be $\geqq 1$. One would expect $\alpha > 1$, but $\alpha \leqq 1$ cannot be excluded in view of the generality of our formulation: processes $P_1, \ldots, P_m$ may really be *unproductive*.

11. In addition, we shall characterize α in two independent ways.

Firstly, let us consider a state of the economy possible on purely technical considerations, expanding with factor α' per unit of time. I.e., for the intensities $x'_1, \ldots, x'_m$:

$$x'_i \geqq 0 \tag{3'}$$

$$\sum_{i=1}^{m} x'_i > 0 \tag{5'}$$

and

$$\alpha' \sum_{i=1}^{m} a_{ij}x_i' \leqq \sum_{i=1}^{m} b_{ij}x_i' . \tag{7''}$$

We are neglecting prices here altogether. Let x_i, y_j, $\alpha = \beta$ be a solution of our original problem (3)-(8') in paragraph 3. Multiplying (7'') by y_j and adding $\Sigma_{j=1}^{n}$ we obtain:

$$\alpha' \sum_{i=1}^{m} \sum_{j=1}^{n} a_{ij}x_i'y_j \leqq \sum_{i=1}^{m} \sum_{j=1}^{n} b_{ij}x_i'y_j ,$$

and threfore $\alpha' \leqq \phi(X', Y)$. Because of (8**) and (13) in paragraph 5, we have:

$$\alpha' \leqq \phi(X', Y) \leqq \phi(X, Y) = \alpha = \beta . \tag{16}$$

Secondly, let us consider a system of prices where the interest factor β' allows of no more profits. I.e., for prices y_1', ..., y_n':

$$y_j' \geqq 0 , \tag{4'}$$

$$\sum_{j=1}^{n} y_j' > 0 , \tag{6'}$$

and

$$\beta' \sum_{j=1}^{n} a_{ij}y_j' \geqq \sum_{j=1}^{n} b_{ij}y_j' . \tag{8''}$$

Hereby we are neglecting intensities of production altogether. Let x_i, y_j, $\alpha = \beta$ as above. Multiplying (8'') by x_i and adding $\Sigma_{j=1}^{m}$ we obtain:

$$\beta' \sum_{i=1}^{m} \sum_{j=1}^{n} a_{ij}x_iy_j' \geqq \sum_{i=1}^{m} \sum_{j=1}^{n} b_{ij}x_iy_j'$$

and therefore $\beta' \geqq \phi(X, Y')$. Because of (7**) and (13) in paragraph 5, we have:

$$\beta' \geqq \phi(X, Y') \geqq \phi(X, Y) = \alpha = \beta . \tag{17}$$

These two results can be expressed as follows:

The greatest (purely technically possible) factor of expansion α' of the whole economy is $\alpha' = \alpha = \beta$, neglecting prices. The lowest interest factor β' at which a profitless system of prices is possible is $\beta' = \alpha = \beta$, neglecting intensities of production.

Note that these characterizations are possible only on the basis of our knowledge that solutions of our original problem exist—without themselves directly referring to this problem. Furthermore, the equality of the maximum in the first form and the minimum in the second can be proved only on the basis of the existence of this solution.

Appendix 4
Game-Theoretic Solution of an Economic Problem

John G. Kemeny

The purpose of this note is to complete the proof of Theorem 2(a) in
[2]. For this purpose we state and solve the following equivalent problem. Another solution to the same problem appears in [3].

Problem: Given a matrix-game P with non-negative entries and positive value, and Q with nonpositive entries and negative value. Find a
convex combination of the two matrices which is a fair game, and for
which there is a pair of optimal strategies x, y such that $xPy > 0$.

We will first prove some theorems about the behavior of games
under small changes in the entries of the game-matrix. We add an
amount ε_{ij} to entry a_{ij} of the game-matrix A. Let $M = \max |\varepsilon_{ij}|$. We
will say "for sufficiently small changes" when we mean "for changes
with a sufficiently small M." A "kernel" of a game is meant in the
sense defined in reference [1].

Theorem 1: For sufficiently small changes, at least one kernel of A
remains a kernel.

Proof: Let us imagine the geometric configuration for the minimizing player. The solutions of subgames are represented by intersec-
tions of hyperplanes or by a hyperplane with a boundary. Such an intersection corresponds to a kernel, unless (1) the intersection lies
outside of probability space, (2) a hyperplane passes below the intersection, or (3) there is another intersection which does not have the
previously mentioned properties and which is lower than the given
intersection.

  An intersection that fails to represent a kernel must fall into one
of the three categories mentioned. We can find a bound on M so that
the intersection will continue to fall into this category and hence will
continue to represent a nonkernel. Thus, for a sufficiently small
change, all nonkernels remain nonkernels. But every game has a kernel, and hence at least one kernel remains a kernel.

QED.

This paper was written in 1955 but was never published by John G. Kemeny, now
President of Dartmouth College. He has kindly given us permission to publish it here.

251

For the following lemma, it is convenient to introduce some auxiliary notation. $\emptyset$ is the sum of the cofactors. $\emptyset_j$ is the sum of the cofactors of column j. A small amount, ε_j, will be added to each entry of column j, and this will be done for each column. $Q = \Sigma \ \varepsilon_j \emptyset_j / \ \emptyset$. The corresponding quantities for the changed matrix will be indicated by primes.

Lemma: Given a square matrix with $D = 0$, if sufficiently small changes are made—with ε_j added to the entries in column j—then the sign of $D'/\emptyset'$ is the same as that of Q.

Proof: $D' = D + Q\emptyset$. $\emptyset' = \emptyset + \varepsilon$, where ε is of the order of magnitude of M. Since $D = 0$, $D'/\emptyset = Q[\emptyset/\emptyset + \varepsilon]$.

For sufficiently small M, the quantity in brackets is positive.

QED.

Theorem 2: Given a fair game A and a row-vector r having the property that for every optimal strategy y of the second player, ry has the same sign (*or* is non-negative *or* is nonpositive). A_ε is formed by adding εr ($\varepsilon > 0$) to every row of A. For sufficiently small ε, the value of A_ε has the same sign as ry (*or* is non-negative *or* is nonpositive).

Proof: Consider a kernel of the game A. Let ε_j be the jth component of εr. ε_j is added to the jth column of the kernel (for all j belonging to the kernel). Since A is fair, the kernel has a zero determinant. Thus the lemma is applicable.

If the kernel remains a kernel, the value of A_ε will be $D'/\emptyset'$, whose sign, for sufficiently small ε, depends on Q. But the basic strategy y_0 of the second player given by the kernel has components $\emptyset_j/\emptyset$ (and 0 outside the kernel); hence $Q = \varepsilon r y_0$. Thus, for sufficiently small ε, if the kernel remains a kernel, A_ε has a value whose sign is that of the ry (*or* is non-negative *or* is nonpositive).

We can choose an ε sufficiently small for all kernels to have this property, and in addition so that Theorem 1 applies.

QED.

It is easy to see how we can extend this to a game of arbitrary value. We need only regard such a game as formed from a fair game by adding the value of the game to every entry.

Theorem 3: Given a game A of the form

B	C
D	E

with $v(A) = v(C) = v(D) = 0$, and B consisting entirely of zeroes. Let F be the game gotten from E by giving to the first player as pure strategies his basic strategies in D, and to the second player his basic strategies in C. (Thus the mixed strategies in F are the optimal strategies of the two players in D and C respectively.)

Then the first player has an optimal strategy for A, in which he makes use of the strategies below the line, if, and only if, $v(F) \geq 0$. And there is an optimal strategy for the second player, in which he makes use of the strategies to the right of the division, if, and only if, $v(F) \leq 0$.

Proof: Suppose that $v(F) \geq 0$. Then there is a strategy x_0 of the first player optimal in D which guarantees this value in E against all strategies y of the second player optimal in C. Let $r = x_0 E$; $ry \geq v(F)$. Let C_ε be gotten from C by adding εr to each of its rows. Now theorem 2 applies. Hence we know that for sufficiently small ε, if $v(F) > 0$, then $v(C_\varepsilon) > 0$, and if $v(F) = 0$, then $v(C_\varepsilon) \geq 0$. Let x_1 be an optimal strategy of the first player for C_ε. Then $x_1 C_\varepsilon = x_1 C + \varepsilon r$ is positive in the former case, and non-negative in the latter.

We now choose as a strategy for A the vector $[1/(1 + \varepsilon)]x_1$ above the line of division and $[\varepsilon/(1 + \varepsilon)]x_0$ below. Since B consists entirely of zeroes and x_0 is optimal for D, we are guaranteed a non-negative amount to the left of the vertical division. To the right the outcome is $(1/(1 + \varepsilon))(xC + \varepsilon r)$. This is non-negative, proving that we have an optimal strategy of the required kind. If $v(F) > 0$, then we know that we have a positive amount guaranteed to the right of the vertical division, and hence the second player cannot have a strategy of the desired kind.

A similar proof for the second player completes the argument.

QED.

We are now in a position to show that our problem always has a solution. We consider convex combinations $pP = qQ$, with non-negative p and q, and $p + q = 1$. If $p = 0$, the value is positive; if $p = 1$, the value is negative. The value is a continuous function of p, hence for some permissible, p we get a fair game.

Since P has non-negative entries and Q has non-positive entries, the value is monotone increasing in p. Thus we get either a unique p or a closed interval for p in which the game is fair. The difficult part of the problem is to fulfill the condition $xPy > 0$. The following theorem shows that this condition can be fulfilled for the extreme values of p. It was shown in the paper cited [2], that the condition can be fulfilled for only a finite number of p-values.

Theorem 4: If p_0 is the largest (or smallest) p for which $pP + qQ$ is fair, then there exists a pair of optimal strategies such that $xPy > 0$.

Proof: We will give the proof for the case where p_0 is the largest p giving a fair game; for the smallest p the proof is exactly analogous. *Let us assume that our theorem is false.*

Rearrange the rows of $p_0P + q_0Q$ so that all pure strategies ever used by the first player are above the division line, and all those used by the second player are to the left of the division in the matrix:

B	C
D	E

If we rearrange the P and Q matrices, we can talk about the corresponding four areas in each of them. We can construct a single optimal strategy for each player using all these pure strategies, hence the B-area of P must consist entirely of zeroes by our assumption. But since the entire game is fair, the B-area of Q must also consist entirely of zeroes. (An immediate consequence of the fact that P has non-negative entries and Q has nonpositive entries.) Since the entire game is fair, $v(C) \geq 0$ and $v(D) \leq 0$.

Suppose that $v(C) > 0$. Since the entire game has negative value for $p = 1$, C must also have a negative value for $p = 1$. Hence for some $p_1 > p_0$, C is fair, and hence the entire game is fair for p_1, contrary to the hypothesis. Hence $v(C) = 0$.

Suppose that $v(D) < 0$. Then the second player has a strategy y_1 to the left of the line, guaranteeing him a positive amount in D. Let y_2 be optimal for the second player in C. There is an upper bound to the amount he can lose with y_2 in E. Hence a combination of y_1 with a small multiple of y_2 will still be optimal, contrary to our assumption. Hence $v(D) = 0$.

We can now apply Theorem 3. There either exists a mixed strategy of the first player using some pure strategy below the line, or one for the second player using a pure strategy to the right of the division, or both. In any case we have arrived at a contradiction from our assumption. Hence the theorem is true.

QED.

This result is of methodological interest, since game theory is used here as a mathematical tool to solve a problem arising in a *non*game-theoretic model. The method also suggests that some further study of the effect of small changes in the matrix entries may be fruitful.

Bibliography

[1] Bohnenblust, H.F., S. Karlin and L.S. Shapley, "Solutions of Dis-

crete Two-Person Games,'' In *Contributions to the Theory of Games*, I: edited by H.W. Kuhn and A.W. Tucker, Annals of Mathematics, No. 24. Princeton: Princeton University Press, 1950.

[2] Kemeny, John G., Oskar Morgenstern, and Gerald L. Thompson, "A Generalization of the von Neumann Model of an Expanding Economy," *Econometrica*, (1956), pp. 115-135.

[3] Thompson, Gerald L., "On the Solution of a Game-Theoretic Problem." In *Linear Inequalities and Related Systems*, H.W. Kuhn and A.W. Tucker, editors. Princeton: Princeton University Press, 1956, pp. 275-284.

Bibliography

The following is a selective bibliography of books and papers relevant to the subject matter of this book. Many of these items are specifically referred to in the text above; however, even those not specifically mentioned in the text influenced our thinking.

[1] Afriat, S.N., "Production Duality and the von Neumann Theory of Growth and Interest," in *Mathematical Systems in Economics*, A. Hahn, Meisenheim a.G., Vol. II (1974) 74 pp.

[2] Balinski, M.L. and H.P. Young, "Interpreting von Neumann Model Prices as Marginal Values," *Journal of Economic Theory*, **9** (1974), pp. 449-463.

[3] Ballarini, K., "Ein Bemerkung zum Morgenstern-Thompson Konsumsmodell," *Zeitschrift für Nationalökonomie*, forthcoming.

[4] Bauer, L., "Consumption in von Neumann Matrix Models," in *Mathematical Models in Economics*, J. Los and M.W. Los, editors, North-Holland Publishing Co., Inc., Amsterdam (1974), pp. 13-26.

[5] Beckmann, M.J., "The Period of Production in a Von Neumann World," in *Contributions to the Von Neumann Growth Model*, G. Bruckmann and W. Weber, editors, *Zeitschrift für Nationalökonomie*, Supplementum 1 (1971), pp. 3-10.

[6] Bernardelli, Harro, Die *Grundlagen der Ökonomischen Theorie*, Tübingen, I.C.B. Mohr, (1933), 100 pp.

[7] Bromek, T., "Equilibrium levels in decomposable von Neumann models," in *Mathematical Models in Economics*, Jerzy and Maria W. Los, North-Holland Publishing Co., Inc. Amsterdam and New York (1974), pp. 35-46.

[8] Bromek, T., "Consumption-Investment Frontier in von Neumann Models," in *Mathematical Models in Economics*, Jerzy and Maria W. Los, North-Holland Publishing Co., Inc., Amsterdam and New York (1974).

[9] Bruckmann, G. and W. Weber, editors, *Contributions to the von Neumann Growth Model, Zeitschrift für Nationalökonomie*, Supplementum 1, Springer-Verlag, New York, Wien (1971), 216 pp.

[10] Burley, S.P., "Calculating von Neumann Trajectories by Simulated

Market Adjustments," in *Contributions to the von Neumann Growth Model*, G. Bruckmann and W. Weber, editors, *Zeitschrift für Nationalökonomie*, Supplementum 1 (1971), pp. 131-138.

[11] Burley, S.P., "Dynamic generalizations of the von Neumann model," in *Mathematical Models in Economics*, Jerzy and Maria W. Los, North-Holland Publishing Co., Inc., New York and Amsterdam (1974), pp. 27-34.

[12] Cantillon, R. *Essay on the Nature of Commerce in General*, Paris (1755).

[13] Cassel, G. *Theoretische Sozialökonomik*, Leipzig (1918).

[14] Champernowne, D.G., "A Note on J. von Neumann's Article" *Review of Economic Studies*, Vol. XII, 1 (1945-1946), pp. 10-18.

[15] Charnes, A. and W.W. Cooper, *Management Models and Industrial Applications of Linear Programming*, 2 vols, Wiley, New York, (1961).

[16] Chipman, J.S., "A Survey of the Theory of International Trade: Part 1, the Classical Theory," *Econometrica*, **33** (1965), pp. 477-519; Part 2, The Neo-Classical Theory," *Econometrica*, **33** (1965), pp. 685-760; and Part 3, The Modern Theory," *Econometrica* 34 (1966), pp. 18-76.

[17] Cremeans, J.E., "Pollution Abatement and Economic Growth: An Application of the von Neumann Model of an Expanding Economy," *Naval Research Logistics Quarterly*, **21** (1974), pp. 525-542.

[18] Dantzig, G.B., *Linear Programming and Extensions*, Princeton University Press, Princeton (1963), *xvi* + 620 pp.

[19] Dell, Alice M., R.L. Weil, and G.L. Thompson, "Roots of Matrix Pencils," *Communications of the Association for Computing Machinery*, **14** (1971), pp. 113-117.

[20] Dorfman, R., P.A. Samuelson, and R.M. Solow, *Linear Programming and Economic Analysis*, McGraw-Hill, New York (1958), *ix* + 527 pp.

[21] Förstner, K., *Wirtschaftliches Wachstum bei vollständiger Konkurrenz und linearer Technologie*, Methods of Operations Research IV, (Hrsg.: R. Henn), Meisenheim a. Glan (1967).

[22] Frisch, H., "Consumption, the rate of interest, and the rate of growth in the von Neumann Model," *Naval Research Logistics Quarterly*, **16** (1969), pp. 459-484.

[23] Gale, D., "The Closed Linear Model of Production," in *Linear Inequalities and Related Systems*, H.W. Kuhn and A.W. Tucker, editors, Princeton University Press, Princeton (1956), pp. 385-403.

[24] Gale, D., *The Theory of Linear Economic Models,* McGraw-Hill, New York (1960).

[25] Gale, D., "On Optimal Development in a Multi-Sector Economy," *Rev. Econ. Studies,* **34** (1967), pp. 1-18.

[26] Gale, D., "A Mathematical Theory of Economic Development," *Bull. Am. Math. Assoc.,* **74** (1968), pp. 207-223.

[27] Gale, D., "Comment," *Econometrica,* **40** (1972), pp. 391-392.

[28] Gaver, D.P. and G.L. Thompson, *Programming and Probability Models in Operations Research,* Monterey, Brooks/Cole Publishing Company, California, (1973), *xiii* + 682 pp.

[29] Georgescu-Roegen, N., "The Aggregate Linear Production Function and its Applications to von Neumann's Economic Model," Chapter IV of *Activity Analysis of Production and Allocation,* T.C. Koopmans, editor, Wiley, New York (1951), pp. 98-115.

[30] Georgescu-Roegen, N., *The Entropy Law and the Economic Process,* Harvard University Press, Cambridge (1971), *xv* + 457 pp.

[31] Georgescu-Roegen, N., "Dynamic Models and Economic Growth," *Economie Appliquée,* XXVII (1974), pp. 529-563.

[32] Goreux, L.M., and A.S. Manne, *Multi-Level Planning: Case Studies in Mexico,* North-Holland Publishing Co., Inc., New York; and American Elsevier Publishing Company, *viii* + 556 pp.

[33] Haberler, G., *A Survey of International Trade Theory,* Special Papers in International Economics, No. 1, Princeton University Press, Princeton, (1961).

[34] Haga, H. and M. Otsuki, "Neumann Model and General Equilibrium," *TCER,* No. 122 (1962), in Japanese.

[35] Haga, H. and M. Otsuki, "On a Generalized von Neumann Model," *International Economic Review,* **6** (1965) pp. 115-123.

[36] Hamburger, M.J., G.L. Thompson, and R.L. Weil, "Computation of Expansion Rates for the Generalized von Neumann Model of an Expanding Economy," *Econometrica,* **35** (1967), pp. 542-547.

[37] Hamburger, M.J., G.L. Thompson, and R.L. Weil, "Computing Results from the Generalized von Neumann Model and Using them for Planning," *Jahrbuch der Osteuropäischen Wirtschaft,* **1** (1969), pp. 107-128.

[38] Hatanaka, M., *The Workability of Input-Output Analysis,* Ludwigschafen a/Rhein (1960), *xxiii* + 310 pp.

[39] Hellwig K. and D. Moeschlin, "A note on a Production Problem in a

multisectoral Economic Model," in *Production Theory,* Eichhorn, Henn, et al, editors, Springer, New York, (1974).

[40] Henn, R., "Expansions Modelle vom v. Neumann'schen Typ," in *Optimales Wachstum and Optimale Standorts verteilung,* E. Schneider, editor, Berlin (1962).

[41] Henn, R., "Makroökonomische Expansions Modelle: v. Neumann'sche Interpretation einiger Wachstumsmodelle," *Unternehmungsforschung,* Vol. 6 (1962), pp. 16-25.

[42] Henn, R., "Lineare Methoden des Operation Research und Makroökonomische Expansionsmodelle," *Zeitschrift für National-ökonomie,* Vol. 21 (1962), pp. 297-310.

[43] Howe, C.W., "An Alternative Proof of the Existence of General Equilibrium in a von Neumann Model," *Econometrica,* Vol. 28, 635-639 (1960).

[44] Hulsmann, J. and V. Steinmetz, "A Note on the Nonexistence of Optimal Price Vectors in the General Balanced-Growth Model of Gale," *Econometrica,* **40** (1972), pp. 387-389.

[45] Idzik, A., "Equilibria in von Neumann Models with compact metric spaces of commodities and processes," in *Mathematical Models in Economics,* Jerzy and Maria W. Los, North-Holland Publishing Co., Amsterdam and New York (1974), pp. 59-62.

[46] Kaewsonthi, S., "A remark on free disposal in von Neumann models," pp. 63-66, in *Mathematical Models in Economics,* Jerzy and Maria W. Los, North-Holland Publishing Company, Inc., Amsterdam and New York (1974).

[47] Kemeny, J.G., "Game-theoretic Solution of an Economic Problem," this volume, Appendix 4.

[48] Kemeny, J.G., O. Morgenstern, and G.L. Thompson, "A Generalization of the von Neumann Model of an Expanding Economy," *Econometrica,* **24** (1956), pp. 115-135.

[49] Kemeny, J.G. and J.L. Snell, *Finite Markov Chains,* Van Nostrand, Princeton (1960).

[50] Kemeny, J.G., J.L. Snell, and G.L. Thompson, *Introduction to Finite Mathematics,* Prentice-Hall, Inc. Englewood Cliffs, first edition (1957); second edition (1966); and third edition (1974).

[51] Koopmans, T.C., "The von Neumann Model of Proportional Growth," Texte d'une conference (1958).

[52] Koopmans, T.C., "Economic Growth at Maximal Rate," *Quarterly Journal of Economics,* LXXVIII (1964), pp. 355-394.

[53] Koopmans, T.C., "On the Concept of Optimal Economic Growth," in *The Econometric Approach to Development Plan-*

ning, North-Holland Publishing Company, Inc., and Rand Mc-Nally (1966), a re-issue of *Pontificiae Academiae Scientiarum Scripta Varia,* **28** (1965), pp. 225-300.

[54] Koopmans, T.C., "Objectives, Constraints and Outcomes in Optimum Growth Models," *Econometrica,* **35** (1967), pp. 1-15.

[55] Koopmans, T.C., "Intertemporal Distribution and Optimal Economic Growth," in *Ten Economic Studies in the Tradition of Irving Fisher,* W. Fellner et al., editors, Wiley, New York (1967), pp. 95-126.

[56] Koopmans, T.C., "A Model of a Continuing State with Scarce Capital," in *Contributions to the von Neumann Growth Model,* G. Bruckmann and W. Weber, editors, *Zeitschrift für National-ökonomie,* Supplementum 1 (1971), pp. 11-22.

[57] Koopmans, T.C. and A.F. Bausch, "Selected Topics in Economics Involving Mathematical Reasoning," *SIAM Review,* topic 5, Vol. I, July (1959), pp. 79-148.

[58] Krelle, W. and G. Gabisch, *Wachstumstheorie,* Lecture Notes in Economics and Mathematical Systems, Vol. 52, Springer-Verlag, Berlin-New York (1972), *vii* + 223 pp.

[59] Kuhn, H.W. and A.W. Tucker, "Nonlinear Programming," in *Proceedings of the Second Berkeley Symposium on Mathematical Statistics and Probability,* J. Neyman, editor, University of California Press (1951), pp. 481-492.

[60] Kuhn, H.W. and A.W. Tucker, "John von Neumann's work in the Theory of Games and Mathematical Economics," *Bulletin of the American Mathematical Society,* **64** (1958), pp. 100-122.

[61] Leontief, W.W., *The Structure of the American Economy,* Oxford University Press, New York (1941), second edition (1951).

[62] Los, J., "A Simple Proof of the Existence of Equilibrium in a von Neumann model and some of its consequences," *Bulletin de l'Académie Polonaise des Sciences,* Serie des Sciences Math. (1971), pp. 971-979.

[63] Los, J., "The Approximative Horizon in von Neumann Models of Optimal Growth," in *Contributions to the von Neumann Growth Model,* G. Bruckmann and W. Weber, editors, *Zeitschrift für Nationalökonomie,* Supplementum 1 (1971), pp. 99-106.

[64] Los, J., "Labour, consumption and wages in a von Neumann Model," in *Mathematical Models in Economics,* Jerzy and Maria W. Los, North-Holland Publishing Co., Inc., Amsterdam and New York (1974), pp. 67-72.

[65] Los, J., "The existence of equilibrium in an open expanding

economy model (generalization of the Morgenstern-Thompson Model)," in *Mathematical Models in Economics,* Jerzy and Maria W. Los, North-Holland Publishing Co., Inc., Amsterdam and New York (1974), pp. 73-80.

[66] Los, J. and Maria W. Los, *Mathematical Models in Economics,* North-Holland Publishing Co., Inc. (1974).

[67] Lovell, M.C., "On the Relative Stability of Growth," *Econometrica,* **38** (1970), pp. 355-359.

[68] McKenzie, L.W., "Maximal Paths in the von Neumann Model," in *Activity Analysis in the Theory of Growth and Planning,* E. Malinvaud and M.O.L. Barach, editors, London (1967).

[69] McKenzie, L.W., "Capital Accumulation Optimal in the Final State," in *Contributions to the von Neumann Growth Model,* G. Bruckmann and W. Weber, editors, *Zeitschrift für National-ökonomie,* Supplementum 1 (1971), pp. 107-120.

[70] McManus, M., "General Consistent Aggregation in Leontief Models," *Yorkshire Bulletin of Economic Research,* I (1956), pp. 28-48.

[71] Malinvaud, E., "Capital Accumulation and Efficient Allocation of Resources," *Econometrica* (April, 1953).

[72] Malinvaud, E., "Programmes de' Expansion et Taux d'Interet," *Econometrica,* Vol. 27 (1959), pp. 215-227.

[73] Malinvaud, E. and M.O.L. Bacharach, editors, "Activity Analysis in the Theory of Growth and Planning," *Proceedings of a Conference held by the International Economic Association,* Macmillan, London-Melbourne-Toronto, St. Martin's Press, New York (1967).

[74] Mardon, L., "The Morgenstern-Thompson Model of an Open Economy, in a closed form," in *Mathematical Models in Economics,* Jerzy and Maria W. Los, North-Holland Publishing Co., Inc., Amsterdam and New York (1974), pp. 81-114.

[75] Mirrlees, J.A., "Optimum Growth When Technology is Changing," *Review of Economic Studies,* 34 (1967), pp. 95-124.

[76] Moeschlin, O., "Eine Importbeschränkung im Morgenstern-Thompson Aussenhandelsmodell," *Zeitschrift für National-ökonomie,* Vol. 31 (1971), pp. 425-442.

[77] Moeschlin, O., "Zur Eindeutigkeit von Lösungen des Morgenstern-Thompson Aussenhandelsmodells," *Zeitschrift f. d. Gesamten Staatswissenschaften,* **128** (1972), pp. 65-71.

[78] Moeschlin, O., "On the Existence of Equilibrium Solutions in a von Neumann Growth Model with Non-negative entries," in *Methods of Operations Research,* XIV, W. Krelle, editor (1972).

[79] Moeschlin, O. and G. Bol, "Applications of Mill's Differential," *Naval Research Logistics Quarterly,* **20** (1973), pp. 101-107.

[80] Moeschlin, O., *Zur Theorie von Neumannscher Wachstumsmodelle,* Springer-Verlag, Berlin (1974), 115 p.

[81] Moeschlin, O., "Derivatives of Game Value Functions in connection with von Neumann Growth Models," in *Mathematical Models in Economics,* Jerzy and Maria W. Los, North-Holland Publishing Co., Inc., Amsterdam and New York (1974), pp. 115-128.

[82] Moeschlin, O. and B. Rahut, "Eine Bemerkung zum Axiomensystem des Morgenstern-Thompson Aussenhandelsmodells," *Zeitschrift für Operations Research,* **16** (1972), pp. 153-155.

[83] Morgenstern, O., "Professor Hicks on Value and Capital," *The Journal of Political Economy,* XLIX (1941), pp. 361-393.

[84] Morgenstern, O., editor, *Economic Activity Analysis,* Wiley, New York (1954), *xviii* + 554 pp.

[85] Morgenstern, O., "Limits to the Uses of Mathematics in Economics," in *Mathematics and the Social Sciences,* American Academy of Political and Social Science, Philadelphia (1963), pp. 12-29.

[86] Morgenstern, O., "Pareto Optimum and Economic Organization," in *Systeme und Methoden in den Wirtschafts- und Sozialwissenschaften,* N. Kloten and others, editors, I.C.B. Mohr, Tübingen (1964), pp. 573-586.

[87] Morgenstern, O., "The Compressibility of Economic Systems and the Problem of Economic Constants," *Zeitschrift für Nationalökonomie,* XXVI (1966), pp. 190-203.

[88] Morgenstern, O., "John von Neumann, 1903-1957," *Economic Journal,* **68** (1968), pp. 170-174.

[89] Morgenstern, O., "Does GNP Measure Growth and Welfare?" in *Social Responsibility and Accountability,* Jules Backman, editor, New York University Press, New York (1975), pp. 57-76.

[90] Morgenstern, O. and G.L. Thompson, "Private and Public Consumption and Savings in the von Neumann Model of an Expanding Economy," *Kyklos,* **20** (1967), pp. 387-409.

[93] Morgenstern, O. and G.L. Thompson, "Un modèle de croissance en économie ouverte," *Economies et Sociétés,* V (1971), pp. 1703-1728.

[94] Morgenstern, O. and G.L. Thompson, "A Note on an Open Expanding Economy Model," *Naval Research Logistics Quarterly,* 19 (1972), pp. 557-559.

[95] Morgenstern, O. and G.L. Thompson, "Long term planning with models of the static and dynamic open expanding economics," in

Mathematical Models in Economics, Jerzy and Maria W. Los, North-Holland Publishing Co., Inc., Amsterdam and New York, (1974), pp. 129-138.

[96] Morgenstern, O. and T.M. Whitin, "The Economics of Input-Output Relations," No. 18, *NBER,* Princeton University Press, Princeton (1955), pp. 128-135.

[97] Morgenstern, O. and Y.K. Wong, "On the Equilibrium of a Linear Economic System with Non-Dominant Outputs," Abstract, *Econometrica,* **24** (1956), pp. 200-201.

[98] Morgenstern, O. and Y.K. Wong, "A Study of Linear Economic Systems," *Weltwirtschaftliches Archiv,* Vol. 79, Heft 2 (1957), pp. 222-241.

[99] Morishima, M., "Economic Expansion and the Interest Rate in Generalized von Neumann Models," *Econometrica,* **28** (1960), pp. 352-363.

[100] Morishima, M., *Equilibrium, Stability, and Growth,* The Clarendon Press, Oxford (1964).

[101] Morishima, M., *Theory of Economic Growth,* The Clarendon Press, Oxford (1969).

[102] Morishima, M., "Consumption-investment Frontier, Wage-profit Frontier and the von Neumann Growth Equilibrium," in *Contributions to the von Neumann Growth Model,* G. Bruckmann and W. Weber, editors, *Zeitschrift für Nationalökonomie,* Supplementum 1 (1971), pp. 31-38.

[103] Morishima, M. and G.L. Thompson, "Balanced Growth of Firms in a Competitive Situation with External Economies," *International Economic Review,* **1** (1960), pp. 129-142.

[104] Morton, G. and A. Zauberman, "von Neumann's Model and Soviet Long-term (Perspective) Planning," *Kyklos,* **22** (1969), pp. 45-60.

[105] von Neumann, J., "Uber ein ökonomisches Gleichungssystem und eine Verallgemeinerung des Brouwerschen Fixpunktsatzes," *Ergebnisse eines mathematischen Kolloquiums,* **8** (1937), pp. 73-83, translated as "A Model of General Economic Equilibrium," *Review of Economic Studies,* **12** (1945-46), pp. 1-9. Reprinted with correction of misprints in *Precursors in Mathematical Economics: An Anthology,* W.J. Baumol and S.M. Goldfeld, editors, London School of Economics (1968), pp. 296-306. Reprinted as Appendix 3 in this volume.

[106] von Neumann, J. and O. Morgenstern, *Theory of Games and Economic Behavior,* Princeton University Press, Princeton (1944), third edition (1953).

[107] Nikaido, H., *Convex Structures and Economic Theory*, Academic Press, New York and London (1968).

[108] Orosel, G.O., "A Linear Growth Model Including Education," *Zeitschrift für Nationalökonomie*, **33** (1973), pp. 251-279.

[109] Pedone, A., "Appunti sull'introduzione della Domanda in un modello generale di Produzione," in *Nuovi problemi di sviluppo economico*, L. Spaventa, editor, Florence (1974), pp. 235-255.

[110] Perroux, F., L'équilibre de von Neumann, une première evaluation, *Economie Mathématique et Econometrie, Cahiers de l'I.S.E.A.*, No. 10, October (1971).

[111] Radner, Roy, "Balanced Stochastic Growth at the Maximum Rate," in *Contributions to the von Neumann Growth Model*, G. Bruckmann and W. Weber, editors, *Zeitschrift für Nationalökonomie*, Supplementum 1 (1971), pp. 39-52.

[112] Ramsey, F.P., "A Mathematical Theory of Saving," *The Economic Journal*, **38** (1928), pp. 543-559.

[113] Robinson, S.M., "Irreducibility in the von Neumann Model," *Econometrica*, Vol. 41, No. 3 (1973), pp. 569-73.

[114] Robinson, S.M., "The linearization technique for solving the irreducible von Neumann economic model," in *Mathematical Models in Economics*, Jerzy and Maria W. Los, North-Holland Publishing Co., Inc., Amsterdam and New York (1974), pp. 139-152.

[115] Scarf, H., with the collaboration of Terje Hansen, *The Computation of Economic Equilibria*, Cowles Foundation for Research in Economics, Monograph 24, Yale University Press, New Haven (1973), x + 249 pp.

[116] Steinmetz, V., "Zur Existenz von Wachstumsgleichgewichten in Wachstumsmodellen vom von Neumannschen Typ," in *Mathematical Systems in Economics*, Vol. 1, Verlag A. Hahn, Meisenheim a.G. (1972), 100 pp.

[117] Sutherland, W.R., "On Optimal Development in a Multi-Sectoral Economy: The Discounted Case," *Review of Economic Studies*, **37** (1970), pp. 585-589.

[118] Thompson, G.L., "On the Solution of a Game-Theoretic Problem," in *Linear Inequalities and Related Systems*, H.W. Kuhn and A.W. Tucker, editors, Princeton, New Jersey (1956), pp. 275-284.

[119] Thompson, G.L., "Computing the Natural Factors of a Closed Expanding Economy Model," *Zeitschrift für Nationalökonomie*, **34** (1974), pp. 57-68.

[120] Thompson, G.L., "A Note on the MT - Consumption Model," *Zeitschrift für Nationalökonomie* (1975).

[121] Thompson, G.L., "Extensions of the Perron-Frobenius Theorem to Generalized Eigensystems," Working Paper, Carnegie-Mellon University (1975).

[122] Thompson, G.L., "Solutions of von Neumann-Leontief expanding Economy Models and a Generalization of the Perron-Frobenius Theorem," Working Paper, Carnegie-Mellon University (1975).

Thompson, G.L., see also [19], [28], [36], [37], [48], [50], [90], [91], [92], [93], [94], [95], [103]

[123] Thompson, G.L. and R.L. Weil, "Further Relations Between Game Theory and Eigensystems," *SIAM Review,* **11** (1969), pp. 597-602.

[124] Thompson, G.L. and R.L. Weil, "Reducing the Rank of $(A - \lambda B)$," *Proceedings of the American Mathematical Society,* **26** (1970), pp. 381-394.

[125] Thompson, G.L. and R.L. Weil, "Von Neumann Model Solutions Are Generalized Eigensystems," in *Contributions to the von Neumann Growth Model,* G. Bruckmann and W. Weber, editors, *Zeitschrift für Nationalökonomie,* Supplementum 1 (1971), pp. 139-154.

[126] Thompson, G.L. and R.L. Weil, "The Roots of Matrix Pencils $(Ay - \lambda B)$: Existence, Calculations, and Relations to Game Theory," *Linear Algebra and its Applications,* **5** (1972), pp. 207-226.

[127] Tintner, G., "Linear Economics and the Boehm-Bawerk Period of Production," *Quarterly Journal of Economics,* LXXXVIII (1974), pp. 127-132.

[128] Truchon, M., "On Some Models of the von Neumann Variety," Management Sciences Research Report 173, Carnegie-Mellon University (1969).

[129] Truchon, Michel, "On the Importance of Lags in Growth Models," in *Contributions to the von Neumann Growth Model,* G. Bruckmann and W. Weber, editors, *Zeitschrift für Nationalökonomie,* Supplementum 1 (1971), pp. 53-62.

[130] Tsukui, J., "Application of a Turnpike Theorem to Planning for Efficient Accumulation: An Example for Japan," *Econometrica,* **36** (1968), pp. 172-186.

[131] Tucker, A.W., "Dual Systems of Homogeneous Linear Relations," in *Linear Inequalities and Related Systems,* H.W. Kuhn

and A.W. Tucker, editors, Princeton University Press, Princeton, New Jersey (1956), pp. 3-18.

[132] Ulam, S., "John von Neumann, 1903-1957," in *Bulletin of the American Mathematical Society*, **64** (1958), pp. 1-49.

[133] Wald, A., "Ueber die eindeutige positive Lösbarkeit der neuen Produktionsgleichungen," *Ergebnisse eines Mathematischen Kolloquiums*, Fasc. 6 (1935).

[134] Wald, A., "Ueber einige Gleichungssysteme der Mathematischen Oekonomie," *Zeitschrift für Nationalökonomie*, VII, (1936), translated as "On Some Equations of Mathematical Economics," *Econometrica*, **19** (1951), pp. 368-403.

[135] Wang, H., *From Mathematics to Philosophy*, London, Routledge (1974), xi + 428 pp.

[136] Weil, R.L., "An Algorithm for the von Neumann Economy," *Zeitschrift für Nationalökonomie*, **24** (1964), pp. 371-384.

[137] Weil, R.L., "Optimal Growth under the Fixed Time, Maximal Distance Objective," *Economics of Planning*, **3** (1966), pp. 251-271.

[138] Weil, R.L., Jr., "Consumption in the Closed von Neumann Model," *Economics of Planning*, Vol. VII (1967), pp. 39-48.

[139] Weil, R.L., "The Generalized von Neumann Model and International Comparison of Productivity," *The Journal of Political Economy*, **75** (1967), pp. 696-705.

[140] Weil, R.L., "The Decomposition of Economic Production Systems," *Econometrica*, **36** (1968), pp. 260-278.

[141] Weil, R.L., "Game Theory and Eigensystems," *SIAM Review*, X (1968), pp. 360-367.

[142] Weil, R.L., "Solutions to the Decomposable von Neumann Model," *Econometrica*, **38** (1970), pp. 278-282.

Weil, R.L., see also [19], [36], [37], [123], [124], [125], [126].

[143] Wong, Y.K., "Some Mathematical Concepts for Linear Economic Models," in *Economic Activity Analysis*, Oskar Morgenstern, editor, Wiley, New York (1954), pp. 283-339.

[144] Wong, Y.K., "An Elementary Treatment of an Input-Output System," *Naval Research Logistics Quarterly*, **10** (1954), pp. 321-326.

[145] Wong, Y.K. and Oskar Morgenstern, "A Study of Linear Economic Systems," *Weltwirtschaftliches Archiv*, **79** (1957), pp. 222-241.

[146] Woodbury, M.A., "Characteristic Roots of Input-Output Matrices," in *Economic Activity Analysis,* Oskar Morgenstern, editor, Wiley, New York (1954), pp. 365-382.

[147] Zauberman, A., "Soviet Work Related to the von Neumann Model and Turnpike Theories and Some Ramifications," in *Contributions to the von Neumann Growth Model,* G. Bruckmann and W. Weber, editors, *Zeitschrift für Nationalökonomie,* Supplementum 1 (1971), pp. 191-216.

Note: Papers [83] [85] [86] [87] [88] by O. Morgenstern and joint papers [49] [90] [91] with G.L. Thompson are contained in: O. Morgenstern: *Selected Economic Writings,* A. Schotter (Ed.), New York University Press, (1976).

Indexes

Author Index

Subject Index

About the Authors

Oskar Morgenstern is Professor of Economics at New York University and Chairman of its Center for Applied Economics. He is author, among other works, of *On the Accuracy of Economic Observations* (second edition 1963) and, with John von Neumann, of *The Theory of Games and Economic Behavior* (third edition, 1953). He is currently working on power games and integral games. Professor Morgenstern is also Chairman of MATHEMATICA, Inc.

Gerald L. Thompson is Professor of Applied Mathematics and Industrial Administration at Carnegie-Mellon University. He is coauthor (with John G. Kemeny and J. Laurie Snell) of *Introduction to Finite Mathematics* (third Edition, 1974), and coauthor (with Donald P. Gaver) of *Programming and Probability Models in Operations Research*, 1973. Besides the area of mathematical economics, his current research is in the area of specially structured integer programming problems which is part of Operations Research.